(A) · BILLET ·

(C) · DOUBLE · CONE ·

(D) · BEAK · HEAD ·

(F) · CAPITAL ·

(G) · PANELS ·

(H) · CAPITAL ·

(E) · SCULPTURE · · ROMANESQUE · ORNAMENT · · ·

(I) · HEAD ·

(J) · DOG · TOOTH ·

(K) · CRESTING ·

(L) · GARGOYLE ·

(M) · SCULPTURE ·

(N) · MOULDING · ORNAMENTS ·

(O) · TRACERY ·

(P) · BOSS ·

(Q) · SHAFT ·

(R) · CAPITAL ·

(S) · CROCKETS · AND · FINIAL ·

(T) · CHOIR · STALL ·

· GOTHIC · ORNAMENT ·

More Praise for Catholic Church Architecture and the Spirit of the Liturgy

"Denis McNamara has accomplished something unique and important in this book: he has reflected on church buildings as the built expression of distinctively theological ideas. This analysis has enabled him to specify precisely why certain churches are adequate to their deepest purpose—and why others are not. In this lucidly written text, he helps us to see how the Garden of Eden, the Jerusalem Temple, the sacrifice of the cross, the communion of saints, and the song of the angels in heaven all have relevance to the way we think about—and more significantly, the way we build—our churches. It is my hope that this marvelous book will find its way into the hands of pastors, educators, architects, renovators, and worshippers all across the country."

Rev. Robert Barron
Francis Cardinal George Chair of Faith and Culture
University of St. Mary of the Lake/Mundelein Seminary
Founder, Word on Fire Ministries

"This wonderful book will lead those who build churches out of the wilderness littered with ugly and misbegotten buildings. Biblical exegesis and patristic, scholastic, and recent theology support McNamara's convincing rereading of documents of the Second Vatican Council. They sanction no particular style but do demand that churches once again shine forth with the beautiful image of the Heavenly Jerusalem. Everyone involved in church building must read it, and take it to heart."

C. William Westfall
Frank Montana Professor
School of Architecture
University of Notre Dame

"Contrary to the impression given by some, the principles of sacred architecture did not begin in the Middle Ages, or even in earliest Christianity. Instead, they are rooted in the liturgy of ancient Israel, embodied in the Tabernacle of Moses and the glorious Temple of Solomon, and fulfilled in Christ and the Church. In this lucidly written and theologically sophisticated book, Dr. Denis McNamara sheds new light on old debates about church architecture by inserting them into salvation history: the three ages of *Shadow, Image,* and *Reality.* By tracing the shape of worship from the paradise of Eden to the heavenly Jerusalem, McNamara has given us something both unique and precious: *a biblical theology of church architecture.* This book needs to be on the shelf of anyone—pastors, seminarians, or laity—interested in what the written Word of God has to say about the spirit of the liturgy and the splendor of worship."

Brant Pitre
Professor of Sacred Scripture
Notre Dame Seminary, New Orleans
Author of *Jesus and the Last Supper:*
Judaism and the Origins of the Eucharist

"Denis McNamara's authorship and scholarship are a tremendous source of inspiration. In this book he illuminates the way forward for art and architecture in true service of the Church and in full participation in God's majestic revelation made present in the Mass. McNamara explains to artists, architects, and their clients the very nature of their work. He establishes expectations for those of us who turn our talents to making the image of the Church. He reveals to us how to think of church building anew, and explains why doing so is absolutely vital to our success in her service. In doing so, McNamara guides the work of bishops, pastors, and the architects and artists who serve them to a more beautiful, more truthful, and infinitely more rewarding manner of making churches."

James McCrery
McCrery Architects
Washington, DC

"Dr. Denis McNamara's *Catholic Church Architecture and the Spirit of the Liturgy* is a must-read for parish councils, building committees, liturgists, pastors, and church architects. Dr. McNamara has a beautiful ability to bring together sacred art, architecture, liturgy, and theology and explain it so that it all makes sense. This book makes clear to us that sacred art and architecture can invoke in each of us a sense of the sacred, and reminds us that when we remove beauty and art from inside our churches we really remove an opportunity for human beings to encounter God. This book will guide parishes to construct churches that not only follow the rules of Vatican II, but the spirit behind Vatican II, and help lead the faithful to more fruitful participation in the earthly and heavenly liturgies."

Denise Ogilvie
Director of Christian Education and Liturgy
Saint Michael the Archangel Church
Leawood, KS

CATHOLIC CHURCH ARCHITECTURE
and the
Spirit of the Liturgy

CATHOLIC CHURCH ARCHITECTURE
and the
Spirit of the Liturgy

Denis R. McNamara

HillenbrandBooks

Chicago / Mundelein, Illinois

Catholic Church Architecture and the Spirit of the Liturgy © 2009 Archdiocese of Chicago: Liturgy Training Publications, 3949 South Racine Avenue, Chicago IL 60609; 1-800-933-1800, fax 1-800-933-7094, e-mail orders@ltp.org. All rights reserved. See our Web site at www.LTP.org.

Hillenbrand Books is an imprint of Liturgy Training Publications (LTP) and the Liturgical Institute at the University of Saint Mary of the Lake (USML). The imprint is focused on contemporary and classical theological thought concerning the liturgy of the Catholic Church. Available at bookstores everywhere, through LTP by calling 1-800-933-1800, or visiting www.LTP.org. Further information about the **Hillenbrand Books** publishing program is available from the University of Saint Mary of the Lake/Mundelein Seminary, 1000 East Maple Avenue, Mundelein, IL 60060 (847-837-4542), on the Web at www.usml.edu/liturgicalinstitute, or e-mail litinst@usml.edu.

Printed in Mexico.

Library of Congress Control Number: 2009935282

978-1-59525-027-8

HCCA

In the past, God spoke in fragmentary and varied ways to our fathers through the prophets; in this, the final age, he has spoken to us through his Son.

—Letter to the Hebrews, 1:1–2

The saints . . . rejoice after their pilgrimage in shadows, and now distinguish the reality from the promise.

—Saint Athanasius, Easter Letter[1]

From the beginning God created man out of his own generosity. He chose the patriarchs to give them salvation. He took his people in his hand, teaching them, unteachable as they were, to follow him. He gave them prophets, accustoming man to bear his Spirit and to have communion with God on earth. He who stands in need of no one gave communion with himself to those who need him. Like an architect he outlined the plan of salvation to those who sought to please him. . . . Through many acts of indulgence he tried to prepare his people for perseverance in his service. He kept calling them to what was primary by means of what was secondary, that is, through foreshadowings to the reality, through the things of time to the things of eternity, through things of the flesh to the things of the spirit, through earthly things to the heavenly things. As he said to Moses: You will fashion all things according to the pattern that you saw on the mountain.

—Saint Irenaeus, *Against Heresies*[2]

Through the Holy Spirit we are restored to paradise, we ascend to the kingdom of heaven. . . . every blessing is showered upon us, both in this world and in the world to come. As we contemplate them even now, like a reflection in a mirror, it is as though we already possessed the good things our faith tells us that we shall one day enjoy. If this is the pledge, what will the perfection be? If these are the firstfruits, what will the full harvest be?

—Saint Basil the Great, *On the Holy Spirit*[3]

Since the daybreak or the dawn is changed gradually from darkness into light, the Church, which comprises the elect, is fittingly styled daybreak or dawn. While she is being led from the night of infidelity to the light of faith, she is opened gradually to the splendor of heavenly brightness. . . . The dawn intimates that the night is over; it does not proclaim the full light of day. . . . It will be fully day for the Church of the elect when she is no longer darkened by sin. It will be fully day for her when she shines with the perfect brilliance of interior light.

—Saint Gregory the Great, *Moral Reflections on Job*[4]

In this age of the Church Christ now lives and acts in and with his Church, in a new way appropriate to this new age. He acts through the sacraments in what the common Tradition of the East and the West calls "the sacramental economy"; this is the communication (or "dispensation") of the fruits of Christ's Paschal mystery in the celebration of the Church's sacramental liturgy.

—*Catechism of the Catholic Church*, 1076

The enemy led you out of the earthly paradise. I will not restore you to that paradise, but I will enthrone you in heaven. . . . I appointed cherubim to guard you as slaves are guarded, but now I make them worship you as God. The throne formed by the cherubim awaits you, its bearers swift and eager. The bridal chamber is adorned, the banquet is ready, the eternal dwelling places are prepared, the treasure houses of all good things lie open. The kingdom of heaven has been prepared for you for all eternity.

—Ancient Homily on Holy Saturday[5]

---

1. Saint Athanasius, Easter Letter (Eph. 14, 1–2: PG, 26, 1419–1420), from the Liturgy of the Hours, Office of the Readings of the Fifth Sunday of Lent.

2. Irenaeus, *Against Heresies* (Lib. 4, 14, 2–3; 15, 1: SC, 100, 542. 548), from the Liturgy of the Hours, Office of Readings, Wednesday of the Second Week of Lent.

3. Saint Basil the Great, *On the Holy Spirit* (Cap. 15, 35–36: SC, 17 bis, 364–370), from the Liturgy of the Hours, Office of Readings, Monday of the Fourth Week of Easter.

4. Saint Gregory the Great, *Moral Reflections on Job* (Lib. 29, 2–4: PL, 76, 478–480), from the Liturgy of the Hours, Office of Readings, Thursday of the Ninth Week in Ordinary Time.

5. Ancient Homily on Holy Saturday, PG, 43, 439, 451.462–463, as given in the Liturgy of the Hours, Office of Readings for Holy Saturday.

Contents

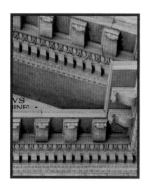

Foreword

After the exodus from Egypt, as Israel sojourned in the desert, God gave Moses "the pattern of the tabernacle and of all its furniture" (Exodus 25:9). And so Moses commanded the construction of this portable sanctuary of God's presence among his chosen people. Centuries later, in Jerusalem, God gave David "the plan of the vestibule of the temple, and of its houses, its treasuries, its upper rooms, and its inner chambers, and of the room for the mercy seat" (1 Chronicles 28:11). To the son of David, King Solomon, God also gave the right to call his temple "the house of the Lord" and "the house of God" (1 Chronicles 28:20–21).

The early Christians saw both the tabernacle and the temple as biblical "types" foreshadowing the Christian Church. They were earthly sanctuaries that would find their fulfillment in the worship of heaven and earth that we find detailed in the New Testament books of Hebrews and Revelation (see Hebrews 8–10 and Revelation 11:19). The Church at worship included what Catholics traditionally call the Church Militant, the Church Triumphant, and the Church Suffering—the great cloud of witnesses—the communion of the Church on earth, in heaven, and in purgatory.

But most of this was invisible to the eye. It was made known, however, through the preaching of the Church fathers, especially those we know as "mystagogues": Ambrose, Cyril of Jerusalem, John Chrysostom, Augustine, Denis the Areopagite, and Maximus the Confessor.

Mystagogy is guidance in the "mysteries," in things hidden since the foundation of the world. The mystagogue guided his congregation, especially the new converts, through the external, material appearances to grasp the unseen reality that is interior, spiritual, hidden, and divine. Thus he could demonstrate that the liturgical and sacramental signs have been foreshadowed in both the Old and New Testaments. He could trace their development from shadow (in the Old) to image (in the New) to reality (in heaven).

Ancient mystagogy was intensely concerned not only with rite and gesture, but with architecture as well. What the tabernacle had been to the Israelites, what the temple had been to the Jews, the church was now for the Christians. The *Apostolic Constitutions* (fourth century) includes a lovely symbolic interpretation of the church building as a ship sailing heavenward. It instructs the bishop thus:

> When you call an assembly of the Church as one that is the commander of a great ship, appoint the assemblies to be made with all possible skill, charging the deacons as mariners to prepare places for the brethren as for passengers, with all due care and decency. And first, let the building be long, with its head to the east, with its vestries on both sides at the east end, and so it will be like a ship. In the middle let the bishop's throne be placed, and on each side of him let the presbytery sit down; and let the deacons stand near at hand, in close and small girt garments, for they are like the mariners and managers of the ship: with regard to these, let the laity sit on the other side, with all quietness and good order.[1]

The redactors obviously believed they could trace the pedigree of such ideas back to the apostles themselves.

But somehow these ideas got lost in the shuffle of the ages—so utterly lost that, in our own age, the popes have issued urgent calls for their recovery. In his apostolic exhortation *Sacramentum Caritatis* (SCar.), Pope Benedict XVI pleads for a "mystagogical catechesis . . . concerned with presenting the meaning of the signs." He continues: "This is particularly important in a highly technological age like our own, which risks losing the ability to appreciate signs and symbols. More than simply conveying information, a mystagogical catechesis should be capable of making the faithful more sensitive to the language of signs" (SCar., 64). Elsewhere in the same letter, he—like his "apostolic" forebears—emphasizes that mystagogy must include the elements of iconography and architecture:

> The profound connection between beauty and the liturgy should make us attentive to every work of art placed at the service of the celebration. Certainly an important element of sacred art is church architecture, which should highlight the unity of the furnishings of the sanctuary. Here it is important to remember that the purpose of sacred architecture is to offer the Church a fitting space for the celebration of the mysteries." (SCar., 41)

I believe that this book by Denis McNamara is the kind of mystagogy Pope Benedict called for. I believe it is the kind of mystagogy the ancient Church fathers would wish for their own churches. Dr. McNamara knows that to contemplate sacred space is not merely to trace influences in an evolutionary diagram back to Vitruvius. To understand a church requires more than a genealogy of tourist postcards. It requires an interior life. It requires a hope of heaven. It requires a revelation. It calls for mystagogy. All of this is evident in the pages of this book.

Dr. McNamara has given us something we desperately need, something rare and great: at once an achievement of scholarship, a work of mystagogy, and an act of piety.

—Scott Hahn

Professor of Theology and Scripture
Franciscan University of Steubenville
Founder and Director, Saint Paul
Center for Biblical Theology

---

1. *Apostolic Constitutions*, 2.57.

Preface

Editor Note: Although you will find this to be a very accessible text, the languages of theology and architecture are very precise and sometimes require a finely nuanced understanding. As an aid to the reader, we have added a small glossary of terms to the text. Items that appear in **bold** will be defined on the bottom of the page where they appear.

Many writings have been released on Catholic liturgical art and architecture in recent years, most notably the revised *General Instruction of the Roman Missal* (2002) and the architectural guidelines given by the United States Conference of Catholics Bishops called *Built of Living Stones* (2000). The value of these official guidelines is inestimable, since they provide normative rules given by the Church. However, these works by nature provide only the minimum for proper building, relying on the living faith of the Church and culture to work out the details of elaboration in every place and time. Since the fields of art, architecture, and theology put the flesh on the bones of the rules, so the health and knowledge of

these professions makes a great impact on the experience of church building. Architects need theological guidance, and clients need to know how to guide their architects. So a small cottage industry has emerged in recent years, producing new books, conferences, and journals on liturgical art and architecture.

But the Church is at an important crossroads in its history. The Second Vatican Council was followed by a period of heady optimism, carried on the winds of a culture eager to break open the riches of the Sacred Liturgy with new love and zeal. But the years after the Council were difficult for the culture into which it was received. The brittle shell of many values and forms was challenged, and society and the Church had not yet formulated new responses to the philosophical demands of Modernity. So for several decades, we have been trying out many things, some genuine and rooted in the Council, others well-intentioned but ultimately a dead end. This process almost always takes forty or fifty years to find its

feet, continuing the rhythm established in the Old Testament of going to the desert and returning from it.

At times the power of culture and hope was so strong that revolution occurred instead of reform. But revolutions never come from thin air. They arise from pent-up frustration, lack of flexibility, and the separation of form from that which gives it meaning. I recall as a child being taught the lyrics to a song in music class that went like this: *"I wish I knew how it would feel to be free, / I wish I could break all these chains holding me. . . ."* These ideas appear to be part of a real, genuine generational experience,

but these were not sentiments that ever meant something to me as I was singing them in middle school in 1982. The chains were already broken by then; all was free and floating where it may. The greater problem was *clarity*. For every 60-year-old who speaks of his or her experience of the Church in childhood as legalistic, rooted in guilt, fear, and inflexibility, there is a 35-year-old who will say that he learned little or nothing of the Faith growing up despite attending Catholic schools or CCD, that her church didn't look like a church, that his priest was at odds with the teaching of the Church, that a large percentage of her peers have left the Church, that his primary thought of a nun is a habitless political radical, and that she discovered her mother's old Baltimore Catechism and pre-conciliar missal and new worlds of clarity and Truth seemed to open up. Add to that the sure, clear teaching of Pope John Paul II, a careful reading of the actual texts of the Council, and the Holy Spirit, and the recipe for faith coming to life was written. So we are at a critical turning point in the history of Vatican II. For anyone born after 1960, Vatican II is not an event, it is a *text*. And for people who read the text, the operative "spirit" of the Council can seem quite far from the text which supposedly inspired it.

This generational process has marked liturgical architecture as well. We are somewhat beyond the period of "anything goes," as the dreamy enthusiasm of the 1960s and 1970s

has turned into the confusion and sometimes bitterness of the 1980s and 1990s. At times, it has even turned into a Romantic escapism, which would retreat to a perceived pre-conciliar golden age because the wounds of ugliness, dissidence, and irreverence were simply still too fresh and too painful. These are not political questions; they are pastoral and theological. We cannot write off souls who try to live in their best understanding of the "spirit" of the Council, nor can we write off those who reject what they believe to be its "poisonous" fruits. The real challenge today is to find a way to help the Church have a serene acceptance of Vatican II. This requires knowing the Council's texts and understanding how to read them. In other words, we need to find out the deep meaning behind the externals and let that meaning become the driving force for our decisions as we live them out in the spiritual order.

This book tries to get at the deep meanings of liturgical art and architecture, and by association, the Sacred Liturgy itself. It is meant to help pastors, architects, artists, members of building committees, seminarians, and anyone interested in liturgical art and architecture come to grips with the many competing themes at work today. The goal then is to drink deeply from the wells of the tradition, to look with fresh eyes at things thought to be outdated or meaningless, and to glean the principles that underlie the richness of the Catholic faith. This work is not intended as a rule book rooted in law and fear, but an idea book rooted in revelation and love. It will not chronicle ecclesiastical legislation; it will help that legislation connect to its deep roots in history and allow for possibilities of future growth in an organic manner. The God who called himself "I AM WHO I AM" wants us to know who he is so we can return to him, and liturgical art and architecture are part of this process. Since Beauty is the splendor of the Truth, we cannot have beautiful churches until we have come to some resolution on the Truth.

The title of this book, *Catholic Church Architecture and the Spirit of the Liturgy*, finds its immediate inspiration in Cardinal Joseph Ratzinger's 2000 book *The Spirit of the Liturgy*, as well as Romano Guardini's book of the same name from the time of World War I. Both of these books address the deep meaning of the liturgy and the nature of Christian liturgical time. Taking his cues from scripture and the Church fathers, Ratzinger speaks of our current age as the "between-time," a period between the "shadowy" typologies that prefigured Christ in the Old Testament, and the time of "reality" when God is all in all and the world has been completely transformed and fully **divinized**. This between time is the time of "image," an "already-but-not-yet" period in which we have real, genuine access to the things of heaven, but *in the mode of sacrament*. The heavenly realities are indeed ours, medi-

ated through material things in the liturgy of the Church. This pattern of shadow-image-reality is a great meta-narrative of the Bible. The Old Testament is filled with persons and things that gave a preparation for the coming of Christ: priests, prophets, kings, and the centrality of the Temple of Solomon. The New Testament shows the shadows being made comprehensible and fulfilled in Christ, but it also tells us that the fruits of Christ's victory are still being applied as this in between time moves forward and we groan for the time when God is "all in all" (1 Corinthians 15:28). We are still "longing to be clothed with our heavenly dwelling" (2 Corinthians 5:2). Though the victory of Christ is assured, the full application of its effects remains in the future, and the book of Revelation gives us insight into these realities. This heavenly future becomes the subject of our present-day participation in "images." In liturgical time, we make present again the events of the past and anticipate the realities of the future. So the term *image* used in this context really means "sacrament," a participation in invisible spiritual realities through the medium of earthly matter.

Church architecture properly belongs in the category of "image," since a church is a sacramental building that makes present to us the realities of heaven and earth at the end of time. In the time of shadow, the Temple of Solomon gave us a look at this future glory. For this reason, a close look at God's

instructions for building the temple teaches us how to understand its fulfillment in church architecture. In the time of reality, the celebrations of heaven will be purely communion and feast without need of material mediation. But now, as beings who perceive through the senses, we humans require the image. The church building, with its liturgical art, tells us in a way that nothing else can, what heaven looks like, who is there, and what the nature of redeemed creation might be like. In short, it gives us a "foretaste" of the realities by way of image. For this reason, the documents of Vatican II could direct that sacred art be "signs and symbols of heavenly realities" (*Sacrosanctum Concilium* [SC], 122). This is the task of all sacramental things, the liturgical arts not excepted. A church building is meant to be an image of heaven in order to fulfill and express its own nature.

---

divinized: to be made like God through his generous and unmerited sharing of his divine life and being with humanity, also known as *theosis*.

The time of the image might also be called the "Age of the Church," the period between the founding of the Church at Pentecost and the point at the end of things when God is all in all. But that latter time has not yet appeared, so the Age of the Church is now "during which Christ manifests, makes present, and communicates his work of salvation through the liturgy of his Church." "In this age of the Church," the *Catechism of the Catholic Church* (CCC) writes, "Christ now lives and acts in and with his Church. . . . He acts through the sacraments. . ." (CCC, 1076). Liturgical art and architecture participate in their own way in this revelation, both by disposing the mind toward the things of God and by using the material "stuff" of the earth to become, by way of analogy, "sacraments" in their own right. Architectural principles in the Age of the Church, then, are not subject to whim, but rather to the same ideas that govern other heavenly realities.

Many people deserve thanks for their help and support in this endeavor. First, I thank His Eminence Francis Cardinal George, OMI, Archbishop of Chicago and founder of the Liturgical Institute, for providing a place for the study and teaching of liturgy in the heart of the Church and with the enriching font of sacramental theology. I thank the faculty, students, and staff of the Liturgical Institute and Mundelein Seminary for their input and support: Father Douglas Martis; Father Robert Barron; Father Thomas Baima; Mrs. Lynne Boughton; Father Edward Oakes, SJ; Father Robert Schoenstene; Mrs. Barbara Nield; and Father John Muir. Much gratitude is offered also to the editor of Hillenbrand Books, Mr. Kevin Thornton, whose enthusiastic support aided in every aspect of writing, as to other professionals at Liturgy Training Publications: Mr. John Thomas, Ms. Anna Manhart, Ms. Carol Mycio, Mr.

Mark Hollopeter, Mr. Jim Mellody-Pizzato, Ms. Kari Nicholls, and Ms. Deanna Keefe. Thanks also to Mr. Duncan Stroik; Mr. Thomas Gordon Smith; Father John Allen; Dr. Scott Hahn; Father Samuel Weber, OSB; Lt. Eric Dean Hutter, USN; Mr. and Mrs. Andy and Sarah Swafford; Dr. Edward Macierowski; Mr. James McCrery; Mr. Michael Franck; Mr. Art Lohsen; Mr. David Meleca; Mr. Leonard Porter; Mrs. Helen Hull Hitchcock; Mr. Patrick Archbold; Ms. Daria Lucas, who was always available for consultation; Dr. John Clabeaux; Father Walter Wagner, OP, and the friars of the Priory of St. Gertrude in Madeira, Ohio; Monsignor William McCumber of the Office of Sacred Worship of the Archdiocese of St. Louis; and the many students of the Liturgical Institute and Mundelein Seminary for their helpful contributions in ideas, concepts, and translations. In particular, I thank Mr. Christopher Carstens of the Diocese of LaCrosse; Father Thomas Petri, OP; and Mr. Catesby Leigh for their close reading and careful critique of the book's manuscript, and for the advice of Dr. David Fagerberg and Father Steve Grunow. Gratitude also to Mr. and Mrs. John and Darcy Powers for their generosity of spirit in helping this project come to fruition. Thanks to my sister, Mrs. Teresa Archbold, for her careful proofreading, and to Mr. Matthew Fish for his provocative theological intellect, as well as to my parents, Denis and Frances McNamara, whose support made my education possible. Many thanks go to those who pledged prayers for this endeavor, including Sister Rosemary and Sister Jane Dominic of the Dominican Sisters of St. Cecilia, Sister Finola Quinn, Mr. Ben Beier, Mr. and Mrs. David and Edi Denton, Prof. James Pauley, Dr. Larry Mueller, and Father Pius Pietrzyk, OP. I also thank Father Dennis Lyle and the Mundelein Seminary Pilgrimage program for allowing me to visit and study the Temple in the Holy Land. I also owe a great debt to the intellectual groundwork laid down by the provocative intellects of Dr. C. W. Westfall of the University of Notre Dame and the late George Hersey of Yale University, whose books have helped make architecture come to life with meaning once again. And finally, I thank the Lord, who in his kindness, reveals the Father to us in the Spirit.

A special note of gratitude goes to Monsignor M. Francis Mannion, founder of the Society for Catholic Liturgy and founding director of the Liturgical Institute at the University of Saint Mary of the Lake. His personal and intellectual generosity introduced me to the world of the Sacred Liturgy and sacramental theology, setting my intellectual life on a course filled with insights and blessings. With admiration for his important contribution to the Church, I dedicate this book to him.

Mundelein, Illinois

·FIG·Ⓐ·TRADITIONAL·GOTHIC·STONE·

·FIG·Ⓑ·CONTEMPORARY·ANGULAR·CONCRETE·

Ⓐ

Ⓑ

·FIG·Ⓒ·CONTEMPORARY·ANGULAR·BRICK·

·FIG·Ⓓ·CONTEMPORARY·CIRCULAR·BRICK·

·ECCLESIASTICAL·CHARACTER·

Introduction

The time of image is the time in which we live, a time when we come to know God through sacramental forms which present earthly images of heavenly reality. It is in the Church, founded at Pentecost with the descent of the Holy Spirit, that God communicates himself to us. Every revelation of God is clear, whole, and ordered. In a word, it is Beautiful, True, and Good because God is himself Beauty, Truth, and Goodness. We know God as he reveals himself: through his Son, in the material things of this world, transformed by the Holy Spirit to become transparent of heavenly things. And we call things beautiful when they reveal to us their inner essence, their reality as understood in the mind of God, who knows no untruth and inspires people to act toward the Good. Any book about liturgical art and architecture therefore must be a book about Beauty, Truth, and Goodness because liturgical art and architecture are about a compelling revelation of God which moves us to grow in conformity to him. Since Beauty is the compelling power of Truth, its splendor and attractiveness draw us out of ourselves to approach and investigate a beautiful thing. We can then be transformed by it. So this is also a book about Goodness, where human acts are made with moral sense, which is informed by a grace-filled reason. The result of these beautiful and good acts is joy and love, and love is willing the good of the other as other, unselfishly so. And what greater good could one wish on another than eternal salvation in the warm embrace of God? So a book about liturgical art and architecture must also be about salvation. And salvation, being perfect, is indeed beautiful. And we start all over again. Amid all of this theological language are the real, tangible objects of liturgical art and architecture, which rightly belong to the spiritual order even as they affect our earthly lives.

Many words have been written about Catholic churches since the Second Vatican Council, and the word *Beauty*, when used at all, has been thrown around rather casually. Many differing theories of post–Conciliar liturgical architecture have emerged, from the most radically avant-garde to the most conservatively traditional. A genuine and good-willed concern for a perceived active participation has steered the conversation and driven the design process. After all, the Second Vatican Council declared that "full and active participation by all the people is the aim to be considered before all else" (SC, 14).

Facing page: Every church building is intended as an image of the Heavenly Jerusalem. This allows for great variety as long as ecclesiastical character is maintained. Ernest Pickering, *Architectural Design,* 1947.

But this notion of active participation has often been worldly and wooden, a hollow shell of its intended meaning. And the desperately poor results we have had in Catholic liturgical art and architecture has both caused and been caused by a lack of the proper understanding of Beauty. An *aesthetic theology* has run rampant over a truly *theological aesthetic,* which is theologian Hans Urs von Balthasar's way of saying that merely human theories have often determined the outcome of liturgical architecture, giving us shallow buildings that ultimately fail to be compelling and convincing of the Truth of the Faith. Beauty is indeed the compelling power of the Truth, yet can many of us claim that our parishes built in recent years provide a very compelling testimony to the Catholic faith? Is our recent liturgical art and architecture so attractive that we bring our out of town guests to see our new Catholic churches? Or do we still make the trek downtown to see the nineteenth-century Gothic romanticisms when we want people to see a church that "looks like a church"? I would suspect that the latter is the case. More ominously, does this lack of Beauty suggest that we have lost our sense of the Truth? In many cases, the answer is yes.

So we must rediscover the meaning of Beauty. Since the Enlightenment we have come more and more to unhinge Beauty from its actual roots, placing it out of the realm of the **object** and the intellect and into the realm of the **subjective perception**, the emotions, or in the hands of dilettante experts. Critics declare that if a thing "moves" the viewer emotionally or shocks the senses, it must be beautiful. Or perhaps we call a building beautiful if a gathering of intellectuals— agnostic if not hostile to Christianity—decides it is a perfect example of its era or the latest linguistic fad growing out of **Derrida's** theories of language or the New York architecture offices. Or have we, as in most institutions of higher learning, simply banished the word *Beauty* from the discussion altogether, considering it indefinable, unknowable, or embarrassingly **bourgeois**? For the average person, the suspicion of the word *Beauty* is in many ways understandable. Art critics repeatedly praise things that the everyday viewer thinks unimaginably arbitrary if not downright ugly. One recent book even praised elephants for painting works of "art" almost indistinguishable from those of the modern masters of the

---

object: something knowable to the senses, which serves as the focus of attention or action.

subjective perception: the understanding in the mind of the individual who experiences the object.

Jacques Derrida: (b. 1930), an Algerian-born philosopher and father of "deconstruction."

bourgeois: of or belonging to the middle class, usually used pejoratively so as to distinguish a social or intellectual elite.

Carthusian Monastery, Gaming, Austria.

Church of the Beatitudes, Tabgha, Galilee.

Sainte-Chapelle, Paris, detail. The Church calls no style her own, yet every church is intended to be a sacramental building, an image of the heavenly Jerusalem to which we journey as pilgrims: Christ-centered, radiant with divine life and filled with heavenly beings.

twentieth century.[1] Another artist recently made the press for his exhibit entitled "Ugly=Beautiful."[2]

Despite our current cultural confusion, the definition of *Beauty* is quite simple. But accepting it changes many things. Beauty is nothing less than the revelation of the **ontological** reality of a thing, the expression in material form of the inner-

most heart of the very identity of its being. It is the manifestation of the "what-ness" of a thing, the dog-ness of a dog, the car-ness of a car, the divinity of the divine liturgy, and most importantly, the full expression of love in the Crucifixion, where God so loved the world that he gave his only Son unto death, even death on a cross. Nothing could reveal God's love for humanity more clearly and fully, and therefore more beautifully. So a great artist is not great because she has a blue period or because he develops a new style or causes a run on brie and merlot in Greenwich Village. A great artist is a great artist because his or her work somehow penetrates the very essence of reality and is capable of manifesting this flash of understanding in a tangible, earthly thing. It reveals this flash to others and attracts them to the very reality of God which the artist somehow saw and portrayed.

---

ontological: from *ontology*, the systematic study of being itself.

Chapel of the Most Blessed Sacrament, Marytown, Libertyville, Illinois.

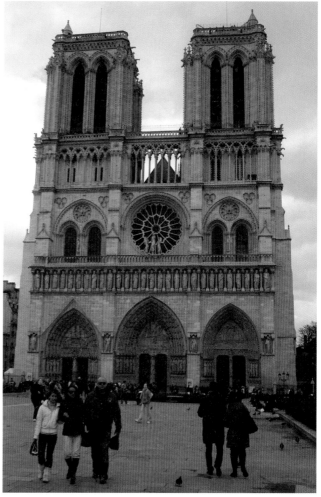

Notre Dame de Paris. Paris, France.

In this light, a rethinking of Catholic liturgical art and architecture is in order. And the only way to develop it properly is to understand it in terms of the very theological realities that it manifests. It must therefore be rooted in sacramental theology, because a church building is first and foremost a sacramental thing, more than a "simple gathering place," as the *Catechism of the Catholic Church* rightly states (CCC, 1180). A beautiful church is the very image of heaven itself made known in material form. *Architecture is the built form of ideas, and church architecture is the built form of theology.* Just as there is right belief and right practice, so there is right building.

But right building is not limited in the worldly sense to one style or another, to modern or traditional, liberal or conservative. In fact, it shatters the supremacy of these terms and finds the middle road. Right building, like all things relating to the transcendentals, has the potential for an infinite variety of beautiful manifestations, provided, of course, that it is indeed manifesting ontological reality in a given situation. For this reason, the Fathers of the Second Vatican Council rightly declared that the Church calls no one style her own, but that the genius of different ages was welcome, *provided that* these styles bring "due honor and reverence to the rites" (SC, 123). If they fail to bring due honor, they are not welcome in church building. The Church has many so-called styles of architecture from early Christian to Gothic Revival, and many have proven suitable for Christian use.

However, it is a fallacy to see the history of styles as a history of novelty alone. The history of ecclesiastical architecture shows us how what was Good, True, Beautiful, and liturgical was known in different times and places, and therefore how Goodness, Truth, and Beauty still exist now as they did then. But not all architecture is suitable for ecclesiastical use just because it supposedly comes from our time. To assume that the latest architectural fads, which often have their intellectual roots in an anti-religious skepticism, are simply the new "new" is to see architecture and faith in relativistic terms. A hymn dedicated to Satan would certainly be novel, but would not be appropriate for liturgical use. Novelty and Beauty are not equivalent.

It is in the very nature of good church architecture to bring due honor and reverence to the rites. If it fails in this task, it cannot make a beautiful church because it fails to manifest the very reason and nature of its existence. And so we say that "this church looks like an airplane hangar" not merely to be flip, but in acknowledgment that the theological reality of the building appears opposed to its built form. We look quizzically and wonder why we are dissatisfied, our minds uneasy. An industrial-looking church is not beautiful, just as a factory dressed up with ecclesiastically derived Gothic trimmings might be interesting for a moment, but ultimately is revealed as a whimsical falsity because its very identity is not manifested in its physical expression (a factory, a place for mechanistic production, with a relatively low status in terms of eternity). And so it is true with the reverse: a church that looks like a factory fails to reveal church-ness, and by definition is not a beautiful church. It might be a mighty fine factory, but as a church, it is not beautiful.

Yet somehow we have spent the last few decades building churches based on experimental theories growing from an inordinate trust in the secular culture and the heady optimism of the immediate post-conciliar era. At the opening of the Council, it seems, many things were up for grabs, and a new liturgical awakening was in its infancy. However, 1963 was almost half a century ago, and Pope John Paul II rightly wrote in 1988 that we were not then in the same situation faced by the Church in 1963, and new approaches were needed to avoid the phenomenon of constant liturgical reform.[3] This is all the more true today. We have an educated faithful, busy in their parish liturgies and governance, following the texts of the Mass and taking their proper parts. But on the other hand, we often face extreme reactions to pre-conciliar excesses devised as if the correctives necessary in 1970 were still necessary. Can we reasonably say that we have even begun to come close to making "an ever deeper grasp of the Liturgy of the Church, celebrated according to the current books and lived above all as a reality in the spiritual order" as John Paul II asked? Or have undoubtedly good-willed liturgy directors sought some sort of continuing reform, kept so busy by all the

Virgin and Child adored by all nations. Cathedral of St. Joseph the Workman, LaCrosse, Wisconsin, ca. 1962. Leo Cartwright, painter.

innovations that the essence of the liturgy in its full ecclesiological, cosmic, and heavenly dimensions has been neglected?

In the field of church art and architecture, the deepest dimensions of the liturgy are widely ignored, and at times, completely forgotten. A theology of liturgical art and architecture is needed, one that steers the course of liturgical design toward the very essence of what the liturgy is and what the liturgical reformers in the decades before the Second Vatican Council hoped we would better understand: through the mercy of God and in the Spirit we use sign and symbol to enter into the worship and praise of the eternal Godhead through the Lord Jesus Christ, a worship that pre-existed us and that we discover in the Church. In sacramental and ritual action, the Christian faithful thus receive the grace that sanctifies them as they gather as Christ's Mystical Body, joining with the eternal cosmic and heavenly worship of God. In this sacramental liturgy, we pass through mere rubrical concerns to participate in the very life of heaven, having the great privilege to experience it in sacramental form of "signs and symbols of heavenly realities." When this earthly liturgy best approximates the heavenly liturgy, grace best transforms us and makes us God-like in a process called divinization.

Art and architecture are critical features of this process. They are not merely neutral backdrops for gathering, nor are they opportunities for sumptuous display alone. Liturgical art and architecture should instead be considered features of the rite itself, part of the cluster of symbols used in a particular order. They form the very symbolic image of the heavenly Jerusalem, the "place" where God dwells and acts with his people. In that sense art and architecture are properly called *sacramental*. Their arrangement should be designed so as to best allow the full, conscious, active, and fruitful participation in the liturgy in its deepest dimensions: the reality of heaven itself.

Entering the heavenly Jerusalem, Notre Dame, Paris.

When liturgical art and architecture are thought of as sacramental and not just a neutral setting or museum of devotional objects, the present-day arguments about these matters from the liturgical left and right are shattered; both are either incomplete or distortions in one way or another. Christ was prefigured in the shadows of the Old Testament, revealing the Father even by veiling his glory while on earth, and now reigns in heaven. So the church-ness of a church embraces the memory of the synagogue and the temple in ancient Jerusalem and reveals the Church **(ekklesia)** gathered today in a time and place. It shows us a sacramental image of the heavenly Jerusalem to which we journey as pilgrims. This heavenly city is described in the book of Revelation in quite specific terms: Christ reigns on the throne, surrounded by an orderly arrangement of saints, angels, the Mother of God, and innumerable multitudes singing God's praises. The city itself has numerous portals, walls with the qualities of gold and gems, and everything radiates the light of God. Churches through the ages have tried in one way or another to capture this image of

heaven, filling sanctuaries with gem-like mosaics, stained glass, and figural and carved imagery in fine stone, gold, and color.

We think of churches that look like this as "churchly" because they capture the qualities of heaven itself: a radiant place filled with the presence of the Trinity and heavenly beings into which we are allowed to enter and pray, participating in the divine life of the Trinity and our destiny to praise God forever (Revelation 4:20). This is exactly the sacramental nature of a church building for which every church architect and artist should strive. Of course heaven is not so much a "place" as a state of restored relationship with God; one cannot attempt to try to replicate heaven in a literal sense because eye has not seen nor ear heard what God has prepared for us (1 Corinthians 2:9). But nonetheless, with sacramental mediation, we use the material of this world to make an image of those heavenly realities to the best of our abilities when aided by the Spirit.

Since architecture is the built form of ideas, only with proper ideas about the very ontological nature of a church building can one even begin to consider building a proper church, a church which reveals its **"ontological secret,"** the very reality of its being. Our task is to build beautiful churches because Beauty makes the Truth of Christ in the liturgy attractive, drawing people toward it, inviting them to engage in it, be transformed by it, and in turn transform the world. Our task is to build beautiful churches that engage us most actively and fully in the liturgy, allowing us to see the presence of the angels, the saints, and even the Trinity itself at an altar that is the very image of the Heavenly Banqueting table. We build beautiful churches to glorify God and grow toward salvation. No other artistic task rises to this level of importance.

---

ekklesia: Greek word now used as "church" to indicate the Mystical Body of the Church's members and distinguished from other meanings of the word *church* such as a church building.

ontological secret: a term used by twentieth-century Thomist Jacques Maritain to describe a thing's depth of being, normally not knowable to the senses but which flashes through in an experience of Beauty.

---

1. Vitaly Komar and Alexander Melamid, *When Elephants Paint* (New York: Harper, 2000).

2. David Foldvari, artist, exhibition entitled "UGLY=BEAUTIFUL," April 3–5, 2005, Rotovz Exhibition Space, Maribor, Slovenia. The artist stated: "Everyone always says I draw ugly people—I don't think I do. I just try to draw people as they really are. I'm not really interested in featureless model types. I'm into grimey inner cities full of grimey inner city people. It's reality as I see it." For an insightful essay on beauty in recent work, see James F. Cooper, "The Problem With Modern Art; or, Why Beauty Matters," *Modern Age* 49 (Fall 2007), 343–350.

3. John Paul II, *Vicesimus Quintus Annus, On the 25th Anniversary of the Promulgation of the Conciliar Constitution "Sacrosanctum Concilium" on the Sacred Liturgy* (1988), no. 14: "The Liturgy of the Church goes beyond the liturgical reform. We are not in the same situation as obtained in 1963: a generation of priests and of faithful which has not known the liturgical books prior to the reform now acts with responsibility in the Church and society. One cannot therefore continue to speak of a change as it was spoken of at the time of the Constitution's publication; rather, one has to speak of an ever deeper grasp of the Liturgy of the Church, celebrated according to the current books and lived above all as a reality in the spiritual order."

Part I

Architectural Theology

Every architectural choice is the result of a theological supposition about the sacramental nature of liturgical objects.

The Catholic Bishops of the United States ended their 2000 guidelines on liturgical art and architecture, *Built of Living Stones* (BLS), by warning that building a new church may cause "the fabric of the assembly to fray and even tear" (#261). As those who have served on church building committees can relate, the difficulties in building a church are many. Every good hostess warns her guests to avoid talking about sensitive subjects like politics or religion, yet the discussion of church architecture by necessity raises firmly held opinions on liturgy and ecclesiology, often with a strain of stubborn inflexibility that can cause people to withhold their dollars from the building fund or move to another parish.

But with the exception of the rare veritable curmudgeon or pure emotion-driven, anti-intellectual, arguments about altars that look like tables, pews that look like benches, or altarpieces that look "pre–Vatican II" are rarely only about the objects themselves. Debates over the location of a tabernacle or a fiberglass baptismal font are not really debates about the objects or their locations at all. These are discussions about the underlying meaning of architectural choices. Every architectural choice is the result of a theological presupposition, whether intellectualized or intuitive. Architectural arguments are really theological arguments, and proper architectural solutions grow from proper theological ideas. So the arguments among building committee members are really about belief rather than architecture. Consider the discussions that sprout today when someone proposes the return of an altar rail to a church. Charges of a so-called "pre-conciliar" mindset fly quickly. But a rail is just a rail. People generally don't despise rails when they appear on icy steps on a winter day. But the design of a church is a theological act, so the insertion or disposal of an altar rail is also a theological act. Theological disagreements occur. So it is with architectural choices. The location of a tabernacle speaks to belief about the place of the reserved Blessed Sacrament in the life of the Church. The design and materials of an altar express the sacramental theology of the person who commissions it. An altar understood as a table for a community meal will look different from one that is believed to be a sacramental image of the heavenly banqueting table of the Lamb. Similar things can be said about liturgical seating arrangements or the way images are used.

Just as words have meaning and grow from an accepted lexicon of connotations, architecture bears meaning as well. The Church holds to the principle of *lex orandi-lex credendi*, that is, the law of prayer is the law of belief. We pray as we believe and also believe as we pray. As an immediate response to an encounter with God, prayer is primary. We then try to articulate this belief in theology books, rituals, and liturgical art

Number and geometry in architectural elements. Church of the Holy Sepulcher, Jerusalem.

and architecture. But these responses to an encounter with God then become opportunities for others to encounter God. The *Catechism of the Catholic Church* (CCC) states it quite clearly: "the Church believes as she prays" because "the Church's faith precedes the faith of the believer who is invited to adhere to it" (CCC, 1126). We pray as we have been taught by the apostles and their successors, and then our prayer conveys that belief forward to the next generation. A properly

Citizens of the heavenly Jerusalem made present. Saint Patrick's Cathedral, New York City.

built church is the faith of the Church in built form, and it precedes those who come to it. For that reason among others, it must adhere to the received Tradition. It can and should be "true." Moreover, it should be compelling in its Truth in the same way convincing rhetoric moves the mind and will. This compelling power of the Truth is, again, called Beauty.

A double equilateral triangle forms the compositional underpinning revealing the double trinity of Christ's earthly and heavenly "families." Mundelein Seminary, Illinois. Francisco Zurbarán, painter.

Art and architecture are therefore never purely neutral. Theologian Edward Oakes, SJ, has said, "Art doesn't lie."[1] It may express wrong ideas, but it is never untrue to itself. Architecture is the built form of ideas, and anything built expresses the ideas its designer gave it. The world's best architects are almost always philosophers as well, and buildings look very different when they are designed by devotees of **Aristotle**, **Aquinas**, **Calvin**, **Nietzsche**, or Ratzinger, now

---

Aristotle: (384–322 BC), Greek philosopher who believed that the form existed with material, so objects as they appear are true and real and able to be understood by the mind.

Aquinas: Saint Thomas Aquinas (ca. 1224–1274), the "angelic doctor," Italian saint, and theologian who built on the Aristotelian tradition while expounding on the nature of reality as revealer of the God who made it as the first agent who produces things which are like him.

Calvin: John Calvin (1509–1564): prominent theologian of the Protestant Reformation, noted for his strong arguments for the absolute sovereignty of God and distrust of the "depravity and corruption" of human nature and the fallen natural world.

Nietzsche: Friedrich Nietzsche (1844–1900): German philosopher known for his unrelenting critiques of Christianity, and who declared the "death of God," which would therefore lead to the loss of any universal norms.

Heavenly beings and the heavenly city surround the Mother and Child. Notre Dame, Paris.

Pope Benedict XVI. An architect who believes that God ordered the world, giving everything number measure and weight (Wisdom 11:20), will search through nature and revelation to design buildings that reflect that divine order. Another who believes that the only knowable thing about the world is its chaotic bondage to disorder, anxiety, and despair will design buildings that, as many deconstructionists do, put chaos into built form. Architecture is the built form of ideas; church architecture is the built form of theology. As go the ideas, so goes the architecture.

The sacramentality of architecture means that belief and design are closely intertwined. No thinking person can separate the two without violence to the integrity of the building itself. When this separation happens, which it does all too frequently, the result is an unsatisfactory church that radiates a sense that something is wrong, that the church doesn't "look like" a church. Because the theological ideas that it should express are not matched by the architecture doing the expressing, a disconnect occurs and the mind cannot rest, forced instead to resolve seemingly irreconcilable differences between the form it sees and the idea it is supposed to represent. In Classical aesthetics, this disconnect is the very definition of a lack of beauty.

So the challenge for today's pastor, committees, and church architects is first to realize that all architectural decisions are theological decisions. Then it must be understood that liturgical architecture is indeed *liturgical*, designed according to not only physical requirements of the ritual action, but to the very theology of the liturgy in all of its many dimensions. By definition, then, church architecture is intimately bound to the teaching of the Church and the traditions handed on from generation to generation. This idea is not fundamentally ideological in the current-day sense of winning arguments and scoring sectarian victories. Rather, it reaches to the very core of the mission of the Church. *There are right things to believe, and therefore right ways to pray and right ways to build.* These three ideas can never be separated. Belief finds its liturgical expression in language, both the language of the spoken word and in the language of liturgical art and architecture.

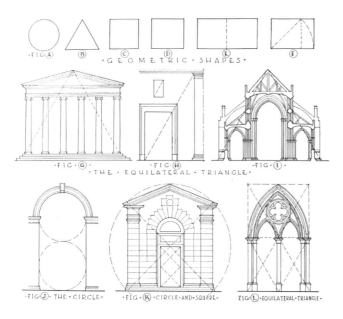

Architecture is the built form of ideas. Architects who believe that God ordered the world, giving everything number, measure, and weight, will search through nature and revelation to design buildings that reflect divine order. Those who believe the world bound to disorder and despair will attempt to put chaos into built form.

A properly built church is the Faith in built form and usually precedes those who use it. For that reason among others, it must adhere to received Tradition. Saint Thomas Episcopal Church, New York City. Cram, Goodhue, Ferguson, architects.

Four foundational statements about the nature of liturgical architecture follow. First, in thinking this way about the revelatory nature of liturgical art and architecture, the law of building is the law of belief: *lex aedificandi–lex credendi*. Second, this principle is true because church architecture can rightly be understood as the *built form of ideas*, with *church architecture the built form of theology*. Third, proper church architecture is *sacramental* in that it signifies in material form an invisible theological reality. Lastly, because there are right beliefs, there is in fact a right way of building. Orthodoxy (*ortho* = right + *doxa* = opinion, glory) leads directly to right liturgical practice, and part of this right practice is right building, which we might call *orthotectonics* (Greek: *ortho* + *technikos*, of art, skillful).[2]

The challenge for us today is to understand which of the many ways of design are fundamentally consonant with Catholic liturgical theology, and therefore Catholic architectural theology. It begs the questions: What *is* liturgical theology and therefore architectural theology? What is beauty? What does God's revelation in scripture tell us about liturgical architecture? What is the liturgical end of an altar, a pew, or a tabernacle? What can the Classical tradition teach us? What are we to make of the turbulent twentieth century?

---

1. Edward Oakes, "Icons and Kitsch" First Things 111 (March 2001): 37–43.

2. In normal language, the term *tectonics* refers to the movement or building up of geological structures as in the phrase "plate tectonics" used to describe earthquakes. Yet the word is derived from the Latin *tectonicus*, itself derived from the Greek *tektonikos*, of a builder. Both words are derived from the Greek *technē*, meaning "art, craft, skill."

Chapter 1

Lex Orandi–Lex Credendi–Lex Aedificandi: Architecture as the Built Form of Ideas

What Is Liturgical Theology?

Theologian David Fagerberg has aptly addressed the question of liturgical theology in his book *Theologia Prima: What Is Liturgical Theology?*[1] One of Fagerberg's fundamental claims is that liturgy is "a faith's grammar in motion," a "genuine theology, but one manifested and preserved in the community's *lex orandi* (law of prayer) even before it is parsed into *lex credendi* (law of belief)."[2] We believe as we pray. The parallels in church architecture are clear. If Catholics believe as they build, then architectural theology may be considered a genuine theology, faith's grammar in built form, preserved in the community's inherited architectural traditions even before any ritual use is made of it. Fagerberg argues strongly that the *lex orandi* is the fount and source of theology, because the encounter with God is primary, and then we try to articulate what that encounter means. The liturgy can indeed serve as this encounter. After seeing faith in motion, the viewer might be inclined to articulate or express what he believes. This principle can be applied to liturgical art and architecture as well. The beauty of a church building, radiant with golden angels, saints, and an altar that speaks of the banqueting table of the Wedding Feast of the Lamb, can also be "lex orandi actualized in stone," making it deeply theological.[3] Liturgical art and architecture, then, can be a source of theology which causes an expressive response. An atheist who responds to the beauty of a church building's perceptible theological content by kneeling to pray has encountered God. He might then go inquire as to the creed that the congregation holds.

Of course, the parallel between architecture and liturgy is not complete. Liturgical art and architecture are clearly subordinate to the liturgy, a component of it, linked to liturgy through the medium of the rite. Architecture is not liturgy, just as texts are not liturgy. Architecture is, however, a medium that not only serves a didactic and functional purpose, but has the high calling to be sacramental and therefore make present and active the spiritual realities of the Faith. The Eastern

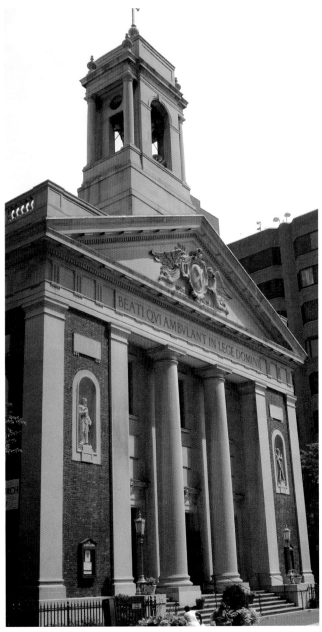

Using architecture theologically. Saint Andrew's Church, Manhattan, New York City.

Christian traditions call this its "Taboric" role, making the **eschatological** glory of heaven knowable to the senses just as the Christ manifested his glory on Mount Tabor at the Transfiguration. In order to be sacramental, architecture must be legible by first conveying its meaning on the earthly level, and then reveal heavenly realities.

Fagerberg starts his book with a chapter called "Deepening the Grammar of Liturgy," which proves useful in setting the framework for deepening the grammar of liturgical art and architecture. First, Fagerberg uses Ludwig Wittgenstein's idea that theology is a grammar, and to "know theological words" is different from "using words theologically."[4] We use words, but given the multiplicity of meanings that the same word can have, its meaning comes not only from knowing a word's definition, but also from how to use a word in Wittgenstein's "language game."[5] Many people use language properly without ever knowing a direct object from an indirect object. The function of language is primarily to convey meaning, though it is sometimes useful to analyze its structure and syntax. It is important to note that analysis of grammar is about grammar rather than about the content of a sentence. The spell checker on a word processor works in the same way whether the written document is a recipe for meringue or a call for political revolution. As Fagerberg writes, "grammar is first of all a tool for use, and second, a subject to examine."[6] Similar things can be said about ritual, and by extension, liturgical architecture.

An architecture that ignores, reverses, or expunges the context developed over history—as did much of Modernism— will have a very hard time making the language of that art and architecture clear. And so some of our churches wind up looking like ski lodges, factories, or high-end retail shops. Liturgical architecture is not *primarily* about styles and engineering, just as liturgical language is not primarily about the rules of grammar. Liturgical art and architecture are about the conveying of information about God and humanity's relationship to him in the sacred liturgy. Central to this relationship is God's sharing of his divine life with his creation, and so liturgical architecture works as the image of heavenly realities: all is glorified, all is restored, all is radiant with grace. Styles, movements, and fads in architecture are relevant only to the degree that the theological content which they express is made clear.

Fagerberg writes about the nature of liturgy and those who study it, claiming that anyone who "does" the liturgy is a liturgist; those who study it are *liturgiologists*. Participating in the liturgy can give the average person without academic theological knowledge the opportunity to experience a real

eschatological: dealing with the *eschaton*, or end times, when the final destiny of the world to be fulfilled and glorified by God is complete; when the time of image gives way to the time of reality.

Physical things like paper, ink, and the voice become the matrix through which the heavenly liturgy is manifested. Sacred art and architecture can be to the eye what public proclaiming and preaching is to the ear. Art engages us, teaches us, and forms us. Saint Meinrad Abbey, Indiana.

theology. Because we believe what we pray (and later pray as we believe), liturgy "creates a Christian grammar in the people of God who live through the encounter with the paschal mystery, and then have something to say. But what they have to say is usually about God and not about ritual!"[7] Similarly, when people feel the impulse to fall to their knees because of the prayerful beauty of a church, they usually aren't thinking of I-beams or architectural theories. The artistic encounter with the Paschal Mystery moved them to experience real theology without necessarily knowing anything about architecture as a science or an art. Here the wisdom of the commonly heard claim that "this church *looks like* a church" can and should be taken seriously.

Distinguishing between the experience of theology and the study of ritual should not be understood to diminish the importance of knowing what the liturgy is and how the ritual of the liturgy should be done. The experience of the liturgy is intricately intertwined with how it is done; compelling and beautiful liturgy depends upon knowing what the liturgy *is*. Since the ritual is the matrix for the theological action, it is indeed important. It is the medium that clarifies the meaning of the words spoken. Orthodox theologian Paul Evdokimov writes that "the liturgy initiates us into the language of the sacred" and the "world of symbols" that represent "a participation in the heavenly with the symbol's very material configuration."[8] Knowing which symbols to use and how to use them (in art and architecture as in all the liturgical arts) lies at the core of a sacramental revelation, and is an outgrowth of faith, not liturgiology. The faithful person in the pew, who, in imitation of Aidan Kavanaugh, Fagerberg calls "Mrs. Murphy," knows intuitively what liturgy is even if the complex lexicon of erudite liturgical studies is completely foreign to her. If she has already encountered God and has been formed in Godliness, she knows that she is creature and God is the creator. Therefore she expresses that relationship in her liturgical acts. She can also assess church architecture, knowing what "looks like" a church even if she can't tell Baroque from Gothic or buttresses from chancels.

As "faith's grammar in action," the liturgy "forms a believer whose life is theological," who may or may not then go on to become a liturgiologist. The liturgy is formative, shaping the lives of those who "transact" the Church's faith. The age-old goal of liturgy is to glorify God and sanctify humanity, and this latter "process of shaping lives" is what we call *asceticism*. Most of the time prayer involves quieting the passions and doing things that are for our own good even if they are sometimes difficult. Liturgy "is the place of communion with God; that asceticism is the imitation of Christ by a liturgist; and that the end of liturgical asceticism is sharing God's life. . . . "[9] While we are becoming more accustomed to thinking to liturgy as theological and formative, we

can now begin to think of liturgical art and architecture in a similar way.

Architectural Theology

If liturgical art and architecture are going to be anything more than pleasant niceties for a worshipping community, then the link between architecture and the theology of the liturgy itself needs to be reestablished. For too long, Catholics (of the Latin rite in particular) have forgotten that liturgical art and architecture are themselves *part of the rite*, not merely a neutral setting for the liturgical action. We still build churches, but more often than not, pastors, architects, and especially liturgical consultants act as architectural liturgiologists rather than architectural liturgists. Their primary concern is often architecture, into which they try to insert a theological rationale. Sometimes they begin with an earthly aesthetic and universalize it, thereby generating an aesthetic theology, rather than begin with theology and find its appropriate aesthetic expression to make a theological aesthetics.[10]

The liturgical-artistic establishment has spent decades talking about (and sometimes inventing) what Vatican II said or implied about liturgical architecture, focusing on seating plans and choosing maximum seating distances from the altar as litmus tests for church plans which supposedly conform with the Council. We've argued over Modernist architecture and "traditional" architecture. We've envisioned churches as hospitable living rooms in comfortable houses, and in reaction have re-made them as examples of a strip mall Gothic Revival-Revival because even poorly-done "traditional" was seen as better than the "empty barns" of the 1970s. We've banished tabernacles, crucifixes, and statues from the sanctuary, then brought them back. The list could go on. In a time of uncertainty in liturgical theology, uncertainty in liturgical art and architecture always follows.

These decisions all have theological consequences and presuppositions, but where is a coherent architectural theology in all of the discussion? Where is the notion that the grammar of liturgical art and architecture is fundamentally theocentric and sacramental? We have often been architectural grammarians instead of architectural theologians. At times we have abandoned our architectural-theological heritage for what amounts to art criticism rooted in the shallowest, most un-theological principles of emotional response or desire not to be "pre-conciliar." Or, on the other hand, we have sometimes replaced a shallow Modernism with a poorly understood and only slightly more theological "traditionalism" based on feelings of nostalgia and reaction. And in all of this, has the formative, ascetic role of art and architecture in the liturgy been considered at all? When a candidate for Holy Orders is ordained to the diaconate, he is admonished by the

Liturgical art can make present those aspects of the worshipping assembly otherwise invisible: angels, saints, and even the persons of the Trinity. Facing Page: University of Notre Dame, Indiana. Above: Serbian Orthodox Monastery, Third Lake, Illinois.

Bishop: "Receive the Gospel of Christ, whose herald you have become. Believe what you read. Teach what you believe and practice what you teach." Most often we have not asked our liturgical artists and architects to do the same.

We can consider liturgical art and architecture "faith's grammar in built form." And of course, architecture will always remain a constituent part of the liturgy rather than liturgy itself. But then again, singing, reading, and speaking are not liturgy, but rise to liturgical use when the content of their use is liturgical. Physical things like paper, ink, and the

voice make present the very liturgical reality they signify, becoming the matrix through which the earthly liturgy is done and the heavenly liturgy is manifested. So it is with art and architecture. They can be to the eye what public reading and preaching is to the ear. Art engages us, teaches us, and forms us, becoming the marker of the presence of heavenly realities. Humans are uniquely, exquisitely created to appreciate the visual beauty which, in the Spirit, reveals God to us and forms us to be more like him and suited to be with him

The Second Vatican Council asked that sacred art be composed of "signs and symbols of heavenly realities." Because it makes the otherwise invisible things of heaven knowable to the eye, iconic liturgical art can be "in a sense, a sacrament" (John Paul II, *Letter to Artists*). Church of the Dormition, Jerusalem.

for eternity. However, in recent decades this approach to Catholic liturgical architecture has rarely even been considered.

Monsignor M. Francis Mannion has rightly called the church a "sacramental building," a thing which acquires its sacredness not only from being inhabited by holy people putting it to good use, but also because a "church building participates in the objective sanctifying and redeeming action of God in the sacramental liturgy."[11] So the building, though not kinetic, is indeed active in that it participates in the action of the ritual. Certainly among Eastern Christian theology, a strong sense of the sacredness of the space defined by a church building has remained strong. The Holy Spirit is invited to dwell within a church and it is consecrated to God, forever changed. If the church building is really to be an "earthly heaven," as is the common phrase in the Eastern traditions, then its theological component must be both true to what we know of heaven and evident to those celebrating the liturgy in the nave.

The Second Vatican Council asked that liturgical art and architecture be composed of the "signs and symbols of heavenly realities" (*Sacrosanctum Concilium* [SC], 122). Similarly, Evdokimov writes, "The Church's liturgy is not simply a copy of the heavenly liturgy but is the eruption of the heavenly into history . . . ."[12] Of course the Incarnation was the supreme bursting of heaven into history, and it established the foundation of the sacramental view of the world, in which matter can bear the weight of heavenly sign and symbol. In our age, the Age of the Church, Christ is mediated sacramentally, and God and humans work in unity to make earthly things transparent of the heavenly. The supreme example of this principle, of course, is the Holy Eucharist, which, in anticipation of our heavenly future, is so thoroughly and completely transformed that it can be *worshipped*. But this idea, by way of analogy, can be applied to art and architecture as well. Sacramental signs make present and active the very reality they signify, and a sacramental building composed of sacramental signs does the same.

Because humans are made in the image of God, they share in God's creative power. Some of us, however, have particular gifts in the arts. In his *Letter to Artists*, Pope John Paul II wrote that artists use special *gifts* to make beautiful art and architecture, not only as a sign of God as "up there" somewhere, but also to reveal his presence on earth in space and time, making art "in a sense, a sacrament."[13] Of course, the point of art and

The church shows her heavenly origins: the dome indicates the unending movement of God, the cubic form the "shape" of heaven given in the book of Revelation, and the golden stone panels the "living stones" of the heavenly Jerusalem.

liturgy are the vehicles for its realization as it uses the natural, conventional, and sacramental signs that humans can perceive.

Our contact with God comes through the sacramental veil in the time of image, the time between Pentecost and Christ's Second Coming. We are not yet suited to see God with unveiled face (2 Corinthians 3:18), as even Christ had to take a human veil in order to be knowable to our senses. Yet the sacramental veil reveals even as it conceals; we are not left orphans. Until Christ comes again, he has sent the Holy Spirit to guide us (John 14:16), and Saint Paul reminds us that the Spirit helps us in our weakness, praying through us, interceding with the Father in sighs too deep for words (Romans 8:26). Similarly, the Spirit can help us in our artistic weakness by painting, carving, designing, and building through us. It is the duty of artists and architects to work with the Spirit to make their craft transparent of the mind of God himself. A daunting task, indeed, but the joyful duty of the artist.

architecture, like the point of all sacramental things, is to lead souls to God and their eternal salvation. So we find the calling of a liturgical artist or architect is higher than a painter of dog portraits or designer of sewage treatment plants, necessary as they might be.

It bears repeating: *Liturgical art and architecture are about salvation* because they are part of the rite of the liturgy, and liturgy is about salvation. Yet liturgy is not some pie-in-the-sky abstraction. It is done with real wine and real bread, in vessels of real metal, by humans of real flesh and blood, in buildings of real steel, brick, and stone. The *Catechism of the Catholic Church* calls liturgy a "sacramental celebration," something "woven from signs and symbols" whose "meaning is rooted in the work of creation and in human culture."[14] Though bound up with human culture, a sacramental liturgy is not merely of human origin, but follows what the *Catechism* calls the "divine **pedagogy** of salvation" (CCC, 1145). In other words, God himself ordained this method by which the grace of Christ is made available to us, and the Church and her

1. David Fagerberg, Theologia Prima: What Is Liturgical Theology? (Chicago: Hillenbrand Books, 2004).

2. Fagerberg, *Theologia Prima*, 4.

3. David Fagerberg, correspondence with the author, March 12, 2008. Like the entire concept of *lex orandi-lex credendi*, ideas move in both directions. One might build a church after encountering God somewhere else, or one might encounter God by visiting a church. What remains primary in e*ach* case is the encounter with God, with an expressive response coming second.

4. Fagerberg, *Theologia Prima*, 3.

5. For more on this topic see Ludwig Wittgenstein, *Philosophical Investigations* (New York: MacMillan, 1958).

6. Fagerberg, *Theologia Prima*, 3.

7. Fagerberg, *Theologia Prima*, 3.

8. Paul Evdokimov, *The Art of the Icon: A Theology of Beauty* (Redondo Beach, CA: Oakwood Publications, 1990), 124.

9. Fagerberg, *Theologia Prima*, 5.

10. Hans Urs von Balthasar, *Glory of the Lord*, volume 1 (San Francisco: Ignatius Press, 1985), 38.

11. M. Francis Mannion, "Toward A New Era in Liturgical Architecture," in *Masterworks of God* (Chicago: Hillenbrand Books, 2004), 145.

12. Evdokimov, *The Art of the Icon*, 120.

13. John Paul II, *Letter to Artists*, no. 8.

14. *Catechism of the Catholic Church*, no. 1145.

pedagogy: strategy or method of instruction.

Chapter 2

An Architecture of Joy: Beauty and Liturgical Art and Architecture

"Beauty enthuses us for work, and work is to raise us up," said Pope John Paul II in his 1999 *Letter to Artists*. Being "enthused" for work may not sound particularly appealing in our age of labor-saving devices, but humans still have much work to do, and the more enthused we are to do it the easier it will be. Liturgical prayer is our most important work, yet it often seems inordinately difficult, taxing, or ugly. There is a good reason that the singing of the divine office is called the *opus Dei*, the work of God. In a fallen earthly condition, humans are easily tired and distracted away from the things they should do, as echoed by the apostle Paul lamenting over his seeming inability to rally his body and will to do what was right and best for him (Romans 7:14–18).

Yet God has not left us unaided, since Beauty comes to help us get motivated. Articulated by great minds like Saint Thomas Aquinas, the Church has called Beauty the "splendor of the Truth," or at times, the *attractive power* of the Truth. Theologically speaking, Beauty is more than an accidental byproduct of artistic production or a social construct that rests in the eye of the beholder. Beauty has a *power*. For confirmation, ask a man who saw his future wife for the first time across a room and found himself inextricably drawn toward her. Ask a tourist who packs heavy luggage and carries it through difficult airport security, then with considerable language difficulty and inordinate expense stays in a hotel just to have a chance to visit the Sistine Chapel or the Mona Lisa. Ask a choir full of singers why the hours of rehearsal were worth it for twenty minutes of flawless polyphony. Ask a gardener who does all the work necessary to produce perfect roses. The power of Beauty enthused them for work; even just the uncertain hope for Beauty enthused them for this work. So it is with liturgical prayer and the art and architecture that serve it.

When Pope John Paul wrote that beauty enthuses us for work, he meant the labor of prayer. And prayer, of course, raises us up to God who then transforms us. The etymology of the word *enthuse* itself confirms this, deriving from *en*, "to

Pope John Paul II wrote that beauty enthuses us for the work of prayer, and prayer raises us up to God.

A church is an image of a glorified future, where Christ is united to his Bride, the Church. Saint Joseph Cathedral, Wheeling, West Virginia.

put into" plus *theos*, "god." So to be en-thused is to have God put into you, to be filled with the animating energy that resonates with the soul. *Beauty has the power to do this*, so conversely, *when things have the power to do this, we called them beautiful*. Beautiful liturgical architecture leads one to God by being liturgical, not only facilitating the ritual action, but by revealing the very sacramental realities of the liturgy itself. The truth of the liturgy is clarified and amplified in beautiful liturgical architecture; the building is a sacramental image of our glorified future, where Christ the Bridegroom is united to his Bride the Church. This symbolic imagery refers to God's entire mission of salvation, in which God becomes "all in all" (1 Corinthians 15:28), completely restoring his creatures through the mission of Jesus Christ.

Art and architecture provide the setting that allows the imaginative reconstruction of this heavenly future, united with otherwise invisible angels, saints, and even the Trinity itself. In this sense, liturgical art and architecture have an eschatological purpose, a revelatory purpose as sacramental things. One can therefore claim a "high" theology of art and architecture, roundly evident in Vatican II, despite much of the architecture that was built in its "spirit." *Sacrosanctum Concilium* claims that sacred art should be made up of images of a transfigured future, that is, the aforementioned "signs and symbols of heavenly realities." Signs and symbols are the very stuff of which sacramental theology is made, so Vatican II makes the strong claim that liturgical art and architecture are sacramental things, the physical expression of an invisible heavenly reality, and by implication, the built (or painted or

A beautiful statue triggers a desire to seek a saint's intercession. Mundelein Seminary, Illinois.

sculpted) form of ideas. And since beautiful things by definition conform most closely in earthly matter to a heavenly prototype understood in the mind of God, beautiful liturgy and its allied arts will always begin with a heavenly component.

So Beauty is more than a cosmetic overlay for a wealthy parish or a nostalgic conceit of a bygone day. It is essential to the mission of all sacred art and architecture because it provides an appealing and compelling way to come to know the Truth by turning "men's thoughts to God persuasively and devoutly" and being "dedicated to God and the cause of His greater honor and glory" (SC, 122). A beautiful church inclines us to kneel and pray. A beautiful statue triggers in us a desire to ask for a saint's intercession. Even a tourist of no faith whatsoever will make the effort to visit a beautiful church, and for thirty minutes is drawn of out self, intensely focused on a thing whose job it is to manifest God to humanity through the very materiality of the world. This thing—be it statue, painting, or column—reveals that a rock or tree or pigment was taken from the earth, and then through the application of will, intellect, energy, and skill was transformed under the guidance of the Holy Spirit to become more than it was. In its Beauty it becomes transparent of the Truth, and the Truth impresses itself on the mind of its perceiver. The Beauty enthuses the viewer to do something, to say something, to be something more than he or she was before encountering this object. He or she leaves changed, whether merely carrying a pleasant memory or turned on to a new course in life.

Beautiful things are therefore *formative*. They inspire us to move toward them to something we perceive as Good. And in Classical thinking, a movement of the will toward the Good is one way of describing love.[1] So beauty inspires love in the viewer. And since all earthly beauty is a partial revelation of the Beauty of God, the inspiration to love Godly things is an invitation to love God himself. Truth can do this, but Beauty makes knowing this Truth delightful.

UNDERSTANDING BEAUTY

One of the great tragedies of the intellectual discourse of recent decades is that the word *beauty* has been either exiled from modern life or so radically redefined so as to be almost lost to comprehension. The results have been obvious in our cities, churches, museums, and art galleries. A renewal of the understanding of Beauty is absolutely required if Catholics are to build appropriate churches once again. But the average parishioner is often befuddled or intimidated by museum curators or liturgical artists who present bizarre creations and tell priests and parishes that they'd better buy them if they don't want to be considered utterly bourgeois. Neither trendiness nor novelty (nor even antiquity) is the same as Beauty.[2]

Modernity and churchliness coexist. Cathedral of Christ the King, Lexington, Kentucky. Edward Schulte, architect, 1967.

The definition of *beauty* is as simple as it is profound: an object is beautiful when it most clearly and fully reveals its ontological reality, the very reality of its being as understood in the mind of God. Dogs should have all the qualities of dog-ness and not cat-ness. Cars should have car-ness and bicycles bicycle-ness. Therefore, things should look like what they are, which is the first step toward revealing what they actually are. Churches should look like churches and not factories with altars placed in them. Churches that use the industrial aesthetic promoted by the leaders of the architectural and liturgical establishments are not so much bad buildings as they are inappropriate churches.[3] Factories have a beauty proper to factories, so we can rightly call them beautiful when they express what a factory is. Churches, however, are not factories. Just as a German shepherd that looks like a Siamese cat might make a fine cat, it makes an awful German shepherd. Cats and dogs belong in different **ontological categories.** So do Catholic churches and factories. For that matter, so do Catholic churches and meeting halls, as the *Catechism of the Catholic Church* reminds us: "these visible churches are not simply gathering places . . ." (CCC, 334). A good bit of ontological confusion arose, for example, when the widely influential 1978 document published by the Bishops' Committee on the Liturgy, *Environment and Art in Catholic Worship*, characterized Catholic liturgical architecture as a "skin for liturgical action" which need not " 'look like' anything else, past or present" (EACW, 42).

In recent years, an interesting phenomenon has occurred. In newly built and renovated churches, a large grassroots movement has arisen with the singular demand that its church needs to "look like" a church. Encapsuled in this claim of the average devoted Mass-goer is the intuitive sense that a church building should express clearly its ontological reality. It should not confuse the viewers by asking them to scratch

---

ontological categories: different kinds or ways of being among things that exist which cannot be reduced to any other class.

Architecture can reveal the order and geometry of the cosmos. Los Angeles Public Library, Bertram Grosvenor Goodhue, architect, 1926.

their heads and wonder what it is, or why it doesn't look like what the sign at the driveway says it is. Their minds want rest from the intellectual work of wondering why their church looks like a factory or a Pizza Hut.® (No offense intended to Pizza Hut,® whose hut-like buildings fit their own ontological category quite nicely.) The faithful want to rest in Beauty and worship their God in a church whose artistic clarity aids in the liturgical participation that Vatican II said was to be promoted above all else. Yet, strangely enough, many of our Catholic churches have done little to nothing to aid in liturgical prayer, while some have become themselves sources of disruption and distraction—all because the ontological reality of the Catholic church building has been ignored or forgotten, with other ontological categories substituted in its place.

This phenomenon is not limited to the Catholic Church or its architects. The theological underpinnings that informed just about everything—marriage, politics, morality, and social justice to name a few—have been unhinged from their expression in society. One has to know what a thing is in its deepest sense to know how it should be made or done. And knowing what a thing is as understood in the mind of God proves no easy task. One turns to the great intellects of the Church who use scripture, tradition, and human reason to begin to tackle the theological problem germane to church

building or any other theological act. To neglect this font of wisdom is to imperil a project with an increased likelihood of banality, drabness, and even wrong-ness. Architecture is the built form of ideas, and church architecture is the built form of theology. And ideas contain either the fullness of Truth or some lesser amount. Beautiful architecture will contain more that is true about church architecture by revealing the ontological reality of church-ness in its very stones, timbers, and windows. A beautiful church brings together the past, the present, and our heavenly future as the living stones of the heavenly Jerusalem.

THE THOMISTIC VIEW OF BEAUTY

We call things beautiful when they reveal their ontological "secret," the invisible spiritual reality of their being as objects of understanding. When we know things easily and deeply because they clearly manifest what they are, we call them beautiful. This cannot be stated too often in our modern world. Because much of the profession of liturgical art and architecture has become unhinged from this simple yet profound definition, our Catholic churches have often demonstrated in recent decades an irrational mishmash of forms that have confused the faithful and lent little credibility to the Church's claims.

Notions of Beauty derived from Plato insist that Beauty is understood first as an idea in the mind, which we then see made in incomplete manifestations on earth. A more Aristotelian view claims that we come to know the full idea of a thing by experiencing many imperfect examples on earth. These top-down or bottom-up theories have their own validity, just as one can study what God is *not* as readily as what God is. A major shift, however, comes when the modern world tells us that Beauty lies in the mind of the individual and is therefore subject only to individual interpretation, removing the possibility for any norms for Beauty. This intellectual legacy is particularly devastating for liturgical art and architecture, since Beauty rises beyond worldly philosophical understandings and engages theological concepts. Claiming no norms for Beauty infers no norms for Truth or Goodness. While there are an infinite number of ways to make a beautiful church (as the history of architecture has shown), all beautiful churches have one thing in common: the theology that underpins their architecture is true. Falsity, distortion, and evil do not present the Truth of the nature of a church building, obscuring rather than clarifying its ontological reality.

Although there are many avenues to approach the question of Beauty, one of the clearest systems comes to us from Saint Thomas Aquinas in the Aristotelian tradition. Thomas never wrote a treatise on Beauty *per se*, but his various writings touch upon the topic, and subsequent authors have summarized his ideas.[4] In Thomistic thinking, Beauty is a perfection of Being. Beauty is therefore a quality that exists in every thing in some degree. Certainly a car cannot be blue if the car does not exist, nor can a church be beautiful if it has not come into existence, either on blueprints or in built form. A thing cannot have characteristics (red, watery, violent, smooth, or beautiful) unless it exists. So it can be said that beauty is *in* the object; the material being-ness of the church is the very bearer of Beauty itself. The viewer understands and turns this Beauty into a facet of the human intellect, and so a perceiver is a necessary component of the experience of the beautiful. But the reality remains that if an object is beautiful, it will be beautiful even if the viewer thinks otherwise. Beauty does not reside in the perception of the individual alone, because the viewer might be uninformed, mistaken, or might oppose beautiful things on principle. A committed Satanist may not see the Beauty in the many facets of the Christian life, yet his lack of perception or even outright rejection does not change the objective beauty of the Christian faith.

One of Saint Thomas's most famous lines reads, "*pulchra dicuntur quae visa placent*," or, "things are called beautiful upon being seen."[5] This phrase has sometimes been mistranslated into "beauty is in the eye of the beholder," suggesting a sort of relativism in which each beholder has his or her own equally valid assessment. However, the verb *visa* implies not merely physical seeing with the eyes, but carries overtones of being perceived or contemplated. Beautiful things that please us do so because we can *know* them. (Consider our fear of the unknown or our suspicion of things we do not understand.) Beauty is an object of intelligence, and the result of its perception for us is joy. We find Beauty in things we come to know and evaluate through the information given to us by the senses, and not the mere stimulation of the senses alone. So a beautiful church will reveal to us the essence of "church-ness" clearly to our intellect, and this Beauty will also necessarily be true, because it is the Truth of church-ness that the beautiful

Icon of the Virgin, detail. Library, Mundelein Seminary, Illinois.

thing conveys. A beautiful church is therefore not only a matter of emotional reaction, but also rational intellectual inquiry. We "feel" that a church is beautiful, reacting with a movement of the heart. And then with a good tour guide, we can "know" the beauty as well.

Beautiful things reveal their own specific ontological realities and do not try to disguise themselves as something else. It is important to note, however, that Beauty as a concept is not a rigid, frozen thing. A Monarch butterfly has a beauty different from a Zebra Swallowtail, yet there is only one butterfly-ness even as there are many species of butterfly and many examples of each species. So there is no one perfect church building to be photocopied and built everywhere for all time. There is only one church-ness, yet it has an unlimited variety of manifestations. A church run by Franciscan friars in Arizona might partake of the local adobe traditions of the southwest, with some reference back to Assisi, and be filled with images of saints of the Franciscan Order. A chapel for Dominican friars in New England might be made of colonial-looking brick but refer to the Gothic architecture of Dominic's birthplace in Spain and rightly contain images of Thomas Aquinas and Catherine of Siena. Each of these churches has a beauty proper to itself, revealing, respectively, Arizonan–Franciscan-ness and New England–Dominican-ness. These

Saint Thomas Aquinas on Beauty

In the tradition of Saint Thomas Aquinas, a beautiful object is understood as one that gives the viewer knowledge of the inner logic of its being. As a quality of being, beauty is therefore not separated from being itself, and is made up of three constituent elements: *integritas*, *consonantia*, and *claritas*. *Integritas*, or wholeness, means that a beautiful thing needs to have all needs to have in order to be what it is. Otherwise, it is deficient and less beautiful than it could otherwise be. *Consonantia*, or proportionality, speaks not only of the physical dimensions of a thing, but also of its correspondence to an ideal, most often to the "end" to which it is put, its purpose in being at all. *Claritas* speaks of the radiant clarity of a thing's inner being, the power of a thing to impress knowledge of itself on the mind of a perceiver.

Integritas, *claritas*, and *consonantia* prove critical in building a church, because as a theological and sacramental revelation of the new heaven and new earth, a beautiful church will provide a fullness of theological ideas by being complete not only in all of its functional parts, but also in its sacred imagery. Moreover, these parts will be proportional to their nature, showing not merely an earthly meeting hall, but an icon of a glorified reality, conventionally understood in architecture through sophistication of design, rich materials, and high levels of craft to be worthy of a church. This worthiness and glorification is made knowable to the mind of the viewer, for whom the church building impresses into his or her mind the signs and symbols of heavenly realities. This participation in the liturgy is the aim to be considered before all else specifically because by perceiving heavenly realities in earthly matter, we have the opportunity to become heavenly ourselves, and we are suited to live happily with God for eternity.

particularities of design are not simply romantic or nostalgic throwbacks to some past age. This legitimate variety clarifies the nature of each building, making the ontological reality of each church evident while still retaining all the markers of "church." Neither church, however, could tolerate a mural glorifying the devil, since this false variety presents something foreign to the nature of the Church and therefore church-ness itself. We could also say that a church is less beautiful than it should be when its tabernacle is not given an appropriate place of honor, where the altar appears like a library table, when religious statuary is distorted, unfinished, trite, or earthbound, or when the empty sea of cream-colored drywall reveals nothing of the cosmic and heavenly dimensions of the liturgy.

Jacques Maritain's famous essay "Art and Scholasticism" claims that a beautiful thing "exalts and delights the soul" and results in a joy in knowing, not because of the knowing itself, but because of *what* we are knowing; namely, the deep, ontological reality of a thing.[6] The beautiful thing delights the mind because the mind is made to know Truth and love the Good, and therefore delights in the Beauty that reveals them both most clearly. Delighting in a beautiful church satisfies this hunger of our minds, which constantly seeks the Truth of things. The heated argument about religion or politics at the Thanksgiving dinner table shows us how natural it seems for us to have our faculties of reason move in discourse and rest in understanding. So it is with beautiful things: our minds rest in the church building that "looks like" a church because it saves us from the mental labor of wondering if it is a church or something else. However, a well-designed church will not only settle the large questions quickly ("What is it?"), but will stimulate the movement of the reason toward a deeper understanding of the Christian mysteries ("What sort of important activity happens here since the building that represents it is so captivating? What would be worthy of this level of craft and material? Who is represented in that statue? What happens at that altar?").

When we experience a beautiful thing, we get a flash of the understanding that God has of that thing, just as Christ's Transfiguration on Mount Tabor gave Peter, James, and John a foretaste of his heavenly glory (Matthew 17:1–3). Because our desire for God is part of our ordered nature, Beauty pleases our souls, which long for an understanding of God. The beatific vision, the vision of the "face" of God, implies in its very wording that God's "face" is beautiful because it clearly reveals knowledge of God and fulfills in us the desire that cannot be completely satisfied on this earth. So the joy of heaven is not a malaise of white-robed harp players on clouds with nothing else to do, but an energizing relationship with an infinite God whose ability to radiate his infinite reality will hold us spellbound in joyful ecstasy for eternity. This is how a properly formed Catholic reacts, in a reduced way, to a beautiful church. The goal of every church architect should be to produce this emotional and intellectual experience in the faithful.

Integritas, Claritas, and Consonantia

Saint Thomas argued that beauty has three constituent elements, all of which are necessary. He called them *integritas*, *consonantia*, and *claritas*, or wholeness, proportionality, and radiant clarity. This triad of Latin words is well known in the circles of theology and philosophy, but it has rarely been applied to the process of present-day church design. Many people make a Thomistic critique unknowingly, saying that their new church seems to be missing something (*integritas*), or doesn't "look like" a church (*claritas*), or seems more appropriate as a meeting hall or parking garage (*consonantia*). We can look further.

Integritas refers to wholeness or completeness, the perfection of the being of a thing. Certainly a painting that is lacking paint could hardly be thought to be complete; the

same could be thought of a house with no walls or a car with no wheels. So a church without an altar would be thought to be lacking, because it is of the nature of churches to have altars, hence the old saying "the altar makes the church." But thinking in terms of sacramental theology, the church building ought to have what it needs in order to be legible as an appropriate sacrament of the glory of the heavenly Jerusalem described in the book of Revelation. So questions of material, imagery, craftsmanship, location, **intellectual content, ornament,** and **decoration** come into play as well. These same attributes of art and architecture also tell of the place of the church building within a culture, and therefore the place of the Church in society. Buildings take the status of the use to which they are put, and important-looking buildings herald important activities. So the wholeness of a building continues beyond the functional requirements of the liturgical action and includes also those architectural embellishments needed to make the building symbolic of its earthly and supernatural realities.

Consonantia similarly carries with it multiple layers of meaning. The standard definitions of the word include terms like "harmony" and "due proportion," but these only scratch the surface of its meaning. The traditional justification for a proper proportionality comes from the scripture passage that credits God with having ordered all things with number, measure, and weight (Wisdom 11:20). It should come as no

Underlying patterns of order, geometry, and mathematics reveal evidence of the mind of the creator which are then discovered and used in architectural design. Above, left: Drawing of the Ionic capital from Ernest Pickering, *Architectural Design,* 1947. Above, right: Ionic capital, Mundelein Seminary, Illinois.

surprise to any believer that God's creative intellect, which actually creates what it thinks and wills, would leave behind echoes of the divine mind in what it creates. This ordering of things is one of the hallmarks of creation, as shown in the underlying patterns of geometry and mathematics in everything from the spirals of snail shells to the double helix structure of DNA. The underlying harmonies of the universe have been discussed from Plato and Pythagoras to our own day.

The Greek term *cosmos* means "order," which is placed in opposition to the disorder of chaos. When sin entered the world, disorder entered the world as well, and humanity's relationship with God was no longer whole and no longer proportionate. Adam and Eve lacked *consonantia* because they ordered themselves to something other than God. The quest to reestablish a properly ordered relationship with God is at the heart of the salvific mission of Christ, and the church building is meant to use art and architecture to give us a foretaste of what this ordered unity with God and all of creation might be like. It is not a statement of the present "story" of the worshipping community without also being a vision of this

---

intellectual content: the capacity of architecture to encapsulate and express knowledge given by its architect.

ornament: as used here, the enrichment of a building so as to clarify use or purpose. See chapter 7.

decoration: as used here, the enrichment of a building in order to clarify structural forces at work. See chapter 6.

Beautiful things reveal their ontological reality most clearly, and therefore a beautiful church reveals its heavenly prototype. Serbian Orthodox Monastery, Third Lake, Illinois.

community's future glory in heaven with all of the other communities of the liturgy: all others on earth worshipping God, the angels, saints, souls in purgatory, and the Trinity itself.

Certainly a thing should have proper proportion within itself, so that all of its various parts fit together in a harmonious whole. The door to a house would be inappropriate and unusable were it to be only six inches high. A person's face would seem somehow wrong, even monstrous, if its eyeballs were the size of salad plates. Consider Frankenstein's monster for a moment: it has the eyes, ears, arms, and legs that humans have, but their proportions are wrong. This disproportionateness of body parts is unnerving to us. More unnerving, however, perhaps is the monster's desire to kill, evidence of a lack of an intellectually rooted moral sense. It not only lacks wholeness, it lacks the knowledge of proportional action in relation to the other beings around it.

Consonantia has deeper implication as well: a thing should also be proportionate in relation to its final end, which

is the goal that God has in mind for it. The final end of a human being is to be united with God for eternity, a tremendous dignity which requires that we be, know, and act a certain way. A church building should not only be proportionate within its own structural and functional requirements, but should also express the innate dignity of its end as a sacrament of heaven and a place for worship. History has shown us that church buildings have typically been at the top of the architectural hierarchy in order to be proportionate to their purpose as a place for the glorification of God and the sanctification of souls. Churches are therefore important, and the level of time, craft, cost, and effort should be proportional to that importance. So *consonantia* demands that church architects make a church something more than a meeting hall or the average secular building. When parishioners evaluate a low-slung church of common domestic materials and utter a phrase like "this church doesn't seem churchy," they are often intuitively referring to *consonantia*. The size, materials, theological

Beautiful things are proportional to their ends and reveal their own nature. A residential building is distinguished from a small chapel, and a chapel from an important church by size, shape, column type, materials, and location. Rome, Italy.

content, and craft often simply do not seem to be proportionate to the importance they know the building should have. Proper *consonantia* has a relative quality, however, in that what is fitting for a cathedral of an important diocese may not be fitting for a small parish church or high school chapel. Decorum, or fittingness, is therefore closely intertwined with *consonantia.*

The last of the three elements of Beauty is *claritas,* the radiant clarity of the reality of a thing, also described as the power of reality to reveal itself to the mind. *Integritas* is about completeness or perfection. *Consonantia* is about order and proportion. But an object needs something else: the power to communicate its wholeness and proportionality to us. How would we know if a thing is orderly and proportionate if it didn't have the power to make that order knowable and perceivable by the senses? (No one can tell us the proportions of the Invisible Man or Wonder Woman's invisible jet because these things lack the power to convey their reality to our eyes.) Since we have the ability to perceive earthly things, the question settles not so much on knowing of their existence, *but on the degree to which they convey the deepest sense of what they are and are meant to be.* In this way, *claritas* depends on *integritas* and *consonantia,* since a thing without all of its parts doesn't manifest its essence as well as one that has them. If the parts are disproportionate to the object itself or its ultimate purpose (as with a church that looks like something else), we tend to think the object is something other than what it actually is.

Here the statement "it doesn't look like a church" finds an explanation. A church that has the conventional[7] architectural markers of churchliness (such as a cross, tower, dome, conventional shapes, and proportions) will be more clearly readable as a church than one that lacks these things. This failure in completeness leads to an inevitable failure in *claritas.* In a similar way, if the design of a church takes on the Modernist notion that the paradigm of all architecture is the factory, and that a church is a machine for praying in, its

materials of concrete, steel, and glass will appear disproportionate to the real importance of the building. Similarly, if one thinks of a church building as a large home rather than a public building of sacramental and civic import—a common mistake of the last few decades, which continues today—its materials of carpet, wallboard, and house plants will seem to follow logically but are, in fact, disproportionate for a church. And in each case, the parishioners who pay for these buildings are told to accept something that they understand to be innately wrong because factory-ness and domesticity do not radiate clearly the essence of church-ness. The question of justice enters here as well, since justice means giving each what is due, and a church building has certain architectural features that are "due" to it. Parishioners have the right to a church that is in fact what it purports to be and therefore opens the sacramental veil of heaven and allows for their full, conscious, active, and fruitful participation in the Sacred Liturgy.

Saint Thomas tells us that when an object has two out of three of these constituent elements of Beauty, it is *pleasant.* When it has all three, it is *beautiful.* A Las Vegas casino may have the marble, paintings, mosaic, and craftsmanship we find pleasant at first blush. But understanding that these materials are disproportionately rich for the relatively low purpose of gambling and secular entertainment means it is not truly beautiful. Similarly, we might like the cozy, secular atmosphere and domestic comfort of a newer church based on the house or ski lodge. After some thought, we realize that this architecture is not proportionate to the final end of a church, which is to rise above the mere domesticity of the everyday house and be a public, ritually festive and sacramental building. One can *like* the pleasant qualities of an un-churchly church even while recognizing that it is not beautiful in the theological sense. One can *like* the concrete church or glass-and-steel cathedral built by the famous *avant garde* architect even while recognizing its complete unsuitableness as a bearer of churchliness. Understanding the theological terminology

Proper liturgical art expresses the attractive power of the Truth rather than exaggerates its historical realities.

of Beauty allows one to discuss the appropriateness of a church building outside of the usual framework of pre– and post–Vatican II polemics and saves parishes from the "I like it—well, I don't like it" stalemate of building committees. "Liking" something is fine, but the more important questions involve Truth, Goodness, and Beauty, and therefore theological inquiry.

Reading about Beauty is a bit like trying to understand the sensation of sitting in a Jacuzzi by reading a book about it. Though we understand beautiful things in the intellect, Beauty must be experienced to be understood because our minds and souls delight in it. This experience of delight is intricately connected to a real object, and therefore with the actual, tangible choices an artist or architect makes. We would never expect anyone to believe a salesperson who tried to redefine the experience of sitting in a Jacuzzi to include frigid water and leave out bubbles in his description. Yet, the art and architecture wings of the liturgical establishment often tell us that the joyless, neutral-beige churches based on an industrial or domestic aesthetic are somehow beautiful. We hear the same of distorted, broken-looking liturgical imagery.

If Beauty is the attractive power of the Truth, then a church building that fails to compel us to come in, visit, contemplate, love, and leave filled with joy has failed to do what it needs to do. It should produce the same upwelling of joy in the heart as the inspirational words that make us want to yell "Amen!" or applaud in the middle of a sermon. A sermon inspires people when its ideas are true and when its delivery expresses those ideas so clearly that the hearer understands fully and completely without effort. And the result is enthu-

siasm (God being put in you!) and joy. A church should do the same. It exalts and delights the soul. Architectural beauty is "not so much a kind of knowledge as a kind of delight,"[8] because the mind likes earthly things to be conformed to God's nature: the completeness of being of *integritas*, the ordered unity of *consonantia*, and the intelligibility of *claritas*.

Author G. B. Phelan made some telling distinctions between Truth and Beauty, which can come in handy when thinking of church art and architecture. Truth is what is "in" things so that they can be known, whereas Beauty is that quality that makes us *enjoy* knowing them. Truth implies a certain likeness to the divine prototype in the mind of God, but Beauty is the power of that likeness to *delight* and *charm*. Truth is seen, but Beauty is seen and *loved*.[9] Many pastors can relate that the money for new church projects will come more easily when the proposed project is beautiful and its theological premises are true. The reason is as simple as it is complex: Beauty produces joy in those who experience it and stirs a desire to move out of self and toward that which is Good. This movement of the will toward the Good is what Christians call love, and it is out of love that people contribute their time and money to a building project. Beauty enthuses them for work (or a donation) by "filling them with God." The correspondence of a beautiful church design with the supernatural realities of heaven tweaks our innate desire to move more quickly and joyfully on our pilgrim journey toward the heavenly Jerusalem.

A discussion of Beauty is decidedly *not* a discussion of mere personal preference, nostalgia, ecclesial politics, or, in most cases, style. Beauty is about making present the ontological reality of the church building as sacramental image of heaven knowable to the minds of those who use it. This will be done in different ways in different cultures and eras of history, but the goal always remains the same because the ontological reality of church-ness always remains the same. Some eras choose to emphasize certain aspects of church-ness over others, and so legitimate variety appears in the splendor of the Christian artistic tradition. Different cultures offer different architectural traditions in which to build, which is why the Second Vatican Council's document on the liturgy stated that "the art of our own days, coming from every race and region, shall be given free scope in the Church" (SC, 123). But, like all true inculturation experiences, the encounter of a church design with the culture that builds it requires that the Catholic theology be held up as a judge to determine if some aspects of the culture need to be purified before being suitable for use. Cultural conventions are always judged by the standard of Truth and appropriateness as known in the Church. John of the Cross reminds us that "love effects a likeness between the lover and the loved."[10] The job of the Church and the ecclesiastical artist and architect is to present things that are loveable not because they embody the latest secular fad, but because they reveal to us the realities of Christ and the redemption he offers.

Since architecture is the built form of ideas, and not all ideas are in conformity with the mission of the Church, not all architecture is suitable for use in building Catholic churches. In fact, one of the country's most famous architects publicly proclaims that his architecture is based on the premise that there either is no such thing as Truth or that Truth is essentially unknowable. Therefore, his argument goes, there can be no improvement of society or the life of people through ordered buildings and cities. So he builds buildings that look like chaotic piles of crumbled up aluminum foil. Mayors of cities clamor for museums designed by him because his buildings look trendy and give a city the appearance of being on the cutting edge of architectural sophistication. However, the premise of this architecture is incompatible with the Christian faith: at its deepest core Christianity is about restoring order to the world, undoing the disorder of sin that entered the world in the Fall, which is the very reason that Christ took human flesh in the Incarnation. To deny that grace can work in architecture to help reorder and transform the world is to deny the value of the Incarnation itself. Architecture that is built on an anti-Incarnational principle will proclaim this denial in architectural terms. It almost goes without saying that an architecture that denies the power of the Incarnation will certainly lack *integritas*, *consonantia*, and most especially *claritas*. The very role of a church building (and all human activities) is to give a foretaste of the ordered perfection of heaven. One would never tolerate a brain surgeon who denied the value of putting nerves and blood vessels in their proper order or that the archetypal model for brain surgery is the healthy brain. Yet for some reason we tolerate architects who put chaos in architectural form.

Even if the average person does not bring this level of architectural knowledge to a building, he or she may have a very strong intuitive instinct that something is indeed wrong with a church that uses a crumbled piece of brown paper or a suburban home as its inspiration rather than the vision of heaven given by God to Saint John in the book of Revelation. Theology must precede architecture, because ideas precede their taking built form. Ideas matter in preaching, writing, teaching, medicine, and also in liturgical art and architecture. And liturgical art and architecture are about, unsurprisingly, the liturgy. They concern not only the functional aspects of the liturgical rites, but they embody the very reality of the idea or essence of the liturgy itself, which exists for the glorification of God and the sanctification of humanity. Beauty makes this activity full, conscious, active, and delightful.

---

1. Saint Thomas Aquinas, *Summa Theologica*, I–II, 26, 4, c. art.

2. In his 1947 encyclical *Mediator Dei*, Pope Pius XII argued that neither unregulated novelty nor an undue respect for antiquity could substitute for liturgical appropriateness. This caution was presented "to protect the purity of divine worship against abuse from dangerous and imprudent" changes. See *Mediator Dei*, especially paragraphs 57–62.

3. Le Corbusier, *Towards a New Architecture* (New York: Dover, 1986), 1–2, "The Engineer's Aesthetic."

4. For more on Thomas Aquinas and Beauty, see Jacques Maritain, *Art and Scholasticism With Other Essays* (New York: Scribers, 1930); Umberto Eco, *The Aesthetics of Thomas Aquinas* (Cambridge: Harvard University Press, 1988); and G. B. Phelan, *Selected Essays* (Toronto: Pontifical Institute of Mediaeval Studies, 1967).

5. Thomas Aquinas, *Summa Theologica*, I, q.5, a.4, ad 1.

6. Maritain, 19.

7. The word *conventional*, as used here, is not meant to imply the common usage, meaning "boring" or "uncreative." Instead, it means that a thing is represented in a generally understood form which allows for common understanding. Examples include the conventional usage of spelling, the way stars and stripes are arranged on a flag, the shape of letters, or the color of stop lights. Because we know that green means "go" and red means "stop," we avoid auto accidents and the result is *consonantia* in traffic flow. Because we put the blue field with white stars on the upper left part of the flag, we know it belongs to the United States of America. Conventions can always be kneaded and given new expressions, as in creating a new font for the same alphabet, where we understand that the letter "A" is the same letter as "**A**," which is the same as "A," which is the same as "**A**," even as each brings a certain clarity of intent, such as solemnity or festivity.

8. Maritain, 21.

9. G. B. Phelan, *Selected Papers*, 169–170. See also Aquinas's *Summa Theologica*, I–II, 9.27, a.1, ad 3.

10. John of the Cross, *The Ascent of Mount Carmel*, chapter 4, paragraph 3, from *John of the Cross Selected Writings* (New York: Paulist Press, 1987), 65.

Part II

Scriptural Foundations

Catholic church art and architecture show the fulfillment of temple ritual and anticipate the heavenly Jerusalem. Church of the Dormition, Jerusalem.

One way to renew liturgical art and architecture is to find its deep theological underpinnings. Questions of style are really secondary, as are many recent-day juxtapositions of supposedly "pre" and "post" Vatican II approaches to liturgy and its art and architecture. The liturgy as a concept cannot be different in 1972 from what it was in 1962 because the earthly revelation of liturgy is just that: a revelation in earthly terms of a heavenly reality that precedes any human attempt to participate in it. As Pope Benedict XVI has argued for decades, the Church does not invent or own the liturgy; rather, she has nurtured and safeguarded it as a revelation. Humans wax and wane in their understanding of the reality of the liturgy and how they should best participate in it, but the sacramental reality of the liturgy itself has a definitive, essential ontological character that cannot be altered in its substance because of human whim, cultural pressure, or

Church as temple on Mt. Moriah above the waters of chaos. St. Thomas Church, Fort Thomas, Kentucky.

scholarly footnotes. What can change, however, are the externals that reveal the inner reality of worship. But these changes must always amplify and clarify the realities they reveal; they should never obscure or diminish the Truth and Beauty of the liturgy.

Here we find the great promise of the Second Vatican Council: the Sacred Liturgy was not meant to be redefined; it was meant to be better understood and lived more deeply. Full, conscious, active, and fruitful participation was intended to be more than adding a few "ministers of hospitality" to the church entrance, helpful as they are. It meant drinking more deeply at the well of grace, the divine life offered in the sacraments of the Church. At times this was aided by greater use of the vernacular, congregational singing, and simplifying the liturgical calendar. However, these changes were never the *goal* of Vatican II, they were its recommended *means* to help people draw divine life from the riches of the liturgy. Similar things can be said of liturgical art and architecture. Changes in seating and altar and tabernacle placement were never to be considered ends in themselves. They were means for aiding in the full and conscious participation in the earthly and spiritual realities of the Church's worship.

Garden imagery signals the renewed heaven and earth. St. Stanislaus Kostka Church, Chicago.

Liturgical art and architecture serve as sacramental things that reveal spiritually those realities in which a worshipper can participate either more fully or less fully, more or less consciously, and more or less fruitfully, and so an investigation of the biblically based ontology of art and architecture is in order.

Tabernacle as microcosm of the heavenly Jerusalem, showing the names of the 12 apostles and 12 tribes of Israel. University of Notre Dame, Indiana.

Two fundamental biblical concepts still inform our understanding of the church building: *synagogue* and *temple*. The synagogue is traditionally understood as a place for verbal prayer and reverent reading and discussion of Sacred Scripture. The temple, on the other hand, was a place of cultic sacrifice and encounter with the presence of God in a restricted, limited way. Much of the post–Conciliar liturgical theology and praxis suggests that Catholics are sometimes more comfortable with thinking of the church building as synagogue than temple. Therefore, a fruitful field of investigation is the temple theology operative in scripture and how it relates to today's Catholic liturgy. A Catholic understanding of the topic brings us back again to the "both/and" approach to these terms. Simply put, a Catholic church building finds its origins in both the synagogue and the temple, yet ultimately it transcends them both.

In his classic work, *Liturgy and Architecture*, Louis Bouyer argued that the synagogue almost exclusively provided the immediate architectural precedent for the church building. He gave the synagogue a high dignity, arguing that late Second Temple era Jews and early Christians understood a synagogue as more than a classroom, but a place for the prayerful hearing of scripture, where its revelations were proclaimed, discussed, and understood. It was, he argued, always associated with ritual celebration and "closely connected with the acknowledgement and the cult of a special Presence of God" and therefore connected to the Temple of Solomon.[1] Its "seat of Moses," which would eventually become the Bishop's throne, formed a natural focus of the teaching authority of rabbis who carried on the living tradition. These synagogues, Bouyer claimed, provided the obvious model for many early Christian churches. Many scholars have agreed with Bouyer, and in recent years, the notion of the temple as origin for the church building has not received much attention. The temple, after all, so closely tied to the Old Law, was a place where God's presence was exclusive and limited, involving the offering of animal sacrifices, which the author of the letter to the Hebrews explicitly would tell us was no longer necessary.

It should not be surprising that we have difficulties understanding the temple in our own day. One could argue that most Christian denominational divisions about liturgy break on how the continuing role of the temple is understood. The Old Testament, of course, says much more about the temple than the synagogue, since the latter finds its great period of growth after the destruction of the temple in the first century. But scripture does seem to set up a certain paradox between the major uses of each building: ritual animal sacrifice on the one hand, and offerings of verbal prayer on the other. Books like Exodus, Leviticus, and Kings are heavy with minute details of the bloody ritual sacrifices of the tabernacle and temple. Yet Psalm 50, Isaiah 1:11, and 1 Samuel 15:22 tell us that God has no need for bullocks and the flesh of animals. Instead, what please him are obedience and an upright heart. This tension was evident between the different groups within Judaism that opposed and promoted the temple worship, and no clear resolution is evident in the Old Testament.

However, as Cardinal Ratzinger writes in *The Spirit of the Liturgy*, the solution to this seeming contradiction is found in the person of Jesus Christ, who reconciles the differing strands of Judaism by being the *Logos incarnatus*, the Word Made Flesh.[2] In Christ, the Word and the sacrificial Victim are brought together into one, and so the Eucharistic prayer spoken at every Mass is in fact a sacrifice of praise, the praise of God by people with upright hearts offering the

Shadow, Image, and Reality

In a longstanding view of Christian history, three major periods appear in salvation history: the time of the Old Testament, the time of the Church after the Resurrection, and the fulfillment in the heavenly Jerusalem at the end of time. These epochs are poetically called *shadow*, *image*, and *reality*.

The time of *shadow* refers to the era of God's revelation in the Old Testament which prophesied in shadowy outlines the Christ who was to come. Notions of presence, kings, prophets, priests, sacrifices, victims, new life, and forgiveness prepared the chosen people in a way similar to seeing the shadow's outline of a person. The shadow gives some idea of the size and shape of the person it reveals, but only in vague indication. In liturgical architecture, the Jerusalem Temple gave the primary shadowy prototype, which, as image of the glorified Garden of Eden and heaven itself, gives today's church builders valuable information about how the church building should be understood.

Reality indicates the fullness of the heavenly glory as it will be known at the end of time when the results of the Fall are undone. The setting for this reality is the heavenly Jerusalem as described in the book of Revelation, a symbolic account of golden, radiant, gem-covered walls that surround a city populated by the angels, saints, and the great multitude of the saved, all praising God for eternity.

The term *image* indicates the sacramental, earthly participation in the fullness of the heavenly reality. This can occur with pictorial images like icons, which reveal the reality of a saint, or in church architecture, which serves as a genuine participation in the setting of the liturgy of the heavenly Jerusalem. For this reason, the Second Vatican Council teaches that participation in the earthly liturgy gives a "foretaste of the heavenly liturgy" (SC, 8), and that sacred art should be composed of "signs and symbols of heavenly realities." Participation in the realities of heaven in the Sacred Liturgy makes us conformed to heaven itself, and for this reason the Council taught that the full, conscious, fruitful, and active participation of the faithful was the aim to be considered before all else.

one sacrifice of Christ to the Father. "Here at last is right worship," Ratzinger wrote, a real sacrifice offered in spirit and truth. He then laments that modern theological discussion has made the synagogue the "exclusive model for the liturgy of the New Covenant . . . in strict opposition to the Temple which is regarded as an expression of the law and therefore as an utterly obsolete 'stage' in religion." The result, he argues, has been "disastrous," because the notions of priesthood and sacrifice "are no longer intelligible" and therefore the "comprehensive 'fulfillment' of pre–Christian salvation history and the inner unity of the two Testaments disappear from view." With true Ratzingerian clarity, he writes: "the Temple, as well as the synagogue, entered into Christianity."[3]

Ratzinger brings the various strands of Old Testament, New Testament, and eschatological thought together by using the aforementioned patristic concept of *shadow*, *image* and *reality*, a trio of words that serves as a handy interpretive guide for the large metanarrative of salvation history.[4] The term *shadow* applies to the Old Testament's preparation through typological precursors, while *reality* speaks of the time when God's restoration of his creation will be complete and all will enjoy heavenly glory.[5] By contrast, our earthly sacramental worship happens in a time of *image*, a sacramental participation in reality, which is something between the Old Testament shadow and unmediated participation in the things of heaven. In the Jerusalem Temple, God gave the chosen people the shadow of the Christ who was to come. Ours is a time of dawn. The rising sun proves to us that the darkness is vanquished, but it has not yet reached its zenith, just as creation still awaits full divinization.[6] This acknowledges that Christ's victory over sin and death is real and operative, and that the veil separating heaven and earth is torn, with grace flowing freely even as the pilgrim Church journeys toward full attainment of its goal. Today, sacramental worship gives humanity the image of a glorious heavenly future as an efficacious means of full, conscious, active, and fruitful participation in the earthly liturgy's foretaste of the reality of heaven.

The image, like the shadow, "is only mediated through the signs of salvation," Ratzinger claims, and therefore "we need mediation," because as "yet we do not see the Lord 'as he is.'"[7] So here we find the essence once again of the "already but not yet" nature of the time of image and its architectural theology.[8] Mediating signs and symbols, that is, earthly matter that reveals spiritual realities, provide the means by which "we learn to see" heaven's openness, because they are the vehicle through which we "know the mystery of God in the pierced heart of the Crucified." In other words, we participate in the heavenly liturgy, not as a shadow as in the Old Testament, nor directly as at the end of time, but in a sort of "in-between" pilgrimage in which heavenly things are mediated through the very material of this earth. Christ's "once for all" is accomplished, but the heavenly Jerusalem is still under construction as salvation history continues to unfold and become complete. "Christ is being brought to fulfillment in his Church, . . . and all of us contribute to its fulfillment, . . . which will reach completion only on judgment day."[9] Here the ministerial role of the liturgical artist and architect finds its greatest dignity: *the liturgical arts are part of the process in making God all in all by showing us what our glorified future looks like*. The temple, whose characteristics in size, proportion, and ornament are inspired in scripture by God himself, form an essential part of this understanding.

This rich layering of meanings in liturgical architecture has found rather little consideration since the Second Vatican Council, which itself grew out of the twentieth-century Liturgical Movement's desire to rebalance the relationship between Word and Eucharist, synagogue and temple, and between priest, rite, and people. However, exaggerations arose that tended to see the church as a de-sacralized synagogue, which was often called a "meeting house" or "skin for liturgical action." A faulty antiquarian mindset often led to the substitution of a domestic model of architecture for the notion of church building as evocation of the synagogue, temple, and the heavenly Jerusalem. Glory was replaced by earthiness, anticipated eschatology by a supposed "sincerity" and commonness. A crucial notion in understanding the relationship between the temple and today's church building remains: we do not imitate the temple today because the temple in itself was glorious. To do so would be like returning to animal sacrifice because it was dramatic. We look to the lessons of the temple because they gave us a foreshadowing knowledge of heavenly glory. Today's church building shows us the temple fulfilled and transfigured as image of the heavenly Jerusalem, and it is as different from the temple as the Mass is from the sacrifice of bulls. Nonetheless, understanding biblical typologies gives us an insight into the very reality we celebrate now, so unveiling the mysteries of the temple can help us recover new aspects of a theology of liturgical architecture that is deep, rich, and rooted in biblical promises.

1. Louis Bouyer, *Liturgy and Architecture* (Notre Dame, IN: University of Notre Dame Press, 1967), 8–24.

2. Cardinal Joseph Ratzinger, *Spirit of the Liturgy* (San Francisco: Ignatius Press, 2000), 47.

3. Ratzinger, 49.

4. Ratzinger, 54.

5. References to the Old Testament time of shadow can be found in Colossians 2:17, Hebrews 8:5 and 10:1.

6. Ratzinger, 54. In his *Moral Reflections on Job*, Saint Gregory the Great writes: "Since the daybreak or the dawn is changed gradually from darkness into light, the Church, which comprises the elect, is fittingly styled daybreak or dawn. While she is being led from the night of infidelity to the light of faith, she is opened gradually to the splendor of heavenly brightness. . . . The dawn intimates that the night is over; it does not proclaim the full light of day. . . . It will be fully day for the Church of the elect when she is no longer darkened by sin. It will be fully day for her when she shines with the prefect brilliance of interior light" (Lib. 29, 2–4: PL 76, 478–480), from the Liturgy of the Hours, Office of Readings, Thursday of the Ninth Week in Ordinary Time.

7. Ratzinger, 60.

8. Jean Corbon, *Wellspring of Worship* (San Francisco: Ignatius Press, 2005), 77–78.

9. Saint John Eudes, *Treatise on the Kingdom of Jesus*, pars. 3, 4: *Opera omnia*, 1, 310–312, as presented in the Liturgy of the Hours, Office of Readings, Thirty-third Week in Ordinary Time.

Chapter 3

The Time of Shadow: The Temple and Salvation

Salvation History and the Sacred Liturgy

Every liturgical act has two ends: the glorification of God and the sanctification of human beings.[1] These ends are the primary considerations in all liturgical decision making, and why Vatican II stated so strongly that "active participation" in the liturgy was the aim to be considered before *all* else. God's mission of restoring his relationship with his creation—that is, undoing the consequences of the Fall—is effected in the action of the liturgy and most especially in the Eucharist (SC, 10). Without its proper end in the sanctification of human beings through participation in this font of divine life, the liturgy loses one of its main reasons for being and becomes vulnerable for takeover by the whim of special interest groups. In the documents of Vatican II, participation is not only described as being active, but also *full, conscious*, and *fruitful*. Without knowledge of the reality of what one participates in, the participation cannot be as full, conscious, or fruitful as it should. One therefore needs to understand how the liturgy is the fulfillment of God's plan of salvation, and this requires knowledge of the Old Testament and its law, which Christ came not to abolish but to fulfill.

The glorification of God and the sanctification of his people have a history longer than last Sunday, the hundredth anniversary of a parish, the years since Vatican II, the centuries since the Council of Trent, or even the Incarnation itself. To understand the big picture of the importance of ecclesiastical art and architecture, we have to start at the beginning, or better yet, start with God who has no beginning. Before creation, the life of the Trinity was already a community of persons, but because of the overflowing of love from God who "does whatever he pleases" (Psalm 115: 3), he chose to create the world and all that inhabits it. The book of Genesis recounts the familiar story of Adam and Eve living in friendship with God, enjoying the fruits of the Garden of Eden in peace with each other. All of creation was in right order: stars,

High priest in the Temple of Solomon wearing symbolic vestments and 12 jewels representing the tribes of Israel. University of Notre Dame, Indiana.

planets, plants, animals, man and woman, oceans, land, frost, chill, sun, and rain. So the "liturgy" began at the first moment of creation, in which all created things obeyed and therefore praised God.

The Fall of our first parents, of course, changed every aspect of human existence, and ushered in a devastating new reality: though not completely corrupted, human nature became seriously wounded. At the Fall, Adam and Eve and their descendants lose the grace of original holiness and become afraid of God, and the "control of the soul's spiritual faculties over the body is shattered." Humans become subject to decay and death, and because harmony with creation is broken, it becomes hostile to humanity (CCC, 399–400). In other words, the harmony and order (*cosmos*) that God had given the world falls into chaos and disorder. Things that were beautiful become less so: lacking the completeness of holiness and perfection, they lack the wholeness of proper *integritas*. Without total ordering toward God and the cause of his glory, things lack proportional relation to each other and their proper end, and therefore lack *consonantia*. And lacking wholeness and proportionality, humanity and nature no longer convey the clarity of the order God intended for them to have, and thus lack the radiance of *claritas*.[2]

But God desired to restore the relationship between himself and his creation. So the Old Testament chronicles God's free and gracious attempts to call his people back to himself, making covenants and promises so that God might be once again all in all. God intervenes repeatedly with Abraham, Moses, and Jacob. In a high point of the salvation narrative, God gives Moses the Ten Commandments, revealing how he wants his people to live. More than the stern dictates of a tyrannical God, the Commandments were a merciful revelation, a loving disclosure of his own inner logic about how to restore Godly order to the world. A world without false gods, theft, adultery, covetousness, and false witnesses is a world that more closely resembles its original state and is therefore more like what God intends it to be. Saint Irenaeus says that the Ten Commandments "prepared man for friendship" with God and harmony with his neighbor, which "raised man to glory because it gave man friendship with God."[3]

But after teaching man how to live, God teaches him how to worship. God tells Moses to build his desert tabernacle (Exodus 25–39), and later tells David how to build the great temple in Jerusalem. In each case, God's presence with his people moves more and more toward inwardness: from things such as burning bushes to persons such as Moses; from fleeting moments in the desert to sustained presence in the temple; from simple presence of action to the joy and peace of communion.[4] Slowly but surely, the Fall becomes reversed as God leads Israel back to himself. Despite the disobedience and punishments of the chosen people, God's self-revelation continues in preparation for another high point of salvation

history: the Incarnation. At the Incarnation, a God who was distant and veiled becomes more imminent and legible, taking on human form. In Christ, God speaks in a language humans understand from a human-divine mouth to humanity's natural ears. Christ promises a glorious heavenly future where God is all in all, later revealed in apocalyptic terms to Saint John in the book of Revelation.

Christ's time on earth was remarkably short, but he did not leave humanity helpless at the Ascension. In fact, he said even greater things would happen after he returned to the Father (John 14:12). After Christ's Ascension, God sent the Holy Spirit to guide the Church at Pentecost. And thus the *Age of the Church* commenced, one in which God's presence is mediated sacramentally in image, with grace bursting into the world through the media of oil, water, bread, wine, paint, stone, glass, and gold. *This Age of the Church is the age in which we live.* It is the time of the image in which heavenly realities are available to us in sacramental form. It is the "you are here" mark on the road map of salvation (see pp. 38–39).

The Church provides the parameters for how we know Christ and how grace comes to us: humans in union with the Holy Spirit tap into their powers given by God in their *imago Dei* to create earthly things, which in their very materiality reveal God himself. As Hans Urs von Balthasar wrote, the maker of truly religious art and architecture is not the genius artist or architect alone, but "God and man in unity."[5] Thus on earth, humans can have a foretaste of heaven mediated by material things. The Eucharist reveals this **anticipated eschatology** most completely, yet all of creation has a "liturgical end" and participates in this eschatological reality to greater or lesser degree.

In the "already but not yet" nature of Christian liturgy, we are not yet fully experiencing the joys of heaven, but we get as close as we can in sacramental form, and therefore experience a foretaste of the heavenly banquet. At the appointed time, God and his creation will be completely united once again. Christ, the Bridegroom, will meet and become completely united with the Church, his Bride. Just as husband and wife become one in Marriage, so to an even greater degree will God and creation become one. This intimate union with God will be complete and unmediated, wholly communion and feast (CCC, 1136). Although the "wedding feast of the Lamb has begun" and his Bride, the Church, is prepared to welcome him (Revelation 19:1–7), this feast of complete union between Christ and his Church is known to us only under the veil of the still fallen material world. In other words, we're not there yet, even though we know there is a "there" there and can experience it as a pledge of future glory.

---

anticipated eschatology: the enjoying now on earth some limited participation in the glory of the renewed world at the end of time, often marked by the phrase "by way of foretaste."

In the meantime, in union with human intellect and will, the things of the earth find their "liturgical end"—their ultimate destiny—in the liturgy. The smell of incense and flowers undoes the stink of decay in the fallen world. The union of many voices praising God in shared liturgical words replaces the usual everyday language of slander and discord. Liturgical books outstrip in beauty and dignity the cheap paperbacks of the world. Vestments of gold and silk replace the ordinary clothes of everyday life. The song of the choir and congregation offer tonal harmonies and deep poetry in comparison to the cheap simplicity of everyday music. Images of angels and saints give us knowledge of the full membership of the Mystical Body of Christ, which praises God with us and would otherwise be unknowable to our senses. Gold and gems are used in the vessels dispensing the Body and Blood of Christ rather than ornamenting the necks and hands of secular millionaires and give us a hint of the glorious radiance of heaven. Most importantly, in the Eucharist we are fed with the heavenly food of the heavenly banquet, which nourishes our souls and fills us with grace. This pledge of future glory containing every manner of sweetness within it, this foretaste of heaven, is the greatest sacramental gift of the liturgy.

It is the job of liturgical art and architecture to be a sacramental bearer of this heavenly future as well. For liturgy to be what it is intended to be, the liturgical arts must "pull" our heavenly future back in time toward us, just as it propels us forward to our heavenly destiny by preparing and informing us what this union with God will be like. It reminds us of God's great deeds in history, yet always pushes us on to a completed, glorified future. It transforms us and prepares us to participate fully in the grace of the Eucharist. A church building is therefore a critically important thing in the life of a Christian. It is part of the sacramentally based plan that God has established to save us, part of the "divine pedagogy of salvation" (CCC, 1145), which allows us to become heavenly even as we remain on our earthly journey.

These notions were echoed by Saint Irenaeus of Lyons: "The Word of God dwelt in man and became the Son of man in order to accustom man to perceive God and to accustom God to dwell in man, according to the Father's pleasure" (CCC, 53). Liturgical art and architecture, designed under the guidance of the Holy Spirit, extend this mission to the human senses and *accustom humans to perceive God* by participating in heavenliness even before they "go" to heaven. Liturgical art and architecture are therefore not neutral, bland, mechanistic, boring, or chaotic, and they should never, ever be determined by artistic theories contrary to the nature of Christ, his Church, and its liturgy. Rather, liturgical art and architecture are properly glorified, perfected, ordered, radiant, lively, colorful, unified, polyvalent, and the built form of orthodoxy, which is the radiant glory of right belief. It is *beautiful* in the deepest sense of the word: it undoes the Fall by showing us

a world restored to wholeness (*integritas*), proper proportionality (*consonantia*), and the clarity of what God's perfection intended the world to be (*claritas*).

The **Kontakion** of the Feast of the Triumph of Orthodoxy states that Christ restored man's fallen image by "uniting it to divine beauty." It is the job of liturgical art and architecture, and therefore the liturgical artist and architect acting in Christ-like manner, to help that happen.

The Temple and the Heavenly Vision

Art and architecture feature prominently in the divine project of salvation history, not only as a human and material adjunct to some gossamer spiritual plan, but with specific architectural directions inspired by God himself. After the Fall, scripture reveals a three-part narrative. First, in the Old Testament, the temple and city of Jerusalem establish an image of God's presence with humanity, which prepared the world for the coming of Christ. Second, Christ comes at the Incarnation to form the Christian community into a temple of "living stones." This "temple" is, in the Age of the Church, made in the image of Christ's Mystical Body. Though it remains bound to the fallen world, it works with and reveals God's grace, slowly restoring the world to the fullness of what God wants it to be. Third, at the end of earthly time, the new heaven and new earth show God's complete indwelling and re-unification with creation.

As beings living in the Age of the Church, we fall into the second of these stages of salvation history. We are the inheritors of the wisdom of God's relationship with his chosen people, but we no longer require the temple as a meeting place with God. Because Christ "tore the veil" of the Holy of Holies, God's grace now flows to all. Rather than meeting God in a singular room in a singular building as in the temple of Jerusalem, the Christian community now forms "living stones" being built into a spiritual house (1 Peter 2:5) built on the foundation of Christ (1 Corinthians 3:10–11). This language marks that God has furthered his movement out of things and into people. In that sense, the actual physical church building is an image of the Christian community as Mystical Body. It has significant sign value because it "signifies and makes visible the Church living in this place, the dwelling of God with men reconciled and united in Christ" (CCC, 1180).

But having a building that signifies "the dwelling of God with men reconciled and united with Christ" refers to a heavenly future in which this process of restoration will be completed. The final state of reconciliation with God is called

---

kontakion: a type of theme-based hymn in the Orthodox and other Eastern Christian churches.

God's Plan of Salvation: Timeline of the History of the World

GOD'S PLAN OF SALVATION

TIMELINE OF HUMAN HISTORY

God Has no Beginning

Life of the Trinity is happy and overflows

Perfect community of love and praise

God Creates the Cosmos and Humanity

Adam and Eve are happy in the Garden, united with God

God is all in all and desires to glorify humanity

The Fall

Adam and Eve rupture their relationship with God when they grasp for glory without him

The history of salvation begins

God wants to be reunited with humanity, bring humans "back to the Garden" and then to glory

Old Testament Revelations

God reveals self and restores order to Adam, Jacob, Aaron, Moses

Ten Commandments: how to live

Tabernacle of Moses and Temple of Solomon: how to worship

Covenantal relationships

Incarnation

God comes to intimate union with humanity

Speaks with human-divine mouth to human ears

Addresses our senses

Involves all types of beings and nature

Christ Prepares the Church

Provides the Eucharist as means to share his Body and Blood

Provides Baptism as means for erasing original sin

Provides the sacramental means for recovering from sin

Establishes leadership in Peter

GOD'S PLAN OF SALVATION

TIMELINE OF HUMAN HISTORY

Passion, Death, and Resurrection

Christ conquers death

Christ reconciles all things to himself, and therefore to the Father

As members of the Mystical Body, we rise again with him

Ascension and Pentecost

Christ sends the Holy Spirit

The Age of the Church commences

Presence and grace come sacramentally through matter

Foretaste of heavenly realities is given

"Already but not yet"

You are here — ### Age of the Church (Time of the Image and Foretaste of Glory)

God's Mission of Salvation Is Complete

"End" of the fallen world

Second Coming

New Heaven, New Earth

Eschaton

ETERNAL HEAVENLY FUTURE

God's Plan of Salvation: Timeline of the History of the World *continued*

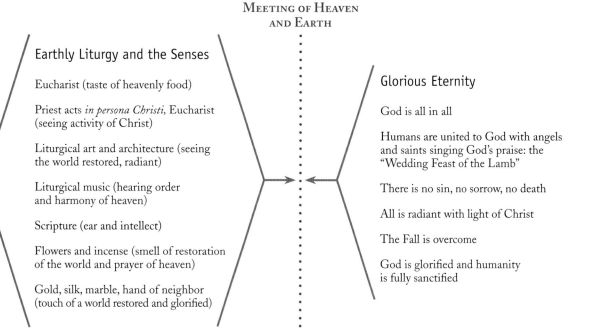

MEETING OF HEAVEN
AND EARTH

Earthly Liturgy and the Senses

Eucharist (taste of heavenly food)

Priest acts *in persona Christi,* Eucharist
(seeing activity of Christ)

Liturgical art and architecture (seeing
the world restored, radiant)

Liturgical music (hearing order
and harmony of heaven)

Scripture (ear and intellect)

Flowers and incense (smell of restoration
of the world and prayer of heaven)

Gold, silk, marble, hand of neighbor
(touch of a world restored and glorified)

Glorious Eternity

God is all in all

Humans are united to God with angels
and saints singing God's praise: the
"Wedding Feast of the Lamb"

There is no sin, no sorrow, no death

All is radiant with light of Christ

The Fall is overcome

God is glorified and humanity
is fully sanctified

a "city," the heavenly city of Jerusalem. Saint John writes: "And I saw the holy city, new Jerusalem, coming down out of heaven from God, prepared as a bride adorned for her husband; and I heard a loud voice from the throne saying, 'Behold, the dwelling of God is with men. He will dwell with them, and they will be his people, and God himself will be with them.'" (Revelation 21:2–3). This earthly church made of stones and steel, then, makes visible the dwelling of God reconciled with men, the glorious city where the decay and death resulting from the Fall are fully transfigured into the radiance of God's divine life. It becomes an *image* of the heavenly realities and therefore "is" heaven itself in sacramental terms.

And so the church we build today is indeed an important theological thing. In its sacramental reality, it does three things: recalls and fulfills the temple; tells of our current condition as earthly, fallen beings living with the grace available in the time of image; and gives a foretaste of our heavenly future. It is concurrently a place of **anamnesis,** imminent experience of God's presence, and anticipated eschatology. Like the liturgy, it contracts time by pulling the past forward and pulling the future backward, all for our sanctification now. How rich and how blessed we are to use art and architecture for such sublime purposes, and how much more it is than a meeting hall!

The abbey church of Bath, England, displays the connection of heaven and earth by showing angels ascending and descending on its towers after the vision of Jacob's ladder.

Facing page: Two reconstructions of Moses' desert camp and tabernacle, which prefigured the Temple of Solomon and the heavenly Jerusalem of the book of Revelation.

THE TEMPLE OF SOLOMON AND THE OLD TESTAMENT

After centuries of theological and historical preparation, the Jerusalem Temple in the time of Solomon became the preeminent place of contact with God and emblem of his presence. Though there had been many smaller temples in the region, under King Solomon these buildings were ordered to be destroyed, and the single Temple of Jerusalem increased greatly in importance. What was one temple among many became central and now also royal, prefiguring Christ, the new temple, as priest as well as king. Christ's body would later be revealed as the new and true temple, and this typological preparation has been read as God's method of bringing the many together as one, the scattered back to the chosen city.[6] Here the 12 tribes of Israel, divided and scattered, find the possibility of a natural focus. The process of unification, which runs through God's mission of salvation, finds its precursors in location, liturgy, government, and architecture.

In the well-known temple ritual, the Jewish high priest entered the small, cubic room at the rear of the temple's interior once a year at the feast of Atonement, bringing the blood of animals to atone for his own sins and thereby make him worthy to act as intercessor for the people of Israel. He brought the prayers of praise and petitions of the people to God, entered the Holy of Holies in clouds of incense, then returned with this blood, pouring and sprinkling it and thereby bringing God's blessing. Because it had been brought into God's presence in the Holy of Holies, it was transformed since "the presence of God is holy and confers holiness."[7] According to God's own direction, this dispensation of holiness required a building and a high priest as mediator. Later, Christians would come to understand that the high priest served as a type of Christ, the true High Priest, and the building signified the "place" of restoration of the relationship of God and humanity: the glorified Garden of Eden and heaven itself. God's restoration of humanity would not simply mean returning to the pleasantries of the garden, but to be glorified beyond even those preternatural gifts into the realm of divinization. An ancient homily used in the Easter liturgy reads: "I will not restore you to that paradise, but I will enthrone you in heaven. . . . I appointed cherubim to guard you as slaves are guarded, but now I make them worship you as God."[8]

Scripture shows us that God gave the design for the temple and the details of its worship, and his purpose in commanding the construction of the temple was to further

---

anamnesis: recalling or representing before God an event of the past so that it becomes present and operative.

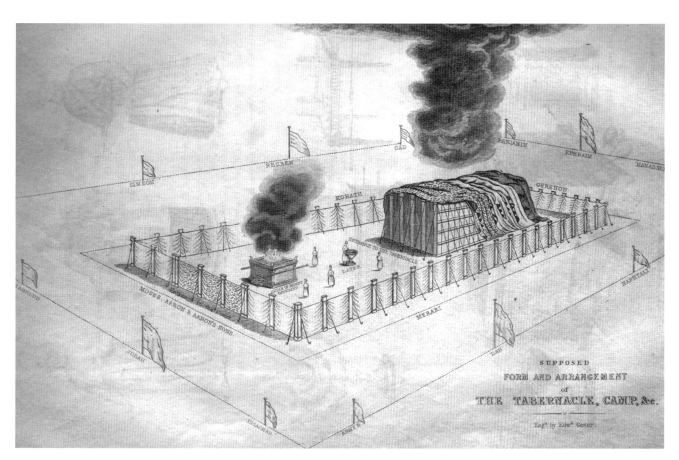

SUPPOSED
FORM AND ARRANGEMENT
of
THE TABERNACLE, CAMP, &c.

Engd by Edwd Gover

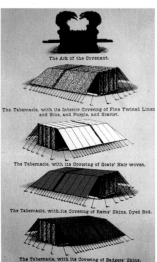

The desert Tabernacle of Moses prefigured Jerusalem's Temple of Solomon and gave a place for the *shekinah*, the glorious presence of God, to dwell.

Left: Scripture reveals that God inspired elaborate instructions for the tent-like desert tabernacle, where every choice of object and material represented the bringing of creation back to God for restoration and divinization.

Later, God tells Moses to build the tabernacle in the desert, so that God may reside among the Israelites. The tabernacle was a semipermanent tent-like structure of several segments that could be taken down and moved. Much of the book of Exodus is filled with painstaking detail as to how it should be built, according to a clear hierarchy of parts. Different materials for the tent-like fabric were specified for different sections, with special mixtures of colored wool and linen, acacia wood, gems, and clasps of bronze, silver, and gold. The three segments of the building's design were directed by God to have specific proportions, with the last two separated by an elaborately woven veil, which included images of cherubim. The most rare and most precious materials were reserved for the cube-shaped inner room called the Most Holy Place or Holy of Holies, the home of the Ark of the Covenant, atop of which God's presence settled down in the form of a cloud between statues of two angels.

God directed that the high priest wear an *ephod*, a colorful, embroidered linen vestment. Moreover, the High Priest was directed to wear a breastplate in which were set 12 gemstones (four rows of three): sard, topaz, emerald; garnet, sapphire, diamond; hyacinth, ruby, amethyst; beryl, carnelian, jasper. These stones represented the 12 tribes of Israel standing in for all of humanity, being brought to into the presence of God for transformation. These mute stones, minerals of exceptional light and color, would later be understood as prefiguring the "living stones" of the Christian era of grace in

advance his indwelling with humanity by his own gracious initiative. Theologian Yves Congar calls it an episode in the story of God's "ever more generous, ever deeper Presence among his creatures."[9] In the history of Israel, God repeatedly appears and gets involved, meeting his people where they pitch their tent. In Genesis, Jacob experiences his famous vision of the ladder or stairs with angels ascending and descending to and from the heavenly temple (Genesis 33:18–20), establishing that heaven and earth could indeed be united. God also appears in the burning bush and on Mount Sinai as fire, cloud, and thunder.

Moses as High Priest with the Tabernacle's golden table with the "Bread of Presence," incense, menorah, and the Ark of the Covenant. Chapel of the Blessed Sacrament, Marytown, Libertyville, Illinois.

which God's presence has moved from fleeting movements to constant communion. Later, heaven itself would be described in similar terms. The walls of the heavenly Jerusalem are described symbolically in Revelation as being composed of these same 12 gemstones, meaning that the city itself is composed of God's redeemed and fulfilled creation. God has filled all with his presence, his divine life, and they have come together in ordered harmony. The heavenly city described above is the completion and perfection of the temple typology.

The preparation of humanity to recognize the heavenly city began here in the time of the Exodus. The Tabernacle of Moses served as a temporary precursor for the permanent temple built by Solomon in the tenth century BC. In a poi-

gnant and instructive turn, the later construction of Solomon's temple grows from the sudden realization by his father David of a breach in architectural decorum. After building himself a house of stone and cedar (2 Samuel 5:11), King David suddenly realizes that the Ark of the Covenant where God dwelled was still housed in a tent like that of Moses. David says to the prophet Nathan: "I am living in a house of cedar, but the ark of God stays in a tent" (2 Samuel 7:1). Later, the Lord visits David and encourages him in this thinking, saying: "Are you the one to build me a house to live in? . . . I have been moving about in a tent and a tabernacle" (2 Samuel 7:5, 6). This problem of decorum occurs later in scripture with the rebuilding of the second temple under the auspices

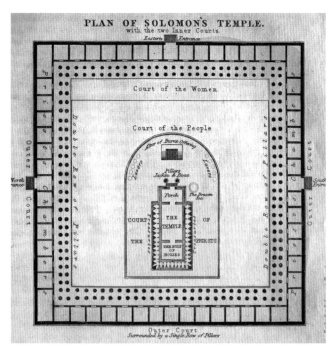

Reconstruction of the first Temple of Solomon with its court and inner rooms.

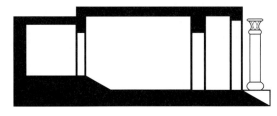

Section of the temple showing the porch, the large inner room or Holy Place, and the cubic Holy of Holies in the rear.

of the Persian King Darius. When facing resistance to the reconstruction of the temple after its destruction by the Babylonians in 586 BC, the Lord spoke through the prophet Haggai, saying: "Is it a time for you yourselves to be living in your paneled houses, while this house remains a ruin?" (Haggai 1:4). This lesson in architectural hierarchy remains potent throughout salvation history and becomes a formative notion: *the architecture in which God dwells and represents his presence on earth deserves to be a place of a higher dignity than that of the secular realm.*

Though David collected money and materials for the temple, it fell to his son Solomon to actually build it. (Solomon himself would later be seen as a type of Christ, since Christ, the "Son of David" [Luke 18:38–39], "builds" the temple of his body, the Church). In both 1 Kings and 2 Chronicles, the directions for building the temple are quite specific. The Temple of Solomon bears a formal similarity to the Tabernacle of Moses, being made up of a porch (the *ulam*); a large rectangular interior room decorated with gold, palm trees, and flowers (the *hekal* or Holy Place); and the most sacred precinct, the Holy of Holies (the *debir* or Most Holy Place), which was a golden, cube-shaped room of 20 **cubit**s on each side in which was placed the Ark of the Covenant guarded by cherubim.

The *hekal* and the *debir* prove most important for the study of contemporary church architecture because, along

---

cubit: an ancient unit of measurement based on the length of the forearm from the elbow to the tip of the middle finger, ranging from approximately 18 to 21 inches.

with Noah's Ark, they represent the earliest use of architectural typologies in Judeo–Christian salvation history and provide the theological foundation for buildings that would follow. They can also help today's architects understand that church buildings come with a revealed and developed intellectual pre-history, which can determine the theological ideas that should go into designing a new church. The temple is not simply a now-defunct building of the Old Testament, but a window into how a loving God desired—and we might even say required—a theology in built form. The temple serves as a precursor that today's Christians can reference, recall, and fulfill, just as Christ came not to abolish the law, but to redeem and fulfill it. The church building today should do in image what the temple did then in shadow: serve as a building that uses matter to communicate the realities of a heavenly future.

To see the temple as something foreign to Christianity is to do it a disservice. The temple served as a touchstone for the earliest Christians who came to understand how God would redeem them by looking at the Old Testament typologies and events of the Gospels that relate to the temple. The New Testament is full of references to the temple, and many of the activities of the earliest Church occurred in its courts. The words *temple*, *priest*, and *offering* permeate the Christological and ecclesiological language of the New Testament as well as the book of Revelation. In understanding the temple, we come to better understand the church.

The Use and Meaning of the Temple

The temple built by Solomon in the tenth century BC made a permanent building based on the plan built by Moses in the desert tabernacle. David planned it atop Mount Moriah, now more often called the Temple Mount in Jerusalem. Though much of the information about the historical setting of the temple remains obscured by the lack of modern archaeological work there, the symbolic importance of the site would not have been lost on Jewish and early Christian thinkers. Every aspect of God's intervention in the life of his people was understood as part of the divine plan to return his lost people

Model of the temple's courts rebuilt by Herod in the time of Christ. The temple proper is the taller building within a set of inner and outer courtyards. The "Golden Gate" is visible at the bottom of the outside wall, where Christ entered Jerusalem during his Passion. Israel Museum, Jerusalem.

to himself by revealing himself in symbolic form. As the early Christians would come to discover, these revelations often came in the form of **typological precursors** to Christ as the means by which God's divine life could be shared with his creation.[10]

In this light, the location of the temple in the heart of David's city is no accident. Scripture tells us that the Lord was displeased with David's plan, incited by Satan, to count the people of Israel while leaving out the tribes of Levi and Benjamin (1 Chronicles 21). David was standing by the threshing floor of Ornan the Jebusite when he suddenly saw a vision of an angel threatening to destroy the city. Because David and the elders repented, the Lord ultimately relented and destruction was averted. Averting the judgment of God would become a critical Christian motif, where Christ becomes the victim offered in humanity's place. The stone on

typological precursors: a figure or symbol of something to come, particularly things in Christian belief represented in the Old Testament.

Holy of Holies   Holy Place

The three-part division of the temple remains in the traditional church plan. The porch is fulfilled in the narthex, the Holy Place (the garden) in the nave, and the sanctuary in the Holy of Holies (heaven).

the threshing floor is said to have become the location for the construction of an altar and eventually the Holy of Holies of the temple itself. This story already tells the reader two things: God's intervention centered on averting humanity's destruction and required the presence of all of the tribes of Israel, later understood as all of humanity.

The location of the temple in the heart of David's city was already charged with meaning based on important events believed to have occurred there. It was understood as the site of Abraham's offering of his son Isaac, the place from where the waters of Noah's flood welled up, and the spot where Jacob's dream and vision of heaven took place.[11] The location of the temple was overlaid with symbolic meaning useful to Israel and later to Christianity: each was a precursor of Christ.[12] On this spot, Abraham was willing to offer his own beloved son. Jacob's dream showed the ladder by which angels traveled between heaven and earth, making the things of

The entire Church, represented by St. Peter's Basilica, is understood as a fulfillment of the temple. Cathedral of St. Joseph the Workman, LaCrosse, Wisconsin.

heaven knowable to humanity. The floodwaters of Noah represented chaos and evil, and the rock that capped them evidenced God's power to keep evil in check, as shown by the repeated mention in the psalms of the Lord as rock of salvation, controlling the waters. As such, the Lord could control the chaos of sin brought about by the Fall and initiate his plan of salvation.

The design inspired by God for the plan, fittings, and furnishings of the temple were quite specific, and author Margaret Barker reminds us that "Israel herself remembered

Garden imagery on the pulpit of the Church of the Nativity, Bethlehem.

Facing page: Garden imagery on the nave walls of St. Monica-St. George Church in Cincinnati, Ohio. Edward Schulte, architect.

that the temple in all its detail was part of the divine plan, revealed, along with the commandments, on Sinai."[13] The specific attributes of the temple were not to be changed arbitrarily. They revealed something specific about God and his plan for salvation.

It goes without saying that building the temple was a large and costly operation. It meant coordinating the movements of people and gathering materials from all around the known world. It required nearly everything that the earth and humanity could offer: stone, timber, gold, silver, bronze, copper, iron, linen, dyes, and wool. It also required human effort and cooperation: quarrying, log cutting, mining, linen making, dyeing, weaving, carving, transport, and so on. It also made necessary international cooperation: cedar from Lebanon, architects and bronze founders from Tyre, and Phoenician transport ships. In a symbolic reading, building the temple meant taking inert matter from around the earth and shaping it through the use of intellect, will, and God's revelation to join an *almost unimaginable number of individual parts into an ordered whole in which God would dwell.* Here again is the typology of the later notion of "God's building" (1 Corinthians 3:9) and the heavenly city of Jerusalem. At the heart of the Christian revelation

is the notion that many will become one, formed into the image of Christ who is the image of the Father and where he dwells. Since many nations were called upon to build the temple and all of Israel was called to worship there, the temple prefigured that time when all nations would be called back to God and divinized to be like him.

The temple was a shadowy architectural sign of a restored relationship between humanity and God, and the present-day church building is meant to be exactly that as well, though now shown in its fullness as image of heavenly realities. *Understanding the meaning of the temple instructs us how to build churches.* If we are going to build and renovate churches, we will need a justification for the time, energy, and expense that this process entails rooted in the fullest possible theological foundation beyond the argument for functional need. Today's church building, like every Catholic church building built until the trend of the neutral, functional "house church" emerged after the Second Vatican Council, was understood as a theological thing that was formative and revelatory. The Temple of Jerusalem forms part of the intellectual genealogy of this revelation.

Even in today's greatly diminished budgets and architectural practice, the analogy between the building and human community is quite clear: thousands of bricks come together to form one wall, then walls come together to form the supports for the beams, which themselves form a single roof, and so on. So in every parish many small individual voices come together to form one great voice of praise of God, and small donations of time, money, and prayer allow for the earthly Church's operation. The ordinary, everyday events of parish life such as bake sales, raffle tickets, and capital campaigns join with the pastoral care of the poor and the sick to form a foundation for the community's life. This human effort finds its source and summit in the divine worship that builds on this foundation, rising to the zenith of human activity: the worship of God and the reception of grace in the sacramental life of the Church. When well-governed and aided by the Holy Spirit, this assemblage becomes a shining beacon of Christ's presence in the world and a foretaste of the heavenly future when there will be no sickness or suffering and when all praise God together in perfect communion.

This assemblage of human parts working in union with the Spirit becomes the analogy for the Body of Christ as "God's building" in the New Testament and the heavenly city in Revelation. A well-governed city is indeed like a well-constructed building or a well-shepherded parish: all the necessary parts are present (*integritas*), in place and strong enough to do what they must (*consonantia*), and form a radiantly perfect image of the Mystical Body of Christ, united with God for eternity (*claritas*). The Temple of Solomon provided an early prototype for understanding this reality, and the city of heaven described in Revelation provides our perfect model

Garden imagery at the south porch of the medieval Abbey Church of St- Denis, Paris.

in its fully divinized completion. Architects and clients in the Age of the Church can look to the past to see God's mighty deeds and to the future to anticipate the perfect realization of his plan of salvation. In the media of art and architecture, and with the revelatory power of the Holy Spirit, we bring the past forward to our day and the heavenly future backward in anticipation. "Already but not yet" remains the order of the day.

The full history and meaning of the temple go well beyond the scope of this book; volumes have been filled, explaining the meaning of the temple ritual, architecture, and implements. Similarly, interpretations of the meaning of the temple run from the most erudite writings of biblical scholars to the most fringe theories of the Internet. But for the practical purpose of this study, most important are the symbolic interpretation of the two major rooms of the temple: the Holy Place (the *hekal*) as garden, the Holy of Holies (the *debir*) as heaven, and the veil that separated them.

The Garden

One of the great temple images is that of the garden. Quite simply, "the temple interior was a garden representing the heavenly garden on the mountain of God, the original Garden

Emblems of the apostles intersect with garden imagery. Church of Our Savior, New York City.

of Eden."[14] Genesis tells that the original garden contained the tree of life, the tree of the knowledge of good and evil, as well as other trees that were "pleasant to the sight and good for food." A river that split into four branches flowed into the garden to keep it watered. Fundamentalist arguments about the literal accuracy and symbolic language of this idyllic description are much less important at the moment than the truth that it reveals about God and creation: there once existed an original state of order, peace, fertility, and right relationship with God. When our first parents ate of the tree of the knowledge of good and evil against God's wishes, this right order was disrupted, and the Lord ordered Adam and Eve forth from the garden. He sent cherubim with a flaming sword to guard the gate to prevent their return. This sword became a potent image of the separation of man from full union with God, and Saint Gregory the Great would later write that the "sacred blood of Christ has quenched the flaming sword that barred access to the Tree of Life. The Christian people are invited to share the riches of paradise."[15] This new access to paradise occurred fully in Christ, but even in the temple the typological preparation for this reality was already at work.

The understanding of the temple as garden is not hard to fathom: the biblical description of the interior of the temple is full of vegetal forms. The scriptures tell us that the cedar within the *hekal* "had carvings of gourds and open flowers" (1 Kings 6:18) as well as "carved engravings of cherubim, palm trees, and open flowers" (1 Kings 6:29). The olive wood doors were also carved with images of cherubim, palm trees, and flowers, all overlaid with gold (1 Kings 6:32, 35).

A symbolic reading of this ornament provides the key to understanding this artistic command of God: in his desire to reunite himself with his creation, God has here invited humanity back into the garden. This time, the creature goes past the cherubim carved in the doors, recalling the same cherubim that had formerly stood at the gate of the Garden of Eden to keep Adam and Eve out and prevent their approach to the tree of life (Genesis 3:24). Now humanity, represented by the Jewish priests, walks around with the angels in the garden as a shadow of a restored earth, making things appear to be again what they once were.

The *hekal*, or Holy Place, serves as a memory of the original Garden of Eden in which God "walked" with Adam and Eve without the necessity of a temple, since the garden itself was already the place where humanity and God met. Interestingly, though, the garden here is not painted with earth tones, but is overlaid with gold, suggesting something higher and better than the original garden, a divinized paradise of heaven. The temple's *hekal* is a splendid recall, but nonetheless only a "shadowy" preparation for the time when the restoration brought about in Christ would be real and effective. That time is now in the Age of the Church. The

The notion of the church building as restored eschatological garden joined with the heavenly Jerusalem unlocks much traditional ecclesiastical symbolism. Angels and saints stand amid golden stone, gem-like mosaic and stained glass. Vegetal forms are not simply reproduced as they exist in nature, but are given an overlay of geometric perfection. The ceiling's vaults and ribs recall a perfected canopy of trees. The nave recalls and fulfills the "garden" of the Temple of Solomon's Holy Place, while the sanctuary fulfills the Holy of Holies. Saint Patrick's Cathedral, New York City.

large room of the temple, the Holy Place, finds its fulfillment in the nave of today's church, a place of invitation back into right relationship with God. Our earthly church, as an image, finds its completion in the realities of heaven.

The Veil

In Solomon's temple, the Ark of the Covenant found a permanent home. It rested in the *debir*, or Holy of Holies, a cube-shaped room in the rear of the temple. Separating the *debir* and the *hekal* was the great veil. This extravagantly rendered tapestry literally obscured the view between the two rooms, but it was understood symbolically to represent all that separated heaven and earth. In order to enter the Holy of Holies and be in God's presence on the feast of the Atonement, the earthly high priest literally had to *pass beyond the veil*, giving us to this day the allegorical phrase used to describe a person leaving this world at death. As Margaret Barker has written, the

> *hekal* represented the earth and the *debir* the heavens; between them was the veil which separated the holy place from the most holy (Exodus 26:33). The veil represented the boundary between the visible world and the invisible, between time and eternity. Actions performed within the veil were not of this world but were part of the heavenly liturgy. Those who passed through the veil were the mediators, divine and human, who functioned in both worlds bringing the prayers and penitence of the people to God and the blessing and presence of God to his people.[16]

Composed of wool and linen, the veil was woven from blue, purple, and crimson threads in a description quite similar to those given to Moses for his desert tabernacle (2 Chronicles 3:14, Exodus 26:31–33). Presumably, like at the Tabernacle of Moses, the veil also had images of the cherubim woven into it, again suggesting those angelic guards of the garden.

The veil was immense, estimated to have been composed of 200 square meters of wool and linen. Because it was sprinkled with blood, it needed to be washed frequently, and it was reported that 300 priests were needed to immerse it. The *Mishnah* tells that 82 young women were necessary to weave each of the two veils made each year.[17] The need for observant Jewish women to be constantly busy weaving new veils has given us the iconic tradition of the Virgin Mary doing weaving or embroidery when Gabriel appeared to her at the Annunciation.[18] The weaving of the veil also signifies the Virgin's role as *Theotokos*, the God-bearer who "wove" the presence of God in her own womb. Like the actual veil in the temple, the Christ woven in her body both revealed and concealed the presence of God.

The Jewish historian Josephus (37–ca. 100 AD), who lived in the time of Herod's temple, believed the veil served as a symbol of the cosmos, and as such, both revealed and concealed God's presence. The scarlet color suggested fire, he

The radiance of the heavenly Jerusalem's gems in stained glass combines with garden figures to symbolize the joining of the new heaven and new earth at the end of time.

said, and the linen represented the earth, blue the air, and purple the sea (as the red blood of fish joined to the blue of the waters).[19] Moreover, Josephus tells that the veil "had also embroidered on it all that was mystical in the heavens. . . ."[20] Elsewhere, Josephus writes that the veil of Moses' desert tabernacle, which would likely have served as a carefully respected model for the temple veil, was "made in way of imitation and representation of the universe."[21] The contemporary Greek-speaking Jewish philosopher, Philo of Alexandria (20 BC–50 AD), wrote that the veil was "woven of such and so many things as the world was made of, [being] the universal Temple which [existed] before the holy Temple."[22] Like the garden, or the Holy Place which presented a new earth, the veil symbolized that all of creation had been brought to divine worship, including the sea and the heavens. Similarly, Josephus writes that the seven-branched candlestick in the temple represented the seven known planets.[23]

Interestingly, when entering the garden-like *hekal*, the high priest wore a garment of materials similar to the veil, symbolically enrobing himself in all of creation and bringing it into the presence of God. Exodus 28 describes these priestly garments of the desert tabernacle made of blue, purple, and scarlet threads. Josephus described the robes of the priests in Moses' tabernacle as being symbolically composed of all creation as

The vestments of the high priest represented his being robed with all of creation, while the stones of his breastplate symbolized the 12 tribes of Israel, who in turn symbolized all of humanity. He prefigured Christ, the true High Priest, who would take on human nature and bring all of creation to the Father.

well. The vestment was also described as "being like lightning in its pomegranates" and with bells sewn on representing thunder. Semiprecious stones called sardonyxes were attached to the shoulders of the high priest's *ephod*, which Josephus tells us were emblematic of the sun and the moon.[24] Each of the 12 gems of the high priest's breastplate were carved with the name of one of the sons of Israel, described in Exodus as being "like a signet," and each engraved "for the twelve tribes" (Exodus 28:17–21). Josephus's commentary on the priestly garments in the Temple of Solomon reveals that they were similar to those of the tabernacle.[25] In the time of shadow, the earthly high priest obediently followed the law in this ritual, but as is evident in the letter to the Hebrews, Christians would later see Christ as the true (or better yet, "real") High Priest who took on human nature, entering the real Holy of Holies in heaven, tearing the veil and bringing heaven and earth together.

In the time of image, we see all of this as the bringing of creation back to God to be made complete once again in the process of "undoing" the Fall. The 12 stones symbolized the 12 tribes of Israel (and therefore all of humanity); the fabrics symbolized the four basic elements of the world, the

power of lightning and thunder (long associated with the majesty of God), and even the sardonyxes as the sun and the moon. Saint Clement of Alexandria, for example, wrote of the mystic meaning of the tabernacle and its furniture in the *Stromata*, echoing Josephus's explanation of the four colors of the woven threads. He called the garment of the high priest the "symbol of the world of sense," which prophesied Christ's "ministry in the flesh" in which he took on the matter of the universe in order to return it to God for transformation.[26] Bringing creation to God meant that God could therefore offer it back divinized and ordered, transformed by his presence.

Interestingly, though, the high priest removed his outer garment and wore only white linen robes into the heavenly *debir*. "In the *debir* he no longer represented the created world, but was deemed one of the heavenly entourage. The white linen garment was the dress of the angels, given to favored human beings upon their ascent to heaven."[27] Clement of Alexandria deciphers this linen garment as evidence of the high priest's purified ascent to a more heavenly state, a precursor of the "bright array of glory" of the "ineffable inheritance of that spiritual and perfect man" after becoming "son and friend" of God once again.[28] Like today's altar servers who wear white albs because they enter into the sanctuary of a church building, the high priest joined the white-robed heavenly beings by crossing the veil and entering the Holy of Holies into the presence of God. Just as the Jewish high priest brought all of creation and all of humanity to God, so today's priest, who acts as Christ, brings all of creation to the Father, wearing above his white alb the vestments of color, gold, embroidered flowers and saints, speaking on behalf of all present and the entire world. He does this by walking through the modern-day *hekal*, which we call the nave, and then enters into our sacramental image of the *debir*, the sanctuary.

The Holy of Holies

The Holy of Holies, or the *debir*, was the innermost region of the temple building, a cube-shaped room in which God chose to dwell and which made present in earthly time and space the timelessness and spacelessness of heaven. Inside the Holy of Holies of Solomon's temple was placed the Ark of the Covenant, which had been carried around with the desert tabernacle since the time of Moses. From all known descriptions, the Ark was a cedar box covered in gold in which were placed a jar with manna from the desert (Exodus 16:33), Aaron's staff which had miraculously flowered into almond blossoms (Numbers 17:8), and the tablets of the Ten Commandments. Guarding the Ark were gold-covered statues of cherubim. These objects would later be described and decoded in the letter to the Hebrews. Though Jewish traditions differ as to some of the details of the Ark and its ornamentation (one calls it God's footstool while another calls it God's throne, for example), it marked the place of God's dwelling and presence, and it gives us one of God's names: the one "enthroned between the cherubim" (Isaiah 37:16). Later called by Luther the "mercy seat," this area atop the Ark is known as the *kapporeth*, a Hebrew word with a double meaning as both a literal cover, as it was for the physical Ark, but also something that covered as in "cleanse" or "wipe out." For this reason, the *kapporeth* is sometimes called the propitiatory or place of atonement, because the presence of God is holy and wipes out the guilt of sin. In the time of shadow, the area atop the Ark was the throne of God on earth. All of this finds its completion in the reality of the *eschaton*, prefiguring the book of Revelation's description of the throne in heaven in which the One was seated and surrounded by angels (Revelation 4:2).

Much has been made of the cubic shape of the Holy of Holies through the centuries. God's directions for making the Holy of Holies in both the desert tabernacle and Solomon's temple insist that the cubic proportion of the 20 cubits be maintained. In Revelation, heaven itself would be described to Saint John as cubic in shape as well; that is, in the "shape" of God. This understanding of the cube as a heavenly shape again comes through in the writings of Josephus, who says that the area within the cubic Holy of Holies in Moses' tabernacle was "a Heaven peculiar to God."[29] Medieval theoreticians of numbers sometimes discussed the Son as the square of the Father, since as the perfect image of the Father, Christ could be understood as a multiplication of him.[30] Taking this idea further and continuing the notion with the Holy Spirit, one might see the nature of God as having similarities with the cube as a qualitative ratio. The number of persons of the Trinity total 3 when added, thereby maintaining three-ness; yet, when cubed, the number 1 ($1 \times 1 \times 1$, or 1^3) still remains as 1. Though it would take the Christian revelation to make this Trinitarian temple numerology more fully understood, the shape of heaven was clearly associated with the cube, which was itself associated with God, and this typology served for later interpretation.

In Revelation, an angel shows John an image of the Church, saying, "Come, I will show you the bride, the wife of the Lamb" (Revelation 21:9). This fully divinized Church (*ekklesia*) is then described as being in the shape of a cube and composed of the 12 gems found on the breastplate of the high priest. In symbolic language, it was described as having been fully conformed to the "shape" or image of God. Because the cube was associated with the "shape" of heaven, and the church building was an image of heaven, many churches throughout history have used the cube as their primary geometric shape. In the Eastern traditions in particular, the dome-on-cube arrangement of the church building represented the circular movement of God (who, like a circle, has no beginning and no end) meeting the cubic shape of the Bride, the Church.

The cubic shape of the heavenly Jerusalem, prefigured in the Holy of Holies of the Temple of Solomon, inspires the shape of many Eastern Christian churches. Holy Trinity Cathedral, Jerusalem.

But in ancient Jerusalem, to enter this cubic room in the temple and step into the presence of God was *to be made holy*. It was here that the high priest entered to perform the atonement rites, sprinkling blood from a slaughtered animal and then exiting the Holy of Holies to pour the blood on the altar in the *hekal*. This atonement ritual signaled God's pledge of fidelity to his covenants with his people and the spreading of his divine life from his heavenly throne to earthly reality. This bloody ritual seems so foreign to modern sensibilities, but was a typological precursor of the coming of Christ, the true High Priest. As Robert Barron has written, the earthly high priest "was acting as the mediator between divinity and humanity, a priest offering sacrifice on behalf of the people and, strangely enough, on behalf of Yahweh himself. In the process, he was making symbolically real the restoration of creation according to God's intentions."[31]

This role of earthly high priest as mediator who crosses beyond the veil into heaven, pleads for his people, and returns with the blessings and divine life of God was understood by the earliest Christians as a preparation for the coming of the true High Priest, Jesus Christ. Christ bridged the great divide between heaven and earth, tearing the veil that separated them, and allowing the sacramental flow of divine life to gush to his creation, slowly causing it to become divinized and

The carved panels of the temple's interior were carved with angels and overlaid with gold, signifying the return of humanity to a divinized Garden of Eden. Cathedral of St. Peter in Chains, Cincinnati, Ohio.

form. The author of the letter to the Hebrews understood this symbolic reality:

> When Christ came as a high priest of the good things that have come, then through the greater and perfect tent, . . . he entered once and for all into the Holy Place, not with the blood of goats and calves, but with his own blood, thus obtaining eternal redemption. . . . For Christ did not enter a sanctuary made by human hands, a mere copy of the true one, but he entered into heaven itself, now to appear in the presence on our behalf. (Hebrews 9:11–12, 24)

The temple, then, was understood as a "copy" of the heavenly sanctuary, and this reality is made present in Catholic liturgy today. The priest makes present the actions of Jesus himself by entering the sanctuary of a church building and pleading and offering the one sacrifice of Christ, which replaced the sacrifice of animals from the old temple. In a great continuity with the Old Testament, today's Catholic priest recalls the shadow of the Jewish high priest by sacramentally re-presenting the reality of Christ as heavenly intercessor. Since Christ did not come to abolish the law, but to fulfill it, the old law of the temple is not erased, but continues in a way entirely transformed by Christ for our own day. As Saint Andrew of Crete wrote, Christ came "not so much to lead us away from the letter as to lift us up to its spirit," because though he "subordinated the law" he "harmoniously united grace with it, not confusing the distinctive characteristics of the one with the other, but effecting the transition in a way most fitting for God."[32] For this reason we still sing the temple psalms at Mass and in the Liturgy of the Hours; we still worship God in his sanctuary and his holy temple. We understand it better and participate in it more fully after the Christian revelation.

In a similar way, the churches we build and the images we put in them are not an unnecessary clinging to the things of worship before Christ. Because architecture is the built form of ideas, it recalls the buildings and events of the Old Testament. However, it presents them to us today in a completely transformed manner. This is fitting for us, as beings who acquire knowledge through our senses. It is also fitting for God, who made us to be so. In the early fourth century, the bishop and historian Eusebius would make this comparison explicit by calling a bishop who built a great church the new Solomon, Zerubbabel, and Bezalel. He also called the altar in the church the "holy of holies."[33] This should remind us that Christianity and Judaism are not enemies, but remain intimately joined.

The temple and its art and architecture also remind us of what our priest is doing at every Mass: acting *in persona Christi*, making present to us again the very action of Christ, the true High Priest. When an earthly priest enters through the front door of a church, past the porch, processing in white alb and circular embroidered vestment through the nave as an

restored to full unity with its creator. When Christ came as the true High Priest, he did not enter into a mere shadowy copy of heaven as did the human high priest. He entered into the reality of heaven itself in the supreme atonement, returning with the blessings of God's presence in a more efficacious image of restored creation, he does what the high priest of the temple did. More importantly, he does what Christ did in coming to earth in the Incarnation, taking on the matter of the universe and walking again with his creation as he once did in the Garden of Eden. This gives a whole new meaning to the vegetal ornament found in churches throughout the centuries, be it the leafy capitals of columns or floral patterns in stone, paint, or stained glass.

When the earthly priest steps from the nave to the sanctuary, he enters again into our sacramental presentation of the heavenly Holy of Holies. He goes to the altar, bringing the prayers and petitions of the people to the Father as well as offerings of grain and wine. In many Orthodox and Eastern Catholic traditions, the altar is not only understood as a heavenly table, but also the throne of God, like the Ark, where his presence remains and where heaven and earth meet. The walls are enriched with images of the angels and saints of heaven. While in the temple, the Ark contained the old law of the Ten Commandments and God's fleeting presence rested atop it as the mercy seat; the fulfillment of the Old Law is found in the Eucharistic presence. This abiding presence in the reserved Blessed Sacrament links directly back to the temple without limiting God's presence to a single place or building. In the time of image, Cardinal Ratzinger wrote, our tabernacle with the reserved Blessed Sacrament serves as the new and fulfilled version of this abiding presence, where "His presence (*Shekinah*) really does now dwell among us."[34] His active presence gushes beyond the veil and out to the world in the people of his church, yet they continually return to his altar for nourishment and restoration.

Instead of bringing the blood of bulls, today's priest offers the symbolic food made of many crushed grains and many crushed grapes, transformed by natural processes and the work of human hands into a new creation of bread and wine. Here, at this divine synaxis, God's presence transforms these humble gifts, making them the heavenly food that nourishes us with his divine life. While the old high priest brought out the blood of bulls, the earthly priest brings the true Body and Blood of Christ to his people. He can do this because he acts *in persona Christi*, acting as Christ who in the true sense "passes through the heavens and enters into the presence of the Father to make him turn in mercy to the human race. . . ."[35] The human priest makes present to our earthly senses the heavenly reality of Christ as true High Priest who pleads with us to the Father.

In the time of image, the high priestly role continues but is completely transformed. Instead of being limited to one man, as in the Old Testament, all of the worshippers in the church, by virtue of their baptismal priesthood, offer themselves in union with the earthly priest. The earthly priest is the head of the earthly body as a sacramental image of the Mystical Body of Christ with its divine Head. Because we are members of the

A pair of angels adoring the reserved Blessed Sacrament shows the fulfillment of the typology of the temple's Ark of the Covenant, where God's presence rested atop the golden Ark between two cherubim. Saint Cecilia Motherhouse Chapel, Dominican Sisters, Nashville, Tennessee.

Body, we are grafted to Christ, and the Father hears us because he hears the Son. So, as a Mystical Body, hierarchically arranged and beautifully ordered, the earthly community brings its prayers to the Father through the mediation of the true High Priest, who then nourishes us with his divine life in his Body and Blood. Pope Pius XII stated it beautifully in his 1947 encyclical *Mediator Dei*:

> The priest is the same, Jesus Christ, whose sacred Person His minister represents. Now the minister, by reason of the sacerdotal consecration which he has received, is made like to the High Priest and possesses the power of performing actions in virtue of Christ's very person. Wherefore in his priestly activity he in a certain manner "lends his tongue, and gives his hand" to Christ.[36]

So the plan of salvation is furthered, and humanity and all of creation become more like what God intended them to be. The role of priestly mediation continues, but as an action of Christ made knowable to the earthly senses by the action of the earthly priest doing in a sacramental form what Christ does in heaven. In ancient Israel, the temple's high priest foreshadowed what Christ would eventually do by "doing" it in shadowy form in the Holy of Holies. In the Age of the Church, we share in the victory of Christ's actions by "doing" them in sacramental form: reliving in ritual form the very mysteries of salvation. This time, however, the victory is not a mere hope, but a reality mediated through the image, and the sharing of divine life has very real transformative effects. This transformation of the temple from building into the living stones of the *ekklesia* should be seen as a fulfillment that does not eradicate the need for buildings, priests, and ritual, but transforms them to the revelation of the New Covenant. As the noted Orthodox theologian Leonid Ouspensky has written, after the apostles were denied access to the synagogues and the temple, "they built Christian sanctuaries, and they did so in strict accord with the revealed character of the place of worship, with the very principle according to which the tabernacle and the Jerusalem temple has been built."[37] It is for elucidation of the new covenant that the old is recalled. The heavenly city is anticipated for the same reason. Throughout history, the temple, as revealed building and prefiguration of heavenly realities, is never far away from the minds of the Church's great builders.[38]

---

1. *Sacrosanctum Concilium* (SC), 10: ". . . and especially from the Eucharist, as from a fountain, grace is channeled into us; and the sanctification of men in Christ and the glorification of God. . . ."

2. For a more detailed description of *integritas*, *consonantia*, and *claritas*, see chapter 2 of this book.

3. Saint Irenaeus, *Treatise Against Heresies*, Lib. 4, 16, 2–5: SC, 100, 564–572, as presented in the Liturgy of the Hours, Office of Readings, Friday of the Second Week of Lent.

4. See Congar, *Mystery of the Temple* (Westminster, MD: Newman Press, 1962), foreword, xi.

5. Hans Urs von Balthasar, *Glory of the Lord*, vol. 1 (San Francisco: Ignatius Press, 1985), 85.

6. For more on Jesus as the new Temple, see Brant Pitre, "Jesus, the New Temple and the Priesthood," *Letter & Spirit* (4), 2008, 49–86 and also Pitre's forthcoming book *Jesus and the Last Supper: Ancient Judaism and the Origin of the Eucharist* (Grand Rapids: Eerdmans).

7. Yves M.-J. Congar, OP, *The Mystery of the Temple* (Westminster: Newman Press, English translation, 1962), 16.

8. *Ancient Homily on Holy Saturday*, Patrologia Greca (PG) 43, 439, 451.462–463, as given in the Liturgy of the Hours, Office of Readings for Holy Saturday.

9. Congar, *The Mystery of the Temple*, preface, x.

10. For more on the typological precursors of the Old Testament, see Aidan Nichols, OP, *Lovely Like Jerusalem* (San Francisco: Ignatius, 2007).

11. Margaret Barker, *The Gate of Heaven* (London: SPCK, 1991), 19.

12. The question of the literal accuracy of scripture is not the concern of this book. I respectfully leave it to biblical scholars to debate the precision of the biblical texts as they see fit. My larger concern in this book is the symbolic importance of the biblical typologies and what they mean for the understanding of the Christian mysteries. I therefore try to assemble a position somewhere between excessively symbolic and fundamentalist readings of scripture. I have chosen to use the traditional language of revelation in scripture for ease of use and clarity of explanation, but I recognize the valid and helpful discoveries of the historical critical method of biblical criticism.

13. Barker, *The Gate of Heaven*, 17.

14. Barker, *The Gate of Heaven*, 27.

15. Saint Leo the Great, *Sermon*, Sermo 15, *De passione Domini*, 3–4: PL 54, 366–367, from the Liturgy of the Hours, Office of Readings, Thursday of the Fourth Week of Lent.

16. Barker, *The Gate of Heaven*, 105.

17. Barker, *The Gate of Heaven*, 106.

18. *The Book of James*, chapter 9. The Book of James, an apocryphal Gospel probably written in the second century, is sometimes also known as the Protoevangelion, and was mentioned by Origen. Though not given the weight of scripture, this document has proven greatly influential over the centuries. It relates that the Virgin Mary, who had been educated at the temple, was chosen by the high priest to work the scarlet and purple threads when the angel Gabriel appeared to her to announce that she was to bear Christ. See *The Ante-Nicene Fathers*, vol. 3, ed. Alexander Roberts (Grand Rapids, MI: Eerdmans, 1951), 361–367.

19. Barker, *The Gate of Heaven*, 109. See also Josephus, *The Antiquities of the Jews*, Book 3, chapter 6; Book 3, chapter 7, in *The Works of Josephus*, trans. William Whiston, (Peabody, MA: Hendrickson Publishers).

20. Josephus, *The Wars of the Jews*, Book 5, chapter 5, in *The Works of Josephus*, trans. William Whiston (Peabody, MA: Hendrickson Publishers).

21. Josephus, *The Antiquities of the Jews*, Book 3, chapter 7.

22. Barker, *The Gate of Heaven*, 109, citing Philo of Alexandria, *Questions on Exodus*, II.85.

23. Josephus, *The Antiquities of the Jews*, Book 3, chapter 7.

24. Josephus, *The Antiquities of the Jews*, Book 3, chapter 7.

25. Josephus, *The Wars of the Jews*, Book 5, chapter 5.

26. Clement of Alexandria, *Stromata*, Book 5, chapter 6, in *The Ante-Nicene Fathers*, vol. 2, ed. Alexander Roberts (Grand Rapids, MI: Eerdmans, 1951), 452–53.

27. Barker, *The Gate of Heaven*, 113.

28. Clement of Alexandria, *Stromata*, Book 5, chapter 6.

29. Josephus, *The Antiquities of the Jews*, Book 3, chapter 6, par. 123.

30. See Otto von Simson, *The Gothic Cathedral* (New York: Harper and Row, 1962), 27, citing Thierry of Chartres's quest to explain the Trinity through geometrical hypotheses: "Thierry recalls that Plato, 'like his master Pythagoras,' identified the metaphysical principles of monad and dyad with God and matter, respectively. God is the supreme unity, and the Son the unity begotten by unity, as the square results from a multiplication of a magnitude with itself. Rightly, Thierry concludes, is the Second Person of the Trinity therefore called the first square."

31. Robert Barron, *The Eucharist* (New York: Orbis, 2008), 74.

32. Andrew of Crete, *Oratio* 1: PG 97, 806–810, as offered in the Liturgy of the Hours, Office of Readings for the birth of Mary.

33. Eusebius, *The Church History*, X.4.44.

34. Ratzinger, *The Spirit of the Liturgy* (San Francisco: Ignatius Press, 2000), 89.

35. Origen, *Homily on Leviticus* (Hom. 9, 5,10: PG 515, 523), as offered in the Liturgy of the Hours, Office of Readings, Monday of the Fourth Week of Lent.

36. Pius XII, *Mediator Dei* (1947), 69.

37. Leonid Ouspensky, *The Theology of the Icon* (Crestwood, NY: St. Vladimir's Seminary Press, 1978), 23.

38. See von Simson also for a seminal exposition on the medieval understanding of the role of the temple in Gothic architecture, esp. pp. 37–38, 95–96. See also Wayne Dynes, "The Medieval Cloister as Portico of Solomon," *Gesta* 12 (1973), 61–69.

Chapter 4

Living Stones: The New Testament and the Temple

Despite the polemics about the sacramental role of architecture which have swirled since the Reformation (and the adoption of the Reformation's theology of sacred architecture in many sectors of the Roman Catholic Church), it is worth noting that the Christian Church was born into a context of highly developed Roman architecture. Though the supposed "Romanization" of the Church is often thought to have come in the fourth century with the conversion of Constantine and the impact of imperial court ritual, the Temple Mount at the time of Christ had been rebuilt under Herod the Great and was one of the largest architectural projects in the entire Roman Empire. Jesus Christ himself taught, prayed, and walked among large Classical columns, marble piazzas, Classical ornamental features, and even a large basilican building called the Royal Stoa, which looked strikingly similar to the earliest Roman churches built under Constantine.

THE CLASSICAL TRADITION, THE TEMPLE, AND THE NEW TESTAMENT

Though Herod is often seen as a local leader, he was a client-king of Judea under the Roman emperor and had traveled to Rome and seen its architecture himself. The buildings he built at Jerusalem's Temple Mount were deeply influenced by the prevailing architectural standards of the empire. Scripture tells us that Christ himself walked in the porticoes and court-yards of Herod's Temple Mount, an ensemble of architectural pieces, elements, and motifs recognizable to any Roman. One of the smaller columns intended but never installed in the Temple Mount was unearthed in Jerusalem in 1871 and gives a sense of the Roman grandeur and scale of the place.

Before the destruction of the temple in 70 AD by forces of the Roman general Titus, New Testament-era Christianity clearly had a significant, ritually public architecture with which Christ and the apostles were intimately familiar. In Christ's own earthly lifetime, the temple courts served as a

A colossal monolithic column intended for a courtyard of Herod's Temple of Jerusalem, excavated in 1871. Jerusalem.

59

significant place for teaching. The blind and the lame came to Christ at the temple (Matthew 21:14), and Christ frequented the temple as a place to preach, admitting himself that "every day" he sat in the temple courts teaching (Matthew 21–23, 26:55; Mark 14:49; Luke 19:47; see also John 5:14, 7:14, 7:28, 8:2, 8:20). It was logical that Christ would teach in the temple precincts. Though only the priests went into the innermost rooms of the temple building, the outer courts served as a place where religious leaders would congregate, as evidenced by Mary and Joseph finding the child Jesus with the rabbis (Luke 2:46–47). And despite all of the prophecy about the temple's coming destruction, the early disciples continued going to the temple precincts for prayer, beginning immediately after the Ascension (Acts 3). Upon returning to Jerusalem from Bethany, the disciples "were continuously in the temple blessing God" (Luke 24:53). Later, Saint John Chrysostom would revel in the fact that the early apostles were "no longer in a house" but "occupied the very temple [in which] they there passed their time!"[1]

Several of the miracles of the early Church occurred in the temple's precincts, but one section in particular stands out in the scriptures: Solomon's portico. The portico was a section of the colonnades on the eastern edge of the Temple Mount, which was believed to have survived from Solomon's original building of the tenth century BC. Long thought to be the location where Solomon performed the dedication rites of the temple centuries earlier, it bore a special significance. Josephus reports that he believed this section of the temple ensemble (alternately called the colonnade, portico, or cloisters of Solomon) to be from Solomon's original temple building campaign.[2] Josephus calls the building a "double cloister" with a roof of cedar and columns of native stone that looked directly into the door of the temple proper and "had been adorned by many kings in former times."[3]

John 10:23 tells us that it was winter, and Christ himself was walking in Solomon's portico when he was asked, "How long will you keep us in suspense? If you are the Messiah, tell us plainly." When Peter cured the lame man in the temple precincts near the "beautiful gate," in his very first steps, the man goes to the crowds in Solomon's portico, following Peter and John. Here Peter gives a major address to the crowds, explaining Christ's place in salvation history (Acts 3:1–26). Acts 5:12–13 tells us that "many signs and wonders were done among the people through the apostles," and that "they were with one accord together at Solomon's Portico."

Solomon's portico was certainly a privileged place, a distinct area of significant size where the early Christians chose to meet, no doubt aware of its association with Solomon the temple builder and executor of its dedication. Saint John Chrysostom's commentary on John 10:22 emphasizes that it was the feast of the Dedication when Christ walked in Solomon's portico, the celebration that recalled and celebrated

Model of the Jerusalem Temple in the time of Christ. The small gateway in the foreground, known as the "Beautiful Gate," is mentioned the book of Acts. Israel Museum, Jerusalem.

"with great zeal the day on which the temple was rebuilt. . . ."[4] Christ's body is soon to be the new Temple, and he is in that sense the new Temple builder, building the Mystical Body which is the Church. Standing in the place where Solomon dedicated the temple on the feast which celebrated that very act, Christ gives quite a long discourse, saying: "My sheep hear my voice. I know them and they follow me. I give them eternal life, and they will never perish. . . . The Father and I are one." Presumably still in Solomon's portico, Christ adds, "The Father is in me and I am in the Father" (John 10:22–30, 39).

If the mute stones of the earthly temple could speak they might have said the same thing: God's presence was in the Holy of Holies of the temple where the high priest entered. Now, temple, high priest, and Father are one in Christ Jesus, and he gives eternal life by his presence. This bringing together of Father with the Son—God with the Mystical Body—finds its symbolic completion in the heavenly Jerusalem described in Revelation, where God and humanity become one for eternity. This coming together is described as a radiant city, and this reality is precisely what today's liturgical art and architecture signify and make present. The biblical language of "being of one accord" in the portico speaks also of the unity of the earliest Christians, which was found in Christ. This sort of language can be read with eschatological

The Royal Stoa of the Temple Mount was described as containing 162 27-foot high columns with a "double spiral" at their base, indicating the two torus moldings used on the Corinthian column's base. Supreme Court Building, Washington, DC. Cass Gilbert, architect, 1928.

overtones: in heaven, the discord and strife that resulted from the Fall is undone and banished forever. Architecture served as its setting and its symbol.

All of this biblical activity, however, occurs within a high-style Roman architecture which rivaled that of the city of Rome. Just a few yards from Solomon's portico stood the Royal Stoa, a building that any Jew who entered the temple precincts or saw the Temple Mount from a distance would have known. Though the basilican churches built by Constantine in the fourth century are often claimed to be a Roman "imperialization" of a supposed house church tradition of the apostolic age, three centuries earlier the apostles already knew of the Royal Stoa, a basilican hall that rivaled anything ever built in Rome. While Herod's temple proper stayed close to the precedent set by earlier buildings and the proportions given in scripture, the surrounding courtyards and structures would have been quite at home in ancient Rome. Josephus had himself been to Rome and had seen its important imperial buildings, but he nonetheless wrote that the Royal Stoa on the Temple Mount deserved "to be men-

tioned more than any other under the sun." He wrote ecstatically of its 162 27-foot high Corinthian columns, which were so large that it took three men with arms outstretched to reach around them.[5] The "double spiral" that he describes at their bases configure perfectly with the typical Roman column base with its two **torus** moldings. These columns were arranged in rows to form a large basilica of the type found in imperial fora in Rome, and he describes the three aisles with the central aisle higher than the sides which characterize the Roman basilica. Josephus also describes the roof of the building as containing figural sculptures in wood.[6] Christ and the earliest Christians found a significant, iconic public architecture an ideal setting for the teaching of the Christian revelation.

This grand public architecture was continued on a lesser scale in the Jewish communities even after the destruction of the temple, as the synagogues of Capernaum and Korazim

---

torus: a rope-like or cushion-like convex molding, commonly the lowest part of a column base, which suggests compression from the column above.

attest, though these buildings are notoriously difficult to date.[7] In fact, scholars divide these synagogues into three types, one of which is called the "basilical" type, while later an apse was added, which earned these buildings the heading "apsidal."[8] Some of these buildings, like the synagogue at Nabratein, show evidence of dating from the second century, using Judaic adaptations of standard high-style Roman forms. The door lintel of the Nabratein synagogue, for instance, shows a menorah image carved inside an otherwise standard imperial wreath.[9] The synagogue at Capernaum, located only feet from the remains of Saint Peter's house, is considered one of the most magnificent of the Palestinian synagogues. Though there is no definite conclusion on the date of its erection, significant evidence leads to a second century date. In similar synagogues dating from the second to the sixth century, Roman-inspired mosaics, columns, capitals, and ornamental motifs were the norm in the life of Palestine. The Romanization of Jewish architecture in the centuries after the destruction of the temple even evidenced itself in the famous tombs of the Jewish cemetery of Bet Shearim after the Sanhedrin moved there in the early third century.

Within this cultural mix, Jerusalem's Christians (which is to say nothing of Greeks and others) would have lived in a highly Romanized culture. Eusebius writes that a large church already stood in Jerusalem before the Second Jewish Revolt of 135 AD.[10] He also writes that by the middle of the third century, large church communities were found throughout Palestine before the emperor Diocletian began the last of the great persecutions. His descriptions imply something more than simple domestic buildings, which certainly would have

Above: The Royal Stoa included Corinthian columns and a roof structure containing sculptural figures in wood.

Facing page, top: The historian Josephus (37–ca. 100 AD) had been to Rome, yet he stated that the Royal Stoa deserved "to be mentioned more than any other under the sun."

Facing page, bottom: King Herod was a client king of Rome, and when he rebuilt the Temple Mount he was deeply influenced by the prevailing architectural standards of the empire. Scripture tells that Christ walked in the porticoes and courtyards of Herod's temple, an ensemble of Classical pieces, elements, and motifs recognizable to any Roman.

been too small to hold the growing communities. Eusebius writes: "We saw with our own eyes the houses of prayer thrown down to the very foundations," (Greek, *prosuktherion*) and later that Diocletian's edicts commanded that "the churches be leveled to the ground."[11] He also speaks of the "stones of the sanctuaries" when speaking of the imperial destruction of church property.[12]

By contrast, Eusebius rejoices greatly in the restoration of church buildings under the reign of the Emperor Constantine, describing "the spectacle for which we all prayed and yearned: festivals of dedication and consecrations of the new houses of worship. . . ." With this language reminiscent of that used for the Feast of Dedication from the Jewish temple, Eusebius writes that the "perfect services were conducted by the prelates, the sacred rites being solemnized, and the majestic institutions of the Church observed, here with the singing of psalms and with the reading of the words committed to us by God, and there with the performance of the

divine and mystic services; and the mysterious symbols of our Savior's passion were dispensed."[13] This "dispensation" of the "mysterious symbols" is no doubt a reference to the Eucharistic liturgy, which was commonly called the *mysterion*, or sacred mysteries.

Acts 2:46 speaks of the Christians breaking bread in their homes as well as continually returning to the temple, and this biblical passage has been the center of arguments since the Reformation about whether the church building is a sacral place or merely a meeting house. Some have argued that the houses where the early Christians met were actually more like palaces with large rooms serving as chapels, and that by living together in common, the apostolic life would be more akin to today's monastery than today's suburban house. Whatever kind of buildings were used in the earliest days of the Church for the "breaking of the bread," the tradition of the Church that church buildings are more than dining rooms in private houses is the presumption made in this book, and the presumption that every builder of a new Catholic church should make. The popularity of the idea of the church building as domestic in character has devastated the field of liturgical architecture since the Second Vatican Council. More will be said on this topic in a later chapter, but the presumptive starting point for any new building project is the *Catechism of the Catholic Church*, which teaches that Christians naturally build churches (rather than limit themselves to a domestic arrangement) when "the exercise of religious liberty is not thwarted," and these "houses of God" show the "truth and harmony of the signs that make it up" in order to give evidence that Christ is "present and active in this place."[14] The church building is more than a domestic dining room grown large; it is a sacramental building.

By the late third century at least, the language of worship was in decided harmony with the temple precursors and later synagogue usages, both of which made use of significant public architecture. Importantly, Eusebius notes that after Diocletian's restrictions were relaxed, "temples" (*neus*) rose again, "receiving a splendor far greater than that of the old ones which had been destroyed."[15] The implication, then, is that the previous churches had some degree of splendor, and the new churches continued an existing current but on a greater scale. Eusebius would go on to include evidence of the theology of the church building in his famous **panegyric** on the building of a "magnificent cathedral" in Tyre given to its bishop, Paulinus. He compared Paulinus to Solomon, the "builder of a new and much better Jerusalem," and also to Zerubbabel, the architect of the second temple "who added a much greater glory than the former to the temple of God."[16]

---

panegyric: a formal public address or essay filled with elaborate praise of a person or thing.

Palm tree imagery in the remains of the Galilean synagogue at Capernaum (possibly second or fourth century), showing the Romanization of Palestinian synagogues after the destruction of the temple in 70 AD.

Moreover, he calls the altar in Paulinus's church the "holy of holies" and suggests that it be enclosed with wooden latticework with elaborate carving so that "it might be inaccessible to the multitude," as was the Holy of Holies in the temple.[17]

In the midst of all of this, of course, Eusebius glories in the architectural magnificence of the church buildings being constructed. He compared the gold-covered ceiling of the Church of the Holy Sepulcher in Jerusalem to a great sea, which caused the whole building to "glitter as it were with rays of light."[18] *Light*, of course, was a loaded word in the early Christian world as it was in the New Testament, and one could easily see this description as an image of the radiant light of the heavenly Jerusalem, which he references elsewhere. Moreover, the word *sea* was also heavy with meaning, since throughout the entire Old Testament the sea served as a symbol of chaos and disorder, yet it was transformed in the New Testament by Christ who calms the storm on the Sea of

Star of David from the pulvinated frieze of the Capernaum synagogue.

Adaption of the Corinthian capital to include a menorah. Synagogue at Capernaum, Galilee.

Galilee, walks on water, uses water for Baptism, and turns it into wine. Later, the book of Revelation speaks of the throne of God as surrounded by a sea of glass (Revelation 4:6) in the heavenly city whose streets where made of gold and were as clear as crystal (Revelation 21:21). So a golden sea on the ceiling of a church can easily be interpreted as a reference to a heavenly realm above.

Eusebius saw that beautiful buildings were needed to be "worthy of the worship of God." Moreover, these beautiful buildings would be evangelical tools, "turning the eyes of those who were strangers to the faith," so that "one being impressed by this might be attracted and be induced to enter by the very sight."[19] The church building was presented "to

all, believers and unbelievers alike, a trophy of [Christ's] victory over death, a holy temple of the true God, . . . which witnesses of eternal life, . . . ascribing victory and triumph to the heavenly Word of God."[20] In the late third and early fourth centuries, then, the building of great churches was seen not as an innovation or unwelcome insertion of imperial architecture into a culture of house churches. In Eusebius's writings at least, the act of church building is directly compared to the act of temple building, and it seems highly unlikely that the Church's liturgical enrichment was a newly adopted sprucing up added to a fellowship meal. Rather than being seen as a wholesale adoption of a new way of thinking about church buildings, Constantinian-era churches give every appearance of being a continuation of a long-desired tradition that finds its roots in the temple and its flowering under imperial patronage.

SPEAKING OF THE TEMPLE OF HIS BODY

In the midst of this rich matrix of architectural thought, Christians had to contend with a new meaning for the Church and the buildings they knew. The typologies of the temple understood in the Old Testament found fulfillment in Christ. As recounted in particular in the letter to the Hebrews, temple worship was seen as an inadequate but necessary precursor to Christian worship. Christ, of course, the new High Priest, not only passed over the veil, but at his death tore the veil that separated heaven and earth (Matthew 27:51). This veil represented the separation of God and humanity resulting from the Fall, and was now opened forever by Christ. With the tearing of the veil, God's presence was no longer limited to the Holy of Holies, because God does not live in shrines built by human hands (Acts 17:24). The question is, then, where does God dwell when the veil is torn? The answer: in the living temple, the Church, as fulfillment of God's plan of salvation. The language of the Old Testament temple prayers spoke of God's covenant plan of salvation, which, through Adam, Noah, Abraham, Moses, and David, Israel grows from a marriage to a family, a family to a tribe, a tribe to a nation, and a nation to a kingdom that is holy, royal, and far-reaching.[21] As Israel grows in its covenants with God, it becomes a clearer sign of God's intention to restore his creation. Christ fulfills this plan as priest, prophet, and king; he offers himself, reveals the truth, and ushers in the reign of justice and new law. Once formed in tangible institutional structures based on the law, God chooses to raise Israel to its next stage in development, moving from the law to the heart, from fearful obedience to love.

The ever-increasing outward movement of God's presence means that God's transformative divine life would expand from temple building and external law to the living temple of the people and internal spirit. God would now not only dwell *with* his people, he would dwell *in* them. Accordingly, the New Testament is filled with allegorical allusions to the Church being a new building where God dwells. The same God who desired intimate union with his creatures now chooses, in his own time, to dwell not in a building alone but also in his creatures, transforming them into his likeness. Just as Christ is often described as going up to Jerusalem and the temple to "take possession" of it, so Christ takes possession of his creatures. The destruction of the old temple building lays "the foundation for the new temple, the Church."[22]

The "building" made of "living stones" can now take God's message and sacramental life across national borders and bring the Gospel to the world to make disciples of all nations, reaching all of the "twelve tribes." As was his will, God's gracious plan of salvation bursts forth from the chosen people and becomes available to Gentile and Jew. Christ himself tells the woman at the well that the time will come when worship of God will no longer be limited to the Temple Mount or even the city of Jerusalem (John 4:21–23). God's plan is to "make the human race, created in his image, a living, spiritual temple in which he communicates Himself and in turns received from it a wholly filial obedience."[23] This sharing of divine life moves from things to persons, from fleeting moments to lasting union, and simple presence to the joy and peace of communion. In our age, the time of image, God dwells in his people, in a lasting relationship for which the temple, rich and wonderful as it was, served as a shadowy precursor meant to accustom the minds of his people to the coming fulfillment.

Some of the most direct allusions in all of scripture are the comparisons of the Church (*ekklesia*) to architecture.[24] Christ's body, of course, is the archetypal building, the new temple where offering and offerer would converge and where being and presence are united and complete. Therefore Christ spoke of raising up the "temple" of his body in three days (John 2:21). Throughout the Gospels, the Church is compared to a new Jerusalem, a new city that God had chosen to show light to the nations (Matthew 5:14–16). This temple is built by Christ and *is* Christ, the true Temple and the builder of the new Temple. After the Ascension, the Age of the Church begins, and it is the apostles who form a new building, each one serving as a living stone. Later, the Church grows and takes on the nature of a large building where each does his or her own part while united in a grand, ordered design.

Peter becomes the rock on which the earthly Church is built (Matthew 16:13–20), though Christ himself is not only the foundation (1 Corinthians 3:11), but also the keystone (Acts 4:11, sometimes translated as "cornerstone"). The keystone is the highest and most central stone in an arch, the one put in place last and without which the entire arch collapses. In a sense it is the "head" of an arch, just as Christ is the

The keystone is in a sense the "head" of an arch, just as Christ is Head of the Mystical Body which is the Church (Acts 4:11).

Facing page: The language of Classicism continued into the Islamic culture of the Holy Land, including this Composite capital in the Dome of the Chain on the Temple Mount, ca. 691.

Head of the Mystical Body made up of many members, which is the Church. Without its head, the body collapses. With its head, the members of the body work together to grow in greater conformity to Christ.

In the time of image, each individual Christian is a living stone in the living temple. Those with a great intellect or highly visible public role might be said to have the brilliance of the golden trimmings atop a church steeple. Others who do the important day-to-day work of the Church might be compared to the subdued earthiness of wooden beams. Others might be foundations, supporting the church secretly in their hidden prayers or anonymous donations. Yet all are necessary for the Church to be what she is and to flourish. A golden tabernacle isn't much good without the marble altar under it, and the walls, roof, floors, and foundation that give them their proper place. As Saint Paul wrote, the foundation of the Church was Christ, and "if anyone builds on the foundation with gold, silver, precious stones, wood, hay, straw—the work of each builder will become visible. . ." (1 Corinthians 3:12).

Some have interpreted this theology of living stones to mean that church buildings no longer need to be sacramental or have any relation to the temple, a notion that lies at the heart of many theologies of church architecture grown up since the Reformation. If God no longer needs animal sacrifices or desires a building limiting his presence to a small room visited once a year—and his presence is found in his people, the Church—then what is the need for an elaborate church building? What can it be said to be? It is three things. First, it is a memory and fulfillment of the temple. Second, it serves as a witness to the Christians gathered in a particular place, which speaks of the newly reordered relationship between

Scriptural references compare holy men and women to columns: "may your daughters be graceful as columns / adorned as though for a palace" (Psalm 144). Porch of the Maidens, Erechtheum, Athens, fifth century BC.

God and humanity, a world groaning as it undergoes the increasing conformity to God in the process of divinization. Third, and most important, the art and architecture of a church building are a foretaste of a glorified heavenly future, revealing to us the beauty of our heavenly destiny, thereby enthusing us for the work of being conformed to Christ.

THE CHURCH LIVING IN THIS PLACE

The *Catechism of the Catholic Church* teaches that church buildings are "not simply gathering places, but signify and make visible the Church living in this place, the dwelling of God with men reconciled and united in Christ" (CCC, 1180). Despite some of the rhetoric of liturgical-artistic professionals since the Second Vatican Council, church buildings still have an important symbolic role beyond the mere meeting house. They *signify*, meaning they convey information to those who encounter them. In this case, buildings are evidence that Christians worship here, just as a private home is a sign of family dwelling, even if at the moment they might be scattered at work or play. The church building, especially one that *looks like* a church, is an architectural sign making visible the invisible: here lives the Mystical Body of Christ, the new, living Temple in which God dwells because he has reconciled humanity to himself. It may seem obvious at first blush to

consider that a church building means that Christians are nearby, but we shouldn't underestimate this important architectural task. Since architecture is the built form of ideas, the idea that God is reconciled with his creatures and that many people live that reality is certainly worth proclaiming—and proclaiming clearly, legibly, and with a level of dignity that matches that very reality.

One of the earliest Christian manifestations of an architectural signification grows from scripture itself. In Galatians 2:9, Cephas, James, and John are called "pillars" of the Church, an allusion which has set architects working with "sacramental" columns ever since. This comparison of columns to people had a long history in the Classical tradition, as the words *capital* (from Latin *caput*-head) and *base* (from Greek *basis*—foot, dance) attest. By the time of Christ it was a long-standing tradition that columns were abstracted people, as attested by many uses of columns in the shape of people, dating as early as the fifth century BC. The architectural writer Vitruvius (ca. 80 BC–25) gives elaborate descriptions of the proportions of columns as those of people of different types: men, maidens, and matrons. Even Psalm 144 prays for "daughters as graceful as columns, adorned as though for a palace" (Grail Psalter). This strong cultural convention of the ancient world was not lost on the Emperor Constantine and his architects, who, when building the Church of the Holy Sepulcher in Jerusalem in the early fourth century, arranged a ring of 12 columns in its rotunda explicitly claiming a relationship to the 12 apostles.[25] So from the earliest days, church architecture served as a representation of the *ekklesia*. Much more will be said of this later.

This idea of church building as earthly proclamation of the kingdom of God can be extended in several ways. The American city, with its many immigrant churches, can be read as a microcosm of the world. Tough granite Irish churches next to delicate German rococo beside an Italian parish of Mediterranean inspiration indeed tells not only that Christians live in this place, but that Christ's call to make disciples of all nations has made significant progress. Moreover, these churches partake of the best and most churchly conventions each culture has to offer. One of my African-born students once told me how offended he was that a well-intended Caucasian pastor designed a church for an inner-city African American parish based on an African hut. In his country, he said, even the poorest people build churches that are recognizable as such and do not worship in huts. The dignity and legibility of the church building makes clear the community gathered in this place as doing something at once proper to their community and something of obvious importance.

When there is a general consensus that a church doesn't "look like" one, the building has usually given up an attempt to make a distinct ecclesial architecture. Every church building is, to some degree, a record of the story of its people, but it should not simply be a projection of the earthly congregation. This would make it a decidedly unsacramental building, revealing only the visible realities of the fallen world. A properly designed church building reveals not only the people who built it, but the pilgrimage of the whole human race journeying toward the heavenly Jerusalem which is strengthened by drinking from the springs of divine life in the sacraments. The church therefore reveals also what the members of the congregation *hope to be* when fully nourished by divine life. As such, the architecture of a church building should not be mediocre, chaotic, or profoundly secular or domestic in character. It symbolizes the gathered community at their prayerful best, and therefore its architecture should be publicly communal, exalted, ordered, and ecclesial. In just the same way that the living stones of the Church are intended to form a harmonious whole, the inert stones of the church building should radiate with the order, peace, and unity of the Mystical Body of Christ.

1. Saint John Chrysostom, Homily XII, *Homilies on the Acts of the Apostles and the Epistle to the Romans*.

2. Josephus, *The Antiquities of the Jews*, 20.9.220-222, from William Whiston, trans., *The Works of Josephus Complete and Unabridged* (Peabody, MA: Hendrickson Publishers, 1987).

3. Josephus, *The Antiquities of the Jews*, 15.11.3 and 8.3.9.

4. Saint John Chrysostom, Homily LXI, *Homilies on the Gospel of Saint John and the Epistle to the Hebrews*.

5. Josephus, *The Antiquities of the Jews*, 15.11.4.

6. Josephus, *The Antiquities of the Jews*, 15.5.5.

7. See Leslie J. Hoppe, *The Synagogues and Churches of Ancient Palestine* (Collegeville, MN: Liturgical Press, 1994). For more on the synagogue's relation to early churches, see also Louis Bouyer, *Liturgy and Architecture* (Notre Dame, IN: University of Notre Dame Press, 1967).

8. Hoppe, *The Synagogues and Churches of Ancient Palestine*, 21.

9. Hoppe, *The Synagogues and Churches of Ancient Palestine*, 28–29.

10. Hoppe, *The Synagogues and Churches of Ancient Palestine*, 62, citing Eusebius, *Demonstratio evangelica*, 3.5.108.

11. Eusebius, *The Church History*, 7, 2.

12. Eusebius, *The Church History*, 10.4.14.

13. Eusebius, *The Church History*, 10.3.

14. CCC, 1180–1181.

15. Eusebius, *The Church History*, 10.2.1.

16. Eusebius, *The Church History*, 10.4.3.

17. Eusebius, *The Church History*, 10.4.44.

18. Eusebius, *Life of Constantine*, 3.36.

19. Eusebius, *Church History*, 10.4.38.

20. Eusebius, *The Oration of Eusebius in Praise of the Emperor Constantine*, ch. 18.

21. See Scott Hahn, *A Father Who Keeps His Promises* (Cincinnati: Servant Books, 1998), 31–38.

22. Hubert Lignee, *The Living Temple* (Baltimore: Helicon, 1966), 12.

23. Congar, *Mystery of the Temple* (Westminster: Newman Press, English translation, 1962), foreword, ix.

24. See 1 Corinthians 3:9–17, 2 Corinthians 5:1–5, 6:14—7:1, Ephesians 2:19–22, 1 Timothy 3:15, 2 Timothy 2:19, Galatians 2:9.

25. Eusebius, *The Life of Constantine*, 3.38: "Opposite these gates the crowning part of the whole was the hemisphere [dome], which rose to the very summit of the church. This was encircled by twelve columns (according to the number of the apostles of our Savior). . . ."

Chapter 5

Architecture of the Sabbath: Church as Image of the Heavenly Jerusalem

Sacrosanctum Concilium states that "by way of foretaste, we share in that heavenly liturgy which is celebrated in the holy city of Jerusalem toward which we journey as pilgrims, and in which Christ is sitting at the right hand of God." Furthermore, it continues, in our earthly churches "we sing a hymn to the Lord's glory with all the warriors of the heavenly army" (SC, 8). So at the heart of the Second Vatican Council's teaching on liturgy is the notion of the liturgy as a sacramental participation in the liturgy of heaven, which takes place "in" the **heavenly Jerusalem**, where humans long to be and for which our earthly life is a preparatory pilgrimage. The language used for the heavenly Jerusalem is poetic and symbolic, yet its meaning is real and its manifestations quite earthly. It lies at the heart of the theology of church art and architecture and represents one of the great avenues of continuity between Vatican II and the Church's great tradition.

Simply put, the earthly liturgy is, ontologically speaking, the re-presentation of the liturgy of heaven in sacramental form, which is itself both the eternal offering of the sacrifice of Christ to the Father and the **Wedding Feast of the Lamb**. Liturgical art and architecture form the sacramental revelation of this setting, providing an image attuned to our gift of sight. Here we find the great paradox of the Incarnation: God made himself knowable to our senses by taking on human form, yet except for a moment at the Transfiguration, the Incarnation also veiled God's glory in the form of an ordinary-looking Jewish carpenter. After the death of Christ, however, we no longer live in the time of shadow, but in the time of image, and our earthly attempts at liturgical art become *vehicles* for revelation of the heavenly reality to come. Through

---

heavenly Jerusalem: the state of fully restored relationship between God and humanity in which God's divine life causes a new heaven and a new earth, foreshadowed by the earthly city of Jerusalem and described as a city in the book of Revelation.

Wedding Feast of the Lamb: In Revelation, chapter 19, it is written that the Wedding Feast of the Lamb has begun, referring to the reunion of God and his creation. The feast speaks of the joyful celebration at the completion of Christ, the Lamb's, mission of salvation for humanity.

The earthly liturgy provides a foretaste of the heavenly liturgy which includes the persons of the Trinity, the angels, and the saints. Madonna della Strada Chapel, Chicago. Melville Steinfels, painter.

the transformative power of the Holy Spirit, matter becomes the means through which the realities of heaven are mediated sacramentally to us just as they were in the Incarnation itself. Therefore, unlike the shadowy precursors of the Old Testament, the sacramental images are now efficacious and transfigured to show heavenly glory. The job of liturgical art is not to recreate the everyday humility of the historical Last Supper, but to show the Last Supper transformed into the Heavenly Banquet, which awaits us at the end of time.

Though discussing liturgical art and architecture in this way might seem new to some,[1] the very basis of the divine pedagogy of salvation depends on the ability of things to be signifiers. All signs by their nature convey information, and humans by their nature come to know information through them. Stop signs tell us to stop, and miters tell us there might be a bishop underneath. This sort of sign is merely informative and conventional. But in the strong sacramental theology of the great tradition of the Church, this basic notion can be raised up a few notches so as to be understood as sacramental signs that make present the reality they signify. The Eucharist is the preeminent example of such a sign. "Real presence" means exactly what it says: under the appearance of bread and wine, Christ's presence becomes real and remains with us in the Eucharist. Vatican II tells us that in "the Liturgy the sanctification of man is manifested by signs perceptible to the senses, and is effected in a way which is proper to each of these signs" (SC, 7). In other words, sacramental signs become the very vehicle through which we know God and share in divine life, which makes us more like him and therefore suited to be happy with him for eternity.

The question justifiably arises: why should the church be like heaven, mediating heaven to us? Why not carry on with a stalwart faith and wait for the afterlife to see heavenly things? The answer: so that we "with unveiled faces," beholding the glory of the Lord, might be "transformed into the same image from one degree of glory to another" (2 Corinthians 3:18). We cannot look at the face of God directly and live, so God comes to us under the veil of material things to make us more God-like. Pseudo-Dionysius writes that it would be impossible to be lifted up to heavenly things without material things, because our nature requires perception through the senses.[2] Being changed into the likeness of Jesus Christ requires encountering Jesus Christ in the material things of this world, just as coming to know scripture requires interacting with paper, ink, and bindings. The church building, too, is a kind of signifier, a deeply theological thing making present to us God's plan of salvation in Old Testament typologies, New Testament fulfillment, and the eschatological promises of the book of Revelation. On one level, proper liturgical art and architecture place us in the context of heaven, disposing us to receive the sacraments with fuller appreciation and understanding, leading to a more full, conscious, and active partici-

pation in the liturgy. But an even greater claim can be made: by analogy, liturgical art and architecture can properly be called *sacramental* because they mediate the mysteries of the Incarnation.[3]

The Vision of Heaven

Outside of some extraordinary mystical revelation, no earthly being truly knows what heaven is like. Our continued status of "not yet" in the "already but not yet" nature of sacramental liturgy means our knowledge of heaven is limited. However, the "already" of the same phrase means that we do know something of heaven just as we know something of God, even if through a glass darkly. In the most general terms, we can rightly postulate that heaven would share many of the revealed qualities of the Trinity itself. Heaven is populated community, hence its common symbolic terminology as a heavenly *city*. More than a mere settlement or strip mall sprawl in the sky, to speak of heaven is to speak of a "place" in which all things are ordered, radiant with the glory of God, theocentric, lacking nothing, and where all relationships are proportionate.

Any more specific descriptions of heaven must come from God's revelation, most typically in the Sacred Scriptures. Christ's comments in John 1:51 explain that Christ himself is that ladder between heaven and earth, prefigured by the angels of Jacob's ladder (Genesis 28:10–22). Saint Paul speaks of a man he knew who had been transported to the "third heaven" and heard "inexpressible things," though he was not permitted to tell of them (2 Corinthians 12:1–4). Second Thessalonians 1:7 speaks of Christ's Second Coming as characterized by the presence of angels and blazing fire. Colossians 3:1 tells us that Christ sits at the right hand of the Father in heaven, and Saint Stephen in the book of Acts was "filled with the Holy Spirit" and "gazed into heaven and saw the glory of God and Jesus standing at the right hand of God," with the "heavens opened and the Son of Man standing at the right hand of God" (Acts 7:55–56).

The great treasure trove of information about heaven, however, comes from the book of Revelation, and for that reason it has been used as the model for church architecture for nearly as long as there have been church buildings.[4] The reason is simple: it is the clearest vision of heaven in all of scripture. Unlike the temple, which was a mere shadow, the church building in the time of the image is a real experience of heaven expressed sacramentally. And to best make the earthly image conform to the heavenly reality (and therefore reveal its ontological reality and be rightly called beautiful), Revelation becomes the most valuable resource available to the church architect or liturgical artist. Without the prayerful transcription of the heavenly images of Revelation into built form, one cannot truly speak of a church as beautiful.[5]

With the architectural profession obsessed in our age with novelty and technology, it may come as a surprise to hear that these texts of Saint John have something to teach us. Our age and culture tend to be cut off from the streams that quench our thirst in church architecture. Our souls do not rest until they rest in God, because nothing else satisfies the deepest longings of the soul. Similarly, our earthly, church-going eyes do not rest until they rest in heaven, and in the Age of the Church, the church building is intended to provide that image. An effective image of heaven need not be archaeologically derived or a literal copy of a historical example. It can always be done in a new way better than before. The tradition of the Church shows us how it has been done, and because every generation of artists and architects have given their best efforts at giving heaven a sacramental form, we hold the great churches of history in high esteem. The tradition informs us with principles and even specific forms to imitate. However, no matter what it looks like, a church must always be an image of the joining of heaven and earth, the dwelling of God reconciled with humanity. As the theologian Paul Evdokimov wrote, it is "perfectly legitimate to search for new forms, but these forms must express a symbolic content that remains the same throughout the centuries because it has a heavenly origin. Modern builders must listen to and appreciate the suggestions of the chief architect, the *Angel of the Temple* (Revelation 21:15)" [emphasis original].[6] The Angel of the Temple is none other than the heavenly tour guide who gives Saint John a mystical excursion through heaven. This supernatural vision should also be every earthly architect's guide as well, the answer to every question about the nature of the church building.

Because it tells us what heaven is like, the book of Revelation is required reading for every liturgical artist and architect.

What Does Heaven "Look Like"?

Heaven shows creator and creation united once again, where the Fall is undone and creation is brought to glory. This is the ultimate goal of salvation history. This is the reason for Christ's Incarnation, Passion, and Resurrection. For this God's great deeds are chronicled in the Old Testament, and for this God chose his chosen people, nourished them, taught them, gave them the revelation of the laws of worship and the temple. For this Christ founded the Church and for this we partake of the heavenly realities in the sacraments offered in the time of the image. This anticipation of heavenly glory, the "already" of the "already but not yet," means that church buildings must participate in what heaven is: complete, ordered, harmonic, and radiantly theocentric. This is the "more than" mentioned in the *Catechism of the Catholic Church's* claim that churches are "more than simple gathering places."

In the church building, God's will is shown done on earth as it is in heaven.

A beautiful church truly provides an "architecture of the Sabbath," which frees us from the fallen ugliness and utilitarian drudgery of strip malls and office towers, and instead gives us a delightfully energizing rest in a sacramental paradise, which enthuses us for the work of prayer. The Sabbath is the "day on which man and the whole created order participate in God's rest, in his freedom."[7] This freedom is relief from the effects of the Fall and from the burden of work resulting from it. Liturgical art and architecture show us what this heavenly rest looks like and make it present to our earthly eyes and prayerful minds.

The book of Revelation begins with John speaking from his exile on the island of Patmos, with his ecstatic vision fittingly and symbolically occurring on the Sabbath, the day that prefigures the heavenly reality he would witness (Revelation 1:10). Its first chapter gives a vision of the Son of Man sitting among seven golden lamp stands, an immediate disclosure of the majesty of God:

> . . . . and in the midst of the lamp stands was one like a son of man, clothed in a long robe and with a golden girdle round his breast; his head and his hair were white as wool, white as snow; his eyes like a flame of fire, his feet were like burnished bronze, refined as in a furnace, and his voice like the sound of many waters, in his hand were seven stars, from his mouth issued a sharp two-edged sword, and his face was like the sun shining in full strength. (Revelation 1:13–16, Revised Standard Version)

This short passage tells the liturgical artist and architect much about the heavenly realities, and therefore what *Sacrosanctum Concilium* asks to be represented in signs and symbols (SC, 122). This seemingly mysterious vision has found many interpretations through the years, but even before any of the particular symbolism is decoded, the image gives the sense of the strength and majesty of God, confirming that Christ is indeed omnipotent, with a powerful majesty that clarifies the relationship between creature and creator.

The Venerable Bede's seventh-century explanation of Revelation 1:13–16 sees this figure as Christ, whose power is not purely intimidating like the Wizard of Oz in the Emerald City, but whose glory is proof of both his victory over death and his ascension into heaven.[8] Other symbolic references speak of his godliness and identity as the promised Savior. The "expression 'Son of Man' originates in Daniel 7:14, where . . . it refers to someone depicted as Judge at the end of time. . . . His 'long robe' shows his priesthood (see Exodus 28:4; Zechariah 3:4); the golden girdle, his kingship (see 1 Maccabees 10:89); his white hair, his eternity (see Daniel 7:9); his eyes 'like flame of fire' symbolize his divine wisdom (see Revelation 2:23); and his bronze feet, his strength and stability."[9] Bede tells us that the word used for bronze, *orichalchum*, refers to a metal, which, when heated and properly

Grand, yet intimate. Mater Dolorosa Chapel, Marytown, Libertyville, Illinois.

The sacramental role of liturgical art: heavenly radiance made present. Sainte-Chapelle, Paris.

treated, undergoes a glorious, resurrection-like transformation and is "brought to the color of gold." These glorious attributes give just a taste of the heavenly Christ and hearken back to the Transfiguration on Mount Tabor when Christ's heavenliness was shown to Peter, James, and John.

Despite its commanding quality, John's vision of Christ is tremendously positive: Christ is the priest who offers himself to the Father, the king of divine wisdom who brings justice, and God from the beginning whose strength and eternity are sure signs of victory over sin and death. Here is an optimistic vision of a Savior who took the form of a slave in the Incarnation but now reigns in glory. Despite this imposing biblical image, Christ's mercy is evident as he lays his hand upon John's shoulder and says, "Fear not, . . . I died and behold I am alive for evermore . . ." (Revelation 1:17). Here human finitude is not denied, but rather invited to return to God for completion.

Similarly, Revelation gives artists and architects their starting point. The church building should be at once imposing, dignified, and glorious; it is "set apart" from everyday things (SC, 122) to remind the creature of his or her properly humble relationship to an omnipotent God whose wisdom far exceeds that of fallen creatures. But at the same time, this imposing building is one to which all are invited to dwell, provided they choose to follow the will of God. So again we face the richly Catholic "both/and" approach to things: Christ is all-powerful yet deigns to reassure us with the phrase "Be not afraid." In his infinite wisdom, he recognizes our limitations, and without those flaming eyes of wisdom, he would in fact not recognize these limitations and instead would become just another capricious god of the pagan world. So Christ's impressive glory and welcoming compassion are two sides of the same coin.

Many of the ideas expressed in recent years about liturgical art and architecture have eschewed artistic grandeur, choosing instead perhaps an overly optimistic model of the intimate, therapeutic, and domestic interior. The lens of Machiavelli, Kant, and Nietzsche has given Modernity its decided distrust of authority as well as power. This move has established a competitive, "either/or" view of things, pitting the glorious against the welcoming, the solemn against the intimate, the ritually public against the domestic, the **domus Dei** against the **domus ecclesiae**. But like this image of the Son of Man, the church building should be a glorious building to which humble creatures are welcomed, a glorified reality in which the touch of the hand of Christ reassures us of his reception, a palatial edifice to which we are nonetheless urged to be at home because we have become co-heirs with the King. The King offers his palace to his creatures and dwells with them and in them. This reality is at the heart of the Christian plan of salvation, and so is at the heart of church architecture. Diminishing God's authority by making a church less like

domus Dei: the house of God, a place where God's presence dwells.

domus ecclesiae: the house of the people of God, the physical structure where the Christian congregation assembles for worship.

Saint John's vision from the book of Revelation revealed in a great liturgical mural. Cathedral of Saint Joseph, Wheeling, West Virginia. Felix Lieftuchter, muralist.

God's house and more like our house entraps us and mires us in the effects of our greatest human temptation: to think ourselves greater than God, or at the very least, to fail to remind ourselves of our real position as creatures at the foot of the creator. Rich marbles, mosaics, columns, paintings, and plasterwork can indeed form rooms both grand and intimate, inviting the worshipper to feel completely at home in a highly ornamented room which is nonetheless human-scaled and welcoming.

For artists, this glorious vision of Christ means that liturgical imagery must rise beyond both the saccharine, porcelain-doll portraits of nineteenth-century holy cards and the hyper-realistic and overly optimistic imagery of Christ as a chummy first-century Mediterranean standing at the plate with our little leaguers. Christ's humanity is real, and must not be denied, and one finds it emphasized in the Church's devotional life. The *liturgical* Christ, however, is "Sovereign Mediator between God and man, the eternal High-Priest, the divine Teacher, the Judge of the living and the dead . . . rapt into the light of eternity, and remote from time and space."[10] The liturgical Christ cannot be domesticated.

In the liturgy, the face of Christ is represented as the face of Christ is represented as the face of Beauty itself: complete glory and complete compassion, a face ordered to the Father and also to the cries of the faithful,

and all radiant with divinity and humanity. The great mural of Christ at the Cathedral of Saint Joseph in Wheeling, West Virginia, by artist Felix Lieftuchter provides one successful example of this representation. Here, despite the evident heavenly glory surrounding his throne, the pleading quality of Christ's eyes and gentle pose of the hands say "come to me." Unlike other representations of the subject, which show a Christ more like Zeus than the Son of Man, Lieftuchter's murals exhibit this glorified humanity. Earth is invited to heaven, but indeed also heaven comes to earth. More will be said on liturgical imagery in a later chapter, but the task of revealing Christ is fundamentally a sacramental act, making visible not simply the Jewish carpenter of Palestine, but the existing reality of Christ's glory in heaven. This task should be daunting to any artist. It is only with the help of the Holy Spirit that the task is even possible, and for this reason, serious iconographers fast and pray so as to better let the Holy Spirit guide their hands.

John's heavenly visions reappear in chapter 4 of Revelation, now with more information about the activities and beings of heaven. Here we find again an image of the glory and majesty of God, made visible to John through the action of the Holy Spirit:

At once I was in the Spirit, and lo, a throne stood in heaven, with one seated on the throne! And he who sat on the throne appeared like jasper and carnelian, and round the throne was a rainbow that looked like an emerald. Round the throne were twenty-four thrones, and seated on the thrones were twenty four elders, clad in white garments with golden crowns on their heads. . . . and before the throne is as it were a sea of glass, like crystal . . . and day and night they never cease to sing, "holy, holy, holy is the Lord God Almighty, who was and is to come!" (Revelation 4:2–4, 6, 8, Revised Standard Version)

This vision of Christ has formed the foundation for images of heaven ever since. Its influence on the apse of the Wheeling cathedral is evident. But more than just an image of Christ, this passage tells us about heavenly *relationships* and the beings who participate in them.

The throne reiterates Christ's majesty and brings with it fulfillment of the Old Testament's entire tradition of enthronement psalms, sung in ancient Israel to speak of God's enthronement above the ark in the Holy of Holies of the temple, and therefore his presence with his people.[11] Christ appears like the gems of jasper and carnelian, suggesting that John could not see an immediate image of God. The emerald rainbow around the throne recalls the gemstone, which Bede tells us signifies water, and the rainbow recalls God's covenant with Noah (Genesis 9:12–17). Surrounding Christ are 24 white-robed elders on their own thrones, sharing Christ's authority as a heavenly council or senate. Their number has been understood to recall the 24 classes of priests mentioned in 1 Chronicles 24:1–19, or perhaps the number of apostles plus the number of tribes of Israel, symbolizing all of creation now transformed into the Church triumphant. Their white robes speak of their heavenly glory and perfection, just as the white linen garment of the high priest worn in the Holy of Holies was understood as the clothing of heaven.

Interestingly, Christ's throne is surrounded by a "sea of glass" appearing "like crystal." Allusions to the sea often refer to God's power over chaos, as in the parting of the Red Sea, the flood of Noah, or Christ walking on water and calming the storm of the Sea of Galilee. Here the sea that surrounds the throne appears as if frozen, completely subject to God's power, but also glorified now into the radiant quality of crystal, becoming like a bridge back to the throne of God for the creatures who had been separated from God by the chaos of the waters.[12] Bede calls this crystal the water of Baptism, "congealed into a precious stone," a symbolic representation of Baptism as glorious bridge back to wholeness in God.

Four six-winged creatures stand at the throne as well, each with a distinct face: one like a lion, one like an ox, one a man, and one an eagle. This image had precedent in Old Testament prophecy, though within about one hundred years of the writing of the book of Revelation, Saint Irenaeus of Lyon (ca. 120–202 AD) understood these four living creatures to be images of the four evangelists, an idea echoed by Saints

Even flooring can reveal liturgical realities: the streets of heaven are described as a sea of glass, clear as crystal, that bridge the waters of chaos and lead back to Christ.

Augustine and Jerome.[13] For this reason, images of these winged creatures are a common motif in properly ornamented churches. More than a simple reminder of the existence of the Gospel evangelists, the images become icons of the heavenly beings present at the liturgy on earth and in heaven. Crucial, however, is that the creatures have a *liturgical role*. These beings provide the model for the earthly liturgy in their theocentric praise with the words "Holy, Holy, Holy is the Lord God almighty, who was and is and is to come!" Amid the glorious flashes of lightning and peals of thunder at God's throne, these heavenly beings offer their eternal prayer in praise of God. It is for just this reason that people at Mass sing the "Holy! Holy! Holy!" in the Sanctus. Humans do on earth what the saints do in heaven so that things on earth might be as they are in heaven, and God becomes more and more all in all. By *seeing* these beings in art as well as joining them in song, we become changed into God's likeness from one degree to the next.

The white-robed elders share in this liturgical role, offering God their praise by throwing their crowns before the throne, falling on their faces, and singing: "Worthy art thou, our Lord and God, to receive glory and honor and power, for thou didst create all things, and by thy will they existed and were created" (Revelation 4:11). The church building and its figural art make present this heavenly reality, and as such are not simply a neutral background for the carrying out of the rubrics of the Mass, but the visual making real of what heaven "looks like," just as the congregation hears and sings what heaven "sounds like." This is truly *liturgical* art, art which makes present the realities of the heavenly liturgy itself. "This angelic chant, performed as it is in heaven and on earth, reminds us of the sublimity of the Mass, where the worship of God crosses the frontiers of time and space and has a positive influence on the entire world."[14]

These winged creatures, however, are joined by the great multitude of the saved. The figurative number of 144,000 symbolizes an unfathomably large number even in its symbolic specificity: 144,000 of the chosen people—12,000 each from the 12 tribes of Israel—as well as countless multitudes, "which no man could count, from every nation, from all tribes and peoples," clothed in white robes and singing, "Salvation belongs to our God who sits upon the throne and to the Lamb" (Revelation 7:4–14). By singing the chants of heaven and looking at those who chant them with us, the earthly worship gives an eschatological flash of the heavenly realities, which is to say, the transformative presence of God. Faithful and willing worshippers leave transformed, more conformed to heaven, and therefore more suited to heaven itself.

THE NEW HEAVEN AND THE NEW EARTH

Chapter 21 of Revelation is the church architect's guide unlike any other. Here Saint John sees an architectural vision of the new heaven and the new earth in a grand tour which involves an angelic guide and a heavenly tape measure. Moreover, before the tour John is given the angelic architect's "program," laying out exactly what he would be seeing. And the vision provides the image of the time when God is in fact all in all, when the Fall is overcome, and Christ's "Bride," the Church, is again united as one with God. Here is the climax of salvation history. The whole of scripture points to this moment, when the goal of God's salvific mission is achieved and his triumphant glory is manifested in his creation, where, as Saint Irenaeus said, "the glory of God is man fully alive," filled again with divine life.[15] Here the Tabernacle of Moses, the Jerusalem temple, the Incarnation, and the Passion find their completion. Here heaven and earth become one, and God's will is finally done "on earth as it is in heaven."

Here the architect sees the role model for a church building.
Here the liturgical artist sees the goal of artistic representation.
Here the faithful find a critical visual component of the liturgy in which they participate.

So what, then, did John see?

> Then I saw a new heaven and new earth . . . and I saw the heavenly city, the new Jerusalem coming down out of heaven like a bride adorned for her husband; and I heard a loud voice from the throne saying, "Behold the dwelling of God is with men. He will dwell with them, and they shall be his people, and God himself will be with them; he will wipe away every tear from their eyes, and death shall be no more, neither shall there be mourning nor crying nor pain any more, for the former things have passed away." (Revelation 21:1–4)

This vision shows the vanquishing of evil, the end of the time of the Fall, and death, sadness, and privation no longer reign. God wipes every tear from his people's eyes. Jerusalem is now new because it is heavenly, transformed, and restored. Unlike the earthly city of Jerusalem, blessed and chosen as it was, the heavenly Jerusalem is transformed and glorified, coming down from heaven and given to humanity. Christ's own words tell the story: "Behold, I make all things new. . . . these words are trustworthy and true. . . . It is done!" (Revelation 21:5–6).

This new Jerusalem is prepared as a bride for her husband, meaning that it is adorned, festive, and intended for union with God. And the term *new Jerusalem* is symbolic language for the city composed of the "living stones" of the People of God, the 12 tribes, all of humanity. So the new Jerusalem is, in fact, the Church, the people in which God dwells completely. Christ is the Bridegroom, the Church is the Bride, and the two become one. For this reason, the heavenly feast is the *wedding* banquet of the Lamb, and the church building is comparable to a place adorned for a wedding feast. It is the greatest banqueting place of all the cosmos. The altar in a church is more than the community's table; it is the glorified table of this heavenly feast made present sacramentally in earthly matter. Liturgical vessels are more than "basket, basin, plate, and cup." They are sacramental representations of heavenly vessels, the paten of Christ's feast and the precious chalice of the eternal banquet, celebrating the end of the Fall and the unity of God with mortals.

Under the old law, God dwelled in the earthly city of Jerusalem, with the temple's Holy of Holies as its focus. In the New Testament, Christ's body is the new Temple, and Christ's Mystical Body is formed by his union of all humanity to himself. The Mystical Body therefore is Christ and people together. But the Mystical Body is also the *Bride* of Christ, the Bridegroom, so in a virtuoso act of unification, the Bride *is* the Groom! Two are made unchangeably one. But the Bride is also the Church, and the Church is the new Temple, and the new Temple is Christ which is also the heavenly Jerusalem where God dwells and all become one. Moreover, Christ is the new High Priest, and since we are part of his Mystical Body, we also share in the common priesthood of the baptized who can offer sacrifices to God. If this multiplicity seems strangely foreign to the fallen intellect, this only shows the power of God to draw all seemingly disparate things to himself. Here all points converge; the symbolism of Christ, his Church, and heaven become interchangeable because Christ and his Church become one in a glorious restored relationship with the Father. And the earthly church building is a sacramental image of Christ, Temple, Mystical Body, High Priest, Bride, and new Jerusalem all at once.

Saint John gets an insider's tour of this new reality when the angel says to him, "Come, I will show you the Bride,

In the thirteenth-century Sainte-Chapelle in Paris, the walls are composed of radiant, gem-like stained glass panels composed of saints, biblical scenes, and holy men and women.

the wife of the Lamb" (Revelation 21:9). Here the architect finds that which has inspired church builders for centuries:

> [The heavenly Jerusalem] had a great high wall, with twelve gates, and at the gates twelve angels, and on the gates the names of the twelve tribes of the sons of Israel were inscribed; . . . and the wall of the city had twelve foundations, and on them the twelve names of the twelve apostles of the Lamb. (Revelation 21:12–14)

So the "walls" of the heavenly Jerusalem are themselves "made of" the twelve entry points back to God: the tribes of the chosen people and the 12 apostles who bring the message of Christ throughout the world. Viewing the city with the angel, John writes:

> And he who talked to me had a measuring rod of gold to measure the city and its gates and walls. The city lies foursquare, its length the same as its breadth, . . . its length and width and height are equal. . . . The wall was built of jasper, while the city was of pure gold, clear as glass. The foundations of the wall of the city were adorned with every jewel; the first was jasper, the second sapphire, the third agate, the fourth emerald, the fifth onyx, the sixth carnelian, the seventh chrysolite, the eighth beryl, the ninth topaz, the tenth chrysoprase, the eleventh jacinth, and twelfth amethyst. And the gates were twelve pearls, each of the

gates made of a single pearl, and the street of the city was pure gold, transparent as glass. (Revelation, 21:15–16, 18–21)

Here we find the cubic shape again, like the inner room of the Tabernacle of Moses and the Holy of Holies in the Temple of Jerusalem. Those rooms foreshadowed the "shape" of heaven, while Revelation shows it in completion. The cube is now the shape of the *Bride*, who has been fully conformed to the shape of God. In other words, the Church, the People of God, has been fully divinized, fully transformed back to beauty, once again having *integritas*, *consonantia*, and *claritas*.

The foundations and walls of the heavenly Jerusalem are symbolically "made" of gems, clearly evoking the 12 gems of the high priest's breastplate in the temple, but also using signs that humans understand. Our natural attraction to gems comes from their clarity, color, and radiance. Now the city itself is composed of the radiant stones of humanity, no longer the dust of Adam or the living stones of the apostolic age, but radiant, glorified, and transformed.[16] In Revelation, the communion prefigured by the temple worship is accomplished. God now dwells with his people as he intended: not once a year in the Holy of Holies, but in the joy and peace of communion among his creation. Felix Lietuchter's remarkable murals at the Cathedral of the Madeleine in Salt Lake City

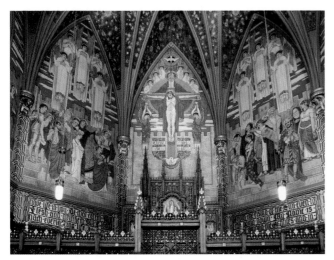

The heavenly Jerusalem. Cathedral of the Madeleine, Salt Lake City, Utah. Felix Lieftuchter, muralist.

The golden walls of the heavenly city portrayed in marble with heavenly beings above. Cathedral of St. Louis the King, Saint Louis, Missouri. Barnett, Haynes & Barnett, architects.

display the heavenly Jerusalem in a slightly different way. Christ's eternal sacrifice appears as a Trinitarian crucifixion scene—not a snapshot of the historical event at Calvary, but the glory of the eternal sacrifice of Christ. Angels in rapt attention to the Father contemplate the sacrifice of the Son. The saints below are enclosed in the golden walls of the heavenly city, with the parapets above explicitly evoking the walls of the earthly Jerusalem under the starry skies of the heavens, which in their order and obedience praise God as well. The Cathedral of St. Louis the King in St. Louis, Missouri, takes the analogy further, covering the walls in courses of golden-colored stone, suggesting that the entire church is contained within the walls of the heavenly Jerusalem, above which the angels and saints stand on a background of golden, gem-like mosaic. In the Blessed Sacrament chapel of the cathedral, Christ is shown as High Priest, wearing the breastplate of 12 gems, signaling his fulfillment of the temple precursors.

In the thirteenth-century Sainte-Chapelle in Paris, the walls have nearly vanished. Except for 12 slender columns, each bearing an image of 1 of the 12 apostles as pillars of the Church (Galatians 2:9), the walls are composed of radiant, gem-like stained glass panels composed of saints, biblical scenes, and holy men and women. Here, without denying the value of material to become the bearer of divinity, the dust of the earth used to make stained glass is transformed through the application of human will and intellect, imitating God the creator who fashioned man from mute dust and made him living and intelligent, then glorified him to radiance. Saint Paul writes, saying that "just as we have borne the image of the man of dust, we shall also bear the image of the man of heaven" (1 Corinthians 15:49), and here stained glass becomes more than a mere painting in light. It reveals in our time the reality of a restored, divinized creation.

This particularly French, medieval way of imaging the heavenly Jerusalem differs from how artists did the same

thing in Byzantium, for instance, yet the theological principal at work in each case is the same. The effective revelation of the heavenly Jerusalem is *the* critical element in sacramental art and architecture whether in the seventh century or the twenty-first. For this reason, the documents of the Second Vatican Council could rightly say that the "art of our own days, coming from every race and region, shall also be given free scope in the Church, provided that it adorns the sacred buildings and holy rites with due reverence and honor" (SC, 123). Due reverence and honor means that the building and its art will reveal the dignity and reality of the liturgy itself: the joining of Bride and Bridegroom and the transfiguration of earthly things into heavenly realities.

Of course, John sees no temple in the heavenly city because the whole city is the temple, the place where God dwells (Revelation 21:22). In earthly terms, the Jerusalem temple was the privileged place of God's dwelling; in the heavenly Jerusalem God dwells everywhere as he had in the Garden of Eden. Saint John sees no sun or moon in the city, for the radiance of God is its light, so bright that any created light source pales in comparison. Toward the end of his vision, Saint John describes an image of the Holy Spirit as the "river of the water of life" flowing from the throne, through the streets of the city, watering the tree of life which produces good fruit and leaves "for the healing of the nations." Here the image of the Garden of Eden returns, where the river flowed from the Garden (Genesis 2:9–10) in which were many fruits that were good to eat. The fruit of the tree that brought about the Fall is hereby replaced in a great biblical bookend by the tree of life, which is the cross. The mural of the Wheeling Cathedral shows this river gushing from the throne penetrating inside the city walls to the people below.[17] Here one visually encounters the river of the water of life, and, as Jean Corbon has noted, "if we let the river of life permeate

Top, left: The Arch of Constantine served as a victorious ceremonial entry to the city. Rome, 315 AD. Bottom, left: The triumphal arch as marker of entry to the heavenly city continues in traditional church design. St. Boniface Church, Evansville, Indiana. Above: In many Gothic cathedrals, a scene of the Last Judgment is placed over the central portal, indicating those worthy to enter the church as image of the heavenly city.

us, we become trees of life, for the mystery that the river symbolizes takes hold of us."[18]

The history of Christian architecture is filled with similar images. The hermeneutic of the heavenly Jerusalem typology brings to life the great portals of the Gothic cathedrals, where Christ the judge sits over the gate-like central doorway to determine who enters the heavenly City, and the unhappy demonic gargoyles and **chimeras** remain always outside. In later centuries, Baroque churches were filled with angels and saints about in a visceral intersection of heaven and earth. Many great twentieth-century reredoses show the orderly array of heavenly beings whom we join in the liturgy. In an earthly recall of conventional signs, many great church entries are based on the Arch of Constantine, recalling the role of the triumphal arch in the ancient world as a symbolic gateway for a military victor into the earthly city. In the church building, however, the victor is Christ, the victory is over sin and death, and the city is the heavenly Jerusalem. This architectural consciousness is not something foreign to our time and place.

So throughout the history of the Church, a critical role of the church building has been its evocation of the heavenly Jerusalem. Though much forgotten today, this theme is completely resonant with the liturgy, even as reformed after the Second Vatican Council. This rich imagery is primarily *liturgical*; it reveals to us the otherwise invisible dimensions of the heavenly and cosmic liturgy. Full, conscious, fruitful, and active participation in the liturgy demands that worshippers know in what they are actually participating! Looking at the sacred liturgical image of our anticipated heavenly glory is no more a distraction from the liturgical action than is singing the Gloria. Singing the texts of the Mass is to participate in the Mass. Looking at the Mass is to participate in it as well, becoming accustomed through the eye to know what heaven is and becoming more suited to dwell there with God for

chimeras: mythical or grotesque figural sculptures best known for adorning Gothic cathedrals, as distinguished from gargoyles, which have a similar form but also serve as terminations of spouts to direct water away from the building.

eternity. Saint Augustine wrote that "no one can be ready for the next life unless he trains himself for it now."[19] Liturgical art based on the scriptural revelation of the heavenly Jerusalem is a crucial sacramental tool in this divine pedagogy of salvation because it recalls the time of the *shadow*, allows us to participate in the victory of Christ by way of *image*, and prepares us for the heavenly *reality*. It waits for rediscovery in our own day.

---

1. Jean Corbon, *Wellspring of Worship* (San Francisco: Ignatius, 2005), 62, ff. 11: "The expression 'heavenly liturgy' is hardly used anymore. Given the concern to demythologize, people prefer to drop it, yet it expresses a purifying insight of faith that opens us to the mystery of the liturgy. To ignore the heavenly liturgy amounts to rejecting the eschatological tension proper to the Church and either settling down permanently in the present world (secularism) or escaping from it (pietism). This leads in turn to a separation of liturgy from life, for the heavenly liturgy is not a different liturgy that either parallels or serves as exemplar for the liturgy we think of as ours in earthly time."

2. Pseudo-Dionysius, *The Celestial Hierarchy,* ch. 1, par. 3, in *Pseudo-Dionysius: The Complete Works* (New York: Paulist Press, 1987), 146.

3. This terminology of grace is normally used for the Church's "seven sacraments," and it is worth being careful not to confuse the effect of liturgical art and architecture with the efficacy of the Church's canonic sacraments. We cannot say that liturgical art or architecture cause grace *ex opera operato* in the same way as the Blessed Sacrament or Baptism, but they do dispose us for the proper reception of grace. Vatican II reminds us that for the liturgy "to produce its full effects, it is necessary that the faithful come to it with proper dispositions, that their minds should be attuned to their voices, and that they should cooperate with divine grace lest they receive it in vain" (SC, 11). The Western Church's thinkers have preferred to preserve the primacy of the Church's seven sacraments by placing liturgical art and architecture in the category of a sacramental, an object that disposes us to receive grace and cooperate with it. In the *Summa Theologiae*, Saint Thomas Aquinas argues that inanimate objects are consecrated because "they acquire spiritual virtue from the consecration, whereby they are rendered fit for the Divine Worship, so that man derives devotion therefrom, making him more fitted for the Divine functions, unless this be hindered by want of reverence" (Tertia pars, q. 83). In the Christian East, the term *sacrament* is often used more loosely to mean anything that uses earthly material to manifest an invisible spiritual reality. In this sense, icons are considered sacraments in that they manifest the very realities of heaven. Pope John Paul II confirmed this idea in his *Letter to Artists* by writing: "in a sense, the icon is a sacrament. By analogy with what occurs in the sacraments, the icon makes present the mystery of the Incarnation" (LA, 8).

4. Eusebius, writing in the early fourth century, refers to the Church as the Bride of the Lamb (Revelation 21:2) when speaking of the basilica at Tyre and quotes Dionysius's writings on the book of Revelation. See Eusebius, *The Church History*, X.4.3 and VII. 25.1–27. In his *Life of Constantine*, Eusebius compares the building of the Church of the Savior (better known as the Church of the Holy Sepulcher) as "the new Jerusalem," even thinking that scripture may have literally referred to this very building as the *actual* new Jerusalem of Revelation 21:2. This pious exaggeration nonetheless reveals the strength of the association between earthly architecture and the heavenly city. See Eusebius, *Life of Constantine*, Book III, ch. 33.

5. It is important to note that this is not a claim that all churches need to look alike. The theological realities expressed by every church are always the same, but the external manifestations of the liturgy can differ within the limits of legitimate variation. The chapel of the Trappist monastery does not need to look like that of an important cathedral or devotional shrine, yet each will always manifest the glory of the heavenly future.

6. Paul Evdokimov, *The Art of the Icon* (Redondo Beach, CA: Oakwood Publications, 1990), 143.

7. Joseph Ratzinger, *The Spirit of the Liturgy* (San Francisco: Ignatius, 2000), 26.

8. Edward Marshall, *The Explanation of the Apocalypse by Venerable Bede* (Oxford: James Parker and Co., 1878), 15–16. It is worth noting that the easily assumed notion of Christ's power as intimidating or competitive is done away with by Bede, who instead sees Christ's majesty as evidence of his heavenly glory and therefore victory of sin and death. Christ's glory is then promised to his creatures.

9. *The Navarre Bible Revelation, Hebrews and Catholic Letters* (New York: Scepter Publishers, 2006), 37.

10. Romano Guardini, *The Spirit of the Liturgy* (New York: Crossroad, 1998), 48–49.

11. For a useful treatment of the meaning of the throne, see Margaret Barker, *The Gate of Heaven* (London: SPCK, 1991), ch. 4.

12. Margaret Barker makes an interesting comment on this sea of glass. First she comments on the temple itself known in Judaic literature as a "firmament in the seas," the throne from which God reigned, as in Psalm 29: "The Lord sits enthroned over the flood, / the Lord sits enthroned forever." Barker also refers to the ca. 100 bc Jewish text *The Life of Adam and Eve*, in which the sea surrounding the paradise was frozen by the Archangel Michael so that Adam could return. See Barker, *The Gate of Heaven*, 65–67.

13. For Old Testament precursors, see Ezekiel chapters 1 and 10 as well as Daniel chapter 7. See also Saint Irenaeus of Lyons, *Adversus Haereses* 3.11.8; Saint Augustine of Hippo *De consensu evangelistarum* 1.6.9; and Saint Jerome, *Preface to the Commentary on Matthew*, 6.1036–1037. The commentary in the Navarre Bible offers this interpretation: "Christian tradition going back as far as Saint Irenaeus had interpreted these four creatures as standing for the four evangelists because they 'carry' Jesus Christ to men. The one with the face of a man is St. Matthew, who starts his book with the human genealogy of Christ; the lion stands for St. Mark: his Gospel begins with the voice crying in the wilderness (which is where the lion's roar can be heard); the ox is a reference to the sacrifices in the temple in Jerusalem, which is where St. Luke begins his account of Christ's life; and the eagle represents St. John, who soars to the heights to contemplate the divinity of the Word." See *The Navarre Bible Revelation and Hebrews and Catholic Letters*, notes, p. 56.

14. *The Navarre Bible Revelation and Hebrews and Catholic Letters*, notes, p. 56.

15. Irenaeus of Lyon, *Adversus Haereses,* IV. 20. 7.

16. The type and meaning of the stones of the high priest's breastplate has been subject to scholarly interpretation for centuries. The translation of the ancient names for each stone varies, and so there is rarely a one-to-one correspondence between the names of the 12 gems on the breastplate and those of the heavenly Jerusalem in most biblical translations. Many scholars have attempted to determine which stone corresponds with which tribe and which apostle. However, for the purposes of this book, the larger symbolic meaning of the gem-covered walls remains primary: the heavenly city is composed of the living stones of the Church, transformed and glorified from the dust of the earth to radiant gem-like glory.

17. For more on the river of the water of life, see Corbon, 62, 69, 78, and also the *Catechism of the Catholic Church*, 1137.

18. Corbon, 29.

19. Saint Augustine, *Discourse on the Psalms*, (ps. 148, 1–2: CCL [Corpus Christianorum Series Latina] 40, 2165–2166) as given in the Liturgy of the Hours, Office of Readings, Saturday of the Fifth Week of Easter.

Part III

The Classical Tradition

OFFERIMVS
TIBI DOMINE

Classical architecture allows for a poetic representation of structure and expresses notions of redeemed creation very effectively.

In the first century BC, a Greek-born architect named Marcus Vitruvius Pollio wrote a treatise that became the most influential architecture book in history, still in print to this day. His *Ten Books on Architecture* had no pictures, being primarily a book about the ideas involved in designing, building, and living. These ideas were not only technical solutions to engineering problems, but dealt with the theory of architecture itself. In chapter 1 of Book 1, Vitruvius claimed rather matter-of-factly that architecture is a bearer of meaning which has two distinct components: first, some sort of invisible idea from the mind of the architect, and second, a physical, tangible building which signifies that idea.[1] Long before the advent of sacramental theology as we know it today, this understanding of architecture by a pre–Christian architect set the stage for a theology of architecture.

Some 300 years before Vitruvius wrote his book, the Athenians had already developed a kind of architecture that embodied knowledge of proportion, beauty, structure, physics, poetry, and even politics. The famous Porch of the Maidens on the Acropolis shows columns taking the shape of women, an artistic and architectural manifestation of the political status of the wives of captured soldiers in one of Athens' many wars. So a column, already a poetic representation of the load–bearing structural component, took on **anthropomorphic** and political significance. In Classical architecture, every **piece, element, and motif**—be it molding, ornament, or

The geometric underpinnings of Santa Maria Novella Church, Florence. Leon Battista Alberti, architect, ca. 1470.

structural device—bears meaning, which has been understood in greater or lesser degrees in the last twenty-five hundred years.

The following chapters will form an investigation into the meaning of the Classical tradition inherited from the Greeks and Romans and developed by Christianity, not merely as a form of nostalgia for pleasant but forgotten forms, but as a way to reintroduce the modern reader to the concept of "reading" architecture. They will then suggest a Christian reading of Classical architecture rooted in history and sacramental theology. Just as Augustine baptized Plato and Aquinas baptized Aristotle, so Christianity baptized Classicism and used it extensively. The arguments presented will not be justified with a claim that "it has always been done that way." The facts are that sometimes it was, and sometimes it wasn't. The more important question arises, however: Are there reasons to use Classicism today beyond mere historical association? The answer given is a very strong yes. This requires a major re-thinking of the current trends in architecture, both for many of the satisfied inheritors of Modernism and for

Sanctuary of the Divine Mercy, Chicago. James McCrery, architect, in progress, 2009.

anthropomorphic: from the Greek, meaning, "in the shape of a human being," often used to ascribe human characteristics to inanimate objects.

piece, element, and motif: a handy terminology developed by historian W. C. Westfall to define the parts of classical architecture. A piece is a small architectural unit such as the capital of a column, which, when joined together with other pieces, forms an element, such as a full column. Motifs are canonical arrangements of elements into something recognizable and symbolic, such as groupings of columns and entablatures in a particular way, such as a temple front or triumphal arch.

Differing views of structural clarity, part 1. Many strains of architectural Modernism insisted on literal displays of structural members and an industrial or engineer's aesthetic (left). On the right, structural clarity is expressed poetically and somewhat ahistorically by suggesting that highly ornamented horizontal "beams" are supported on small projections from the vertical "posts."

those post–Moderns or New Classicists who have embraced Classical architectural forms once again.

Since the advent of Modernism, the Classical tradition in architecture has been labeled by many as a deficient sort of "copyism" which was once relevant but that no longer speaks to the modern mind. Its forms have been compared to a dead corpse of another era, its practitioners some sort of slaves to the past who refuse to recognize that the modern world was dominated by industry, the machine and technology. The questions then for Christians, and anyone interested in the inheritance of history, is how to reconcile the past with current practice.

Could that which was once Beautiful, True, and Good be no longer so, simply because the standard-bearing philosophers of Modernity have claimed a radical break between "then" and "now"? Can the primacy of discontinuity, which has so completely dominated the profession of architecture and architectural history for nearly one hundred years, continue to be credible when Modernism's products have proven so unsatisfying to so many, and its movement has been shattered into hundreds of post–Modernisms, including today's important revival of Classical architecture? Can it simply be ignored that every Christian society in the history of the world has happily embraced the Classical tradition in one form or

another? Is it some sort of supreme arrogance to believe that Constantine, Justinian, Charlemagne, Abbot Suger, Brunelleschi, Michelangelo, Bernini, von Erlach, Wren, Gibbs, Jefferson, Stanford White, John Russell Pope, and countless others were simply misguided puppets of their ages? Of course we could ask a similar question of today's New Classicists, great thinkers and practitioners like Allan Greenberg, Duncan Stroik, Demetri Porphyrios, C. W. Westfall, Thomas Gordon Smith, James McCrery, Franck & Lohsen, David Meleca, Dino Marcantonio, and so many others. If Classical architecture is merely a product of its age (which, theoretically, was long ago) how, then, could the New Classicists come from the Age of the Machine and Modernism and yet still embrace the Classical tradition? Are they dupes who are retarding the advance of civilization by clinging to the past?

Here we begin to find an answer: Classicism represents not so much a set of architectural forms as it does a philosophy of the nature of things as expressed in art and architecture. Those who think most deeply about Classicism recognize it as a system of building that goes far beyond nostalgia and copyism. For some, intuitive knowledge and common sense argue for an architecture of continuity that is humane in scale and rich in poetic allusion. All architecture does this to some degree. However, Classicism does these things with *specificity*

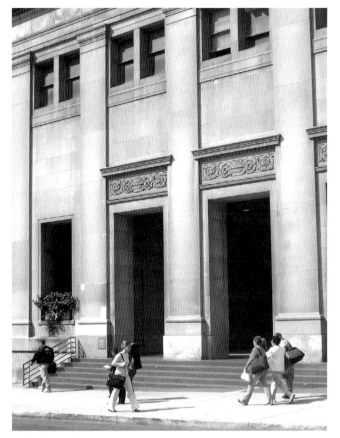

Differing views of structural clarity, part 2. Though the steel structure of each building is covered, a poetic overlay of vertical and horizontal members in stone reveals a "virtual" or poetic representation of structure while maintaining an architectural continuity with the Classical tradition.

as well as an almost endless variety. Classicism trusts precedent explicitly, growing from the rich humanist tradition, with heroes like Plato, Aristotle, Augustine, and the Christian humanists. Classicism values the enduring, the tested, and the poetic representation of what is true. In the Classical worldview, Truth exists and is knowable through intellectual inquiry and revelation. Skepticism is welcomed on a limited scale to test the inherited tradition for current-day use, but it is never the primary lens for looking at the world. This approach is decidedly different from many of the prevailing philosophies of Modernity, and people find Classicism appealing or repulsive based upon their preexisting conceptions of Modernity's ideas.[2] Classicism provides the familiar mode for the world's great monuments, respects received tradition, takes proportional systems and patterns of creation to its very core, bears strong strains of anthropomorphism, and grows from a tradition of ritual festivity. The natural sympathies between a Christian, sacramental worldview, and Classical architecture are strikingly clear.

The intent here is not to find fault with Modernism. Many others have done that with greater and lesser success. The point here is to find the strengths of the Classical tradition and to connect them to sacramental theology. Modernity brings its gifts as does any philosophical system, but in

Christian architecture, anything new must be tested according to the standards of Christ and the Church. That which is antithetical or harmful to Christianity is discarded; that which is good is retained. There is much to praise about a spirit that values new expressions and uses conventional signs appropriate to time and place. However, there is also much to retain in the Classical tradition as a bearer of that which is enduring. Because the Classical tradition seems best capable of living up to the aesthetic challenge of Hans Urs von Balthasar mentioned earlier. It is worth repeating in full:

> The real problem [is] how to construct a theory of beauty (*Aesthetica in nuce*) in such a way that, in it, the total aspiration of worldly and pagan beauty is fulfilled while all the glory is at the same time given to God in Jesus Christ.[3]

One of the premises of Christianity is that God ordered the world and history so as to prepare it for Christ. The Israelites, as chosen people, provided the primary seedbed for the expression of typologies of the Son of God. But the pagan world gets its share of credit as well, developing theories of philosophy, law, governance, art, Beauty, nature, and being, all of which could be read as providing the tools for Christianity to flourish and understand its own revelation. Balthasar's challenge, then, is seen in a new light. Any theory of art and architecture today should absorb the sum phrase, and local conventions. Language reserved for ritual behavior retains archaic forms that distinguish it from everyday speech ("Our Father, who *art* in heaven, *hallowed be Thy name . . . .*"). Language expresses and conveys ideas, and the kind of words used depends on what is being said and to whom. In a similar way, ritual architecture depends upon a stable architectural lexicon and careful choice of forms that express its ritual quality and place in the architectural hierarchy. Moreover, word choice can convey festivity. Words can be extravagant, ceremonial, or joyous. Architecture can be the same, and Classical architecture was born of a desire to express ritual festivity.

If architecture is to be understood as the built form of ideas that reveals knowledge by conveying information, it should use a form, which, like language, is composed of rec-

Monumental Corinthian capital, Union Station, Chicago. Daniel Burnham, architect, 1925.

New Classicism in church design. St. Michael the Archangel Church, Leawood, Kansas. David Meleca, design architect, completed 2009.

Facing page: Chapel at Thomas Aquinas College, Santa Paula, California. Duncan Stroik, architect, completed 2009.

total of knowledge and tradition from the past and fulfill it while still remaining intensely Christocentric. Just as grace does not destroy nature, but purifies and glorifies it, so a Christian theory of architecture does the same. Christianity helps fulfill and illuminate the Truth wherever it is found.

Architectural Classicism might be better compared with language, which has conventionalized structure, syntax, and rules necessary to best convey meaning. Language can be flexible but requires stability, poetic yet precise, mundane yet convey transcendent ideas. Words can be everyday slang or reserved for sacred occasions. Language by its very nature conserves, relying on stability to make it understandable. New words are invented as the need arises, but they are always within the stable context of a common grammar and lexicon. Language has differing accents, regional turns of

ognizable conventions capable of expressing both the most grand and most subtle statements. Where would rhetoric or preaching be if the leaders of the field said that subject matter could not use allusion, convention, or tradition except in only the most vague and distant terms? Where would the compelling power of the Truth be if the only philosophers that could be cited were agnostics, atheists, and spiritualists? Moreover, how persuasive would the faith sound if preachers were to be satisfied with mere utility, seeing their art as merely the most efficient solution to a linguistic problem? We can ask the same questions of liturgical art and architecture: Has the substitution of the meeting house or factory for sacramental building removed the compelling

DUNCAN G. STROIK.   THOMAS AQUINAS COLLEGE CHAPEL   FEB 11, 2003

Seminary of Our Lady of Guadalupe, Denton, Nebraska. Thomas Gordon Smith, architect, under construction 2009.

power of liturgical architecture? Has the substitution of distorted, expressionist, or abstract forms simply turned liturgical imagery into strange "art pieces" recognized by the museum curators but completely unconvincing to the faithful? Has Modernity supposedly true to its age simply provided a set of forms foreign to the people of this age because Modernity doubted the value of inherited conventional, natural, and sacramental signs?

The challenge of Classicism is that it often seems to be "other," from another place, another time, and so on. And yet it remains with us. What are we to make of this? In 1988, in the thick of post–Modern architecture's re-embrace of Classical architecture, art historian George Hersey asked a series of perfectly reasonable questions:

> Why do we still use the classical orders? Practically every town of decent size in the Western world has its quota of Doric, Ionic and Corinthian. And some of the greatest modern buildings, from the Panthéon in Paris, to the Capitol in Washington, to the Imperial Palace in Tokyo, across Southeast Asian countries that have practically nothing to do with classical civilization, and back around the world to government structures of Leningrad, Warsaw, and Brussels, are monumental essays in the use of the orders. Greco-Roman classicism was not only the architecture of the Greeks and Romans and of their empires, it was also the architecture, *mutatis mutandis*, of Romanesque Europe and of Byzantium, of the Renaissance and the Baroque, of Neoclassicism, the Baroque Revival, the Beaux-Arts, and fascism; and it is even, in a peculiar but strong way, a contributor to post modernism. Why?[4]

As one of the twentieth century's leading architectural historians who taught at Yale University for some forty years, Hersey tells us much in recognizing that Classicism is a way of design that seems to have been ubiquitous throughout Western (and some non–Western) history.[5] I would take Hersey's characterization even further to recall that the architecture of Jerusalem in the time of Christ, including the

Jerusalem Temple Mount itself and the many synagogues that were built in Palestine after the temple's destruction, partook of high-style Roman Classicism. Furthermore, we can add the architecture of late medieval Europe, what we call today Gothic, to this litany. Anyone who has seen the prominent display of Corinthian columns lining the nave of Notre Dame de Paris or has read of Abott Suger's desire to send couriers to Rome to gather columns from the ruins of the Roman Empire in order to construct the world's first "Gothic" building at St- Denis in Paris knows that the glory of Classicism captured the minds of the medievals as well. Copies and ideas from Vitruvius's *Ten Books on Architecture* are known to have been available in the Middle Ages.[6]

Unless we are to think of the world's greatest builders as simpletons who simply didn't know what else to do, we must assume that Classical architecture meant something throughout history. It could mean structural stability, figurative legibility, or credibility by association. We know that in the ancient world, at least the best architects understood the history and meaning of Classicism, and that this knowledge existed to a greater or lesser degree throughout Western history until only very recently. Except when based on the

Benedictine Monastery, Clear Creek, Oklahoma. Thomas Gordon Smith, architect, under construction 2009.

most skeptical, deterministic art historical methodology, a history of architecture is much like a history of salvation: it is a history of continuity, and the bearer of that continuity is Classical architecture, glorying in its many variations and manifestations. The attempted departure from Classicism in the Modernist movements of the twentieth century really wasn't one at all. The great modern architects who "invented" Modernism were Classically trained, and evidence of their Classical training has been identified even in their "Modernist" works. A properly trained Classical architectural theorist could argue that Modernism isn't a new thing; it is simply Classicism badly done. Many Modernist architects, for instance, compared the columns of the Greek temples to the

"Ironic" or post-Modern use of classical motifs. Chicago.

steel I-beams of Modernism. Here, the Classical principle of evident structural logic remains, but is impoverished by the denial of the value of ornament, decoration, precedent, craftsmanship, proportional ratios, anthropomorphic allusions, and traditional materials. A steel beam, concrete pole, or deconstructed exterior skin is simply is not equivalent to a properly used column.

Classical architecture certainly engages the affect, giving a satisfying emotional response. The sense of overwhelming drama of the Doric colonnades of the piazza of St. Peter's Basilica in Rome gives the visitor a valid and visceral sense of the importance of the place. But after the initial emotional response has passed, good architecture should then stand the test of the intellect analyzing the knowledge given by the senses. *Claritas* is at the heart of Classical architecture, not in the literal sense of showing its wires and beams, but in the more important sense of revealing its Truth, that which is real about what it represents. It seeks to follow the patterns in nature set by its creator and to give a privileged place to continuity and tradition. It uses ornament to represent clarity of purpose, and decoration to express clarity of structure and its forces. But Classicism is never satisfied with utilitarianism or mere aestheticism. Without doubt, to be done well, a Classical building must satisfy its function. But added to the concept of function are purpose and ontology, and Classical architecture addresses these notions as well. We are reminded here of the famous Vitruvian triad of qualities needed for building well: *commoditas, firmitas,* and *venustas.*[7] *Commoditas* has been translated as a "commodity" or "convenience" that has a certain parallel to *integritas,* meaning a building is fitting, appropriate, or has all that it needs, such as enough rooms of proper size, for instance. *Firmitas* or "firmness" means that a building is structurally strong enough to do what it must do, support use and endure

the weather. *Venustas,* as the name implies, literally means "Venus-ness," having the attractive beauty, loveliness, and charm of the goddess Venus. Beauty, then, is not the result of functional planning of structure and function, but actually something intentionally designed into a building as one of its constituent elements.

Classical architecture seeks to raise the human activity of architecture to *glory* through the clear revelation of reality. It portrays the poetry of structure and purpose, removing them from the everyday functionalism in the same way that the liturgy causes words, gestures, and material things to rise beyond themselves. Because Classicism, properly used and understood, has the goal of participating in that which is eternal and true, and because we are currently in the midst of a large-scale Classical revival in the Roman Catholic Church today, an investigation into its theological possibilities is in order. This result is decidedly not to develop one narrow way of making churches, but to open up again the theological richness that surrounds us in many of our buildings and to inform the architects and clients who are already using the forms once again.

1. Vitruvius, *The Ten Books on Architecture,* I.1.iii. ". . . *quod significatur et quod significat. significatur proposita res, de qua dicitur; hanc autem significat demonstratio rationibus doctrinarum . . .*" or "In all matters, but particularly in architecture, there are these two points:—the thing signified, and that which gives it its significance. That which is signified is the subject of which we may be speaking; and that which gives significance is a demonstration on scientific principles." One of the more popular editions of the work is a reprint of the 1914 edition: Morris Hicky Morgan, trans., Vitruvius, *Ten Books on Architecture* (New York: Dover, 1960). Most recently, a well-illustrated edition was released: see Thomas Gordon Smith, *Vitruvius on Architecture* (New York: Monacelli Press, 2003).

2. For a clear explanation of contrasting views of intellectual inquiry, see Robert Barron, *The Strangest Way* (Maryknoll, NY: Orbis, 2002), 19. Speaking of René Descartes's *Discourse on Method,* Barron writes: "The wrecking-ball our philosopher chooses is the powerful one of systematic doubt: if a proposition or conviction *can* be doubted, it *should* be doubted." Barron has also described the four dominant presuppositions of modernity as methodical doubt, scientific rationalism, radical dualism, and anti-traditionalism in an article entitled "Beyond Beige Catholicism," *Antiphon* 6 (2001), 14–22.

3. Hans Urs von Balthasar, *The Glory of the Lord,* v. 1, (San Francisco: Ignatius Press/Crossroads, 1983), 81–82.

4. George Hersey, *The Lost Meaning of Classical Architecture* (New Haven: Yale University Press, 1988), 1.

5. The subject under consideration here is Classicism in the Western tradition. It is the limitations of the knowledge of the author and the size of the book that prevents the discussion of "Classical" architecture of various age and nations. The Classical traditions of Asian architecture are rich and varied, for instance, and despite their regional conventional usages, share much in common with the Western approach to its "high architecture," notably the attempt to establish an architecture of ritual significance, the elaboration of structure, and the legibility of ornament.

6. See for example, Kenneth J. Conant, "The After-Life of Vitruvius in the Middle Ages," *The Journal of the Society of Architectural Historians* 27 (March 1968), 33–38.

7. Vitruvius, *Ten Books on Architecture,* Book I, ch. 4, par. 2.

Chapter 6

Decoration: Clarity through Revelation of Structure

In modern parlance the terms *ornament* and *decoration* are used interchangeably, generally thought to belong to the realm of Martha Stewart and well-appointed homes and hotel lobbies. But as with many things in popular culture, our everyday understanding grows from origins that carry with them a great deal of meaning, which many have forgotten how to see. In order to "read" Classical architecture once again, we must return to the sources of its meaning. And once defined in architectural terminology, this rediscovery can be investigated for significance in the Christian worldview. We begin with decoration, which can be understood to express invisible natural realities through the poetic representation of a redeemed creation.

Decoration is an enrichment of architecture that adds to *claritas* (and therefore Beauty) by making the structural systems at work more legible.[1] This is not, however, the frank exposing of the engineering "guts" of a building, with steel I-beams and bolts giving the so-called "truth" of structural expression. Decoration is a *poetic* expression of structure, one which gives knowledge of things beyond the mere facts of engineering by beautifully revealing the forces of nature that would otherwise be invisible. Decoration is not satisfied with the earthly "engineer's aesthetic," to borrow a term from Modernist architect Le Corbusier's famous 1927 book *Towards a New Architecture*. It is interested in the *poet's* aesthetic, one which takes the cold facts of the engineer and completes and glorifies them with an overlay of poetic representation. In proper decoration, "the power of mythical fiction presides," writes Demetri Porphyrios, meaning that the intentionality of the *idea* made present in the building presides over the mere contingencies of the facts of its construction. In this sense, it allows for the "convergence of the real and the fictive so that the real is redeemed" and "in a moment of rare disinterestedness, rejoices in the sacramental power it has over contingent life and nature."[2] *Decoration, then, shows architecture as elevated and redeemed, freed, at least in part, from the effects of the Fall.*

Unadorned structural system of vertical posts and horizontal lintels. Stonehenge, Salisbury Plain, England, ca. 4000 BC.

Vertical and horizontal structural units poetically expressed and ornamented. Left: United States Supreme Court. Cass Gilbert, architect. Right: Mundelein Seminary, Illinois. Joseph McCarthy, architect.

DECORATION AND ELEVATED EXPRESSION

In proper decoration, the clarity of structural logic is always present. However, the poetics of architecture rise beyond the technical facts of physics and the strength of materials. Proper decoration provides for the elevated expression of the forces found in a building. In a similar way, prayer uses the rules of correct grammar even as it partakes of elevated language to make the reality of the relationship between creature and creator more clear. If a poem reads like a technical manual it ceases to be poetry. Poetry adds to the mere expression of words, using allegory, allusion, rhythm, or an unusual word choice. In one sense, poetry distorts the facts (for example, calling one's wife "my queen" when she isn't really reigning anywhere) to make the Truth more evident ("I love you enough obey your every wish").

One could read the Crucifixion this way. God could have snapped his fingers and redeemed the world. Instead he did something extraordinary: sent his only Son to earth as a slave to die, even death on a cross. This seeming "excess" showed the immensity and proportionality of God's love for his creatures, and thus the clarity of that same love. The history of salvation is a long poem of love, full of twists and turns seemingly in excess of the "functional" necessities of

redeeming humanity. But without it, the story of salvation would be much less compelling and less true to the nature of God who is love itself. If we look at decoration through a similar lens, we see it as something added to the facts of structure to let the viewer know something more about the building. Since it reveals the nature of the structural system, it adds to *claritas*. Since it is necessary for a complete, well-designed building, it adds to *integritas*. Since the way it is used makes a building properly proportionate to its end, it adds to *consonantia*. And so decoration is intimately related to Beauty. It makes an engineering solution into a poem about structure. It makes the Truth compellingly attractive.

The definition of decoration can seem a bit slippery. As an enrichment that adds to clarity of the structural system, it is indeed something "added." However, it is not dispensable. Architecture always has a certain factual reality: some sort of material is arranged to make a building do what buildings do; namely, stand up, enclose space, and express some transcendent idea. That a building stands up means that the laws of physics are involved, including the forces of pushing or pulling in different directions being put in balance, and order is brought out of chaos. The pull of gravity always exerts a downward force on buildings, and the inherent strength of materials in proper arrangement provides an equal and opposite force. The vertical supports of a building therefore support a beam

Fundamental structural units, vertical, horizontal and spanning, bound with rope and unadorned.

in a purely "up" direction, to use Aristotle's categorization of the direction of forces.

If a horizontal beam is to span the distance between two verticals, then the beam must have a certain amount of strength to resist the pull of gravity as well. This sort of strength is called tensile because the beam is held in tension at its two ends like a clothesline attached to two poles and engages forces pulling from "side to side" as well as up and down. Without enough tensile strength, this beam would sag in the middle like a hammock or fall down completely. In this situation, the nature of things comes to the fore. Gravity pulls down, and architecture resists in several different ways: where the horizontal of the ground meets the vertical of a post, and where the vertical of a post meets the horizontal of a beam it supports. Roof beams then rest on the horizontals and carry their forces up in a diagonal combination of up and down and side to side. Where the verticals meet the horizontals, some sort of attachment is usually required, and this should be strong enough to hold the pieces together.

The forces of physics here can be quantified by engineers who can tell you exactly what sort of material strength is needed to span certain distances and support certain weights. But the details of structural engineering are not of primary concern here. More important is the recognition that nature, as created by God and revealing the divine mind,

works in a certain way. Heavy things hold up light things and not vice versa; verticals support horizontals, strong things support weak things, solids support voids, and so on. This is the Truth of things as found in their nature, given by God who ordered all things by giving them number, measure, and weight. This ordering of things to obey gravity and work according to their nature, then, speaks of the "will" of things to obey the divine order. When things move that aren't supposed to move, as in the case of an earthquake, we realize how completely we depend on nature to work the way it is supposed to. Disorder (*chaos*) in the natural realm is associated with evil, which needs to be restored to order (*cosmos*).

To understand the concept, a hypothetical example proves handy. Imagine a hut as found on a tropical island. To build this hut, the first thing needed would be some stable foundation, typically the earth, the great horizontal which provides stable support. The builder then goes and cuts a large bamboo pole and inserts it vertically into the ground. The density of the soil is strong enough to keep it in place, and the bamboo has enough strength under compression to avoid falling in on itself. (Cherry gelatin, for example, which can be compressed quite easily, would not make a very good vertical support.) Another bamboo pole is erected ten feet away, and then a third pole is placed on top of the two, attached somehow, perhaps by tying them together with vines or wedging

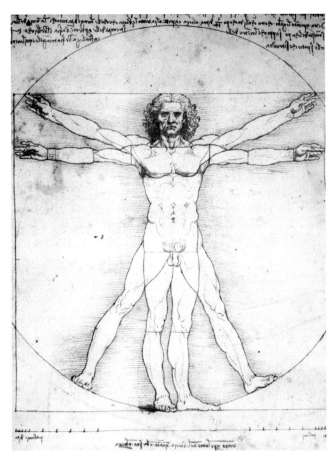

Geometric underpinnings of the human body, Vitruvian Man. Leonard Da Vinci, ca. 1487.

Traces of structural origins can be found in the decorative systems of traditional architecture.

them together with pegs or nails. This is repeated three times to enclose a four-sided room. Then some sort of enclosure is made to fill in the gaps between the poles and make a sort of wall that keeps out wind and weather. Typically, this enclosure does not bear weight; it either hangs from the poles like a straw mat or holds itself up like a pile of bricks. This is the basic system of construction, and everything needs to be strong enough to do what it needs to do or else the whole construction will fall down. One could also substitute steel I-beams for the bamboo poles and glass plates to keep out the weather, and we would have the basic unit of the modern skyscraper. Or we could substitute two beautifully designed columns spanned by a proportioned entablature and we have a glorified version of structure.

This primitive hut provides a good start for understanding the very basics of structural logic, which, again, is rooted in the nature of things in a world created by God. But suppose a period of stability succeeded the initial need for shelter, and something better could be built. The bare minimum might seem inadequate as society develops and the natural human aspiration for higher and better things finds material expression. The builder might desire to cluster bamboo poles together at the corner, tying them together with rope, because the corner bears weight from two side walls and the roof, and

needs more strength than that supplied by one pole alone. He might arrange the poles in a square plan, giving the structure already an expression of geometry that goes beyond itself. Many poles become one corner support, expressing the tensions between unity and diversity, singularity and plurality, for instance, as well as the question about the nature of that which binds them. It cannot help but participate in the nature of things. The square plan speaks of a geometric shape loaded with inherent symbolism, since human beings are created in the image of God and fit into a square, being as tall as they are wide, as expressed so well by Leonardo da Vinci's *Vitruvian Man.* As already discussed in chapter 3, the square is understood as the figure of Christ, who is a multiplication of the Father. Something as simple as the support for a hut becomes a microcosm of the largest questions in society and the nature of the divinity (even if the builder isn't doing it intentionally).

It is here that the nature of decoration starts to come into focus. The rope that ties the poles together reveals something of how the structural system works. The rope serves a literal function, and in that sense, reveals literal structure. It highlights the necessity of the inward force of the rope to hold the many poles together. Suppose, however, that the builder wants to arrange the rope in geometric patterns by using three different colors of rope, braiding it and wrapping

A square plinth under a column base composed of cushion-like moldings.

The decoration of this column suggests the binding of structural components.

Ornamented brackets highlight where forces of different directions meet.

Addition of ornament to a column connotes importance and festivity.

Change of materials highlights the center entrance of a building.

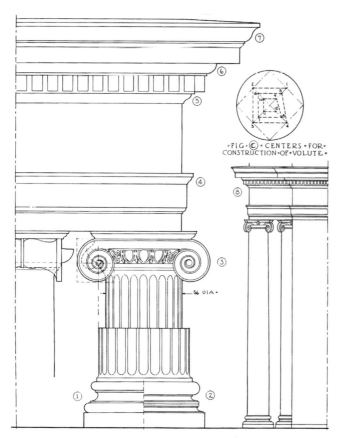

·FIG·ⓒ·CENTERS·FOR·
CONSTRUCTION·OF·VOLUTE·

Above and right: In a feature called *entasis*, columns suggest compression by decreasing in diameter as they rise.

festive, speaking to the nobility of the structure itself, all the while maintaining structural function. Now this little construction is a signifier of structural logic, and does more than the bare minimum needed to hold the building together. It becomes a signifier not only of the physics at work, but also of the aspirations of the builder. It does something "extra." We are reminded of Vitruvius's claim that architecture, like all things, is composed of things that signify (bamboo poles) and ideas that are signified (festivity).[3]

This example can be taken further, however. Suppose the builder finds a strong, thick tree whose trunk can support the corner by itself, and he no longer needs to tie small poles together. The tree is cut down, the log is put into place, yet somehow it seems too unfinished, so he strips off the bark and sands down the lumps. The builder then carves the exterior surface of the log into the shape of four round poles to give it more interest and to recall the local building tradition of years gone by. The tradition has also been to wrap rope around vertical supports, weaving them together with style and grace, so the builder does this to the log even though it is structurally unnecessary. This bit of decoration is now in the realm of virtual structure, no longer literally structural, but still growing from the structural logic of the building. The carved log speaks of the otherwise invisible reality that this one log has the strength of four bamboo poles, and the rope speaks of the fact that the log still needs enough compressive strength not to fall in on itself. Here, decoration has kept alive a memory or "ghost" of a method no longer practiced, which in turn keeps alive a culture's artistic traditions in the community's collective memory. This enrichment lets the viewer know that the same forces that were at work before are still at work.

it around the poles many times. Perhaps the rope gets tied into knots in regular intervals. Suddenly, this otherwise functional thing takes on a new sort of role: it is enriched and

Column base variation within conventional rules. Chicago, Illinois.

Through carving and rope-tying, the invisible forces of physics are made visible. We can call this a revelation of the otherwise invisible forces of nature, giving the architecture an almost sacramental character as revealer of invisible natural realities. Here is the essence of decoration.

The builder might also choose to place his new log on a square stone plate, something akin to the size and shape of first base in baseball. This stone base keeps the corrosive action of the soil from causing the log to rot, raises the log off the ground a few inches, and is wider than the log itself. A similar piece might appear at the top of the log between the vertical and the horizontal beam. The builder might even put a brace or a bracket diagonally between the inside of the log and the horizontal beam to stabilize the joint by helping the weight transfer from the beam to the vertical log. What has happened here? Suddenly the transition from vertical to horizontal has been made more gradual, as the weight of the log is spread over a wider surface area on the ground. The

The seams of the stone pieces indicate the logic of structural support. Supreme Court, Nashville, Tennessee.

weight of the beam is now transferred from vertical to horizontal with a softened transition.

Again, the builder, responding to the desire of the human soul to rise above mere functionality, might add some carving to the stone on the bottom as well as the brace on the diagonal. Then, in order to distinguish between his private house and the house of the tribal leader next door, a decision is made to give the leader's house more development and an enriched expression of this structural logic. Suddenly, a hierarchical relationship emerges between houses, making visible the otherwise invisible hierarchy in the societal structure in the body politic. Just as the tribal leader might wear a special uniform or headdress to signify his or her leadership in the society, so the architecture becomes legible as well.

Decoration and Ornament

Decoration and ornament are both means of enriching architecture, yet each has a proper nature and function in clarifying the meaning of a church building, and in doing so, contribute to the Beauty of a building.

Decoration is an enrichment of architecture that clarifies the structural forces at work in architecture in poetic fashion and usually appears in places where forces change direction. Examples include the tapering of a column as it rises to suggest compression (*entasis*) or the moldings of a column's capital which appears to bend and ease the transition from vertical to horizontal.

Ornament is an enrichment that clarifies the purpose or function of a building. Examples include inscriptions, coats of arms, crosses, shields, carved swags or flowers, logos, or other identifying marks. Ornament typically appears as "added to" a building and does not indicate its structural logic.

This basic example provides the starting point for understanding decoration. Decoration always makes the material qualities of a building more evident.[4] First, it reveals the "character of the material's use," by showing how pieces come together and the quantity of craftsmanship required to make that joint. Second, it clarifies the structural forces at work by highlighting the points where structural forces of different directions come together. While always remaining tied to the inherent structural logic necessary in literal structure, decoration can be fictive and is always poetic. Poetry, by definition, prefers the expression of Truth over fact. Distorting the facts to make the Truth more evident tends to run contrary to much of modern society, which sees *accuracy* (the literal presentation of facts) as equal to Truth. Facts are merely the generally agreed-upon features of a thing, which, when

Canonic base moldings serve as structural and symbolic indicators.

taken together, begin to give only the outline of what is True about something.

ARCHITECTURAL ICONS

Columns are deeply multivalent things, and they will be the subject of much discussion later in this book. At its basic level, however, a column is a vertical support. It meets the horizontal of the ground and rises up to meet a horizontal beam. But a column is not a pole. A pole is an unadorned vertical support, usually round in plan, of a consistent width, and with no particular proportioning system other than that based on the mass of material needed to support a certain weight. A column, on the other hand, varies in its diameter in a condition called *entasis*. A column with entasis (from Greek *teinein*, "to stretch tight") has an optical correction, which is characterized by a narrowing of the column's diameter as it rises to its top, sometimes with a slight bulge at one section of a column's rise. There are different methods of entasis, the most common of which today is shaping the bottom one-third of a column with a consistent diameter, then slowly decreasing that diameter until it meets the capital at five-sixths the width at the bottom. The column does something different from what a pole does; it does something that comes in response to the nature of things in Nature. Since the column is (or appears to be) stronger at the bottom than at the top, it reveals how things work: heavy things hold up lighter things, and the effect of compression usually means that things at the bottom widen as forces press down upon them. Here the invisible forces of physics become visible. When we speak of the invisible becoming visible, we are coming enticingly close to the language of sacramentality. Entasis is a purposeful distortion, but a distortion based on numerical ratios which work with the nature of things to clarify the Truth about how things hold up other things. This, then, is decoration, a clarification of the structural forces at work.

Ionic entablature (bottom to top): architrave divided into three fascia, cymatium ornamented with beads and leaves, frieze ornamented with acanthus and flowers, dentils. Mundelein Seminary, Illinois.

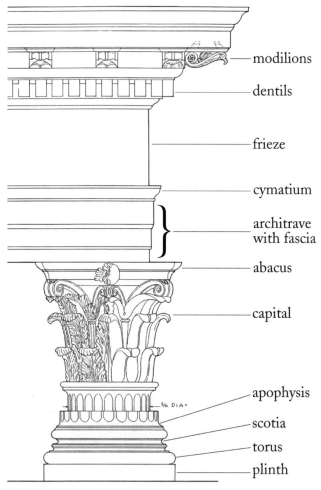

Corinthian order with major parts labeled.

Triglyphs signify the end of a structural beam and are therefore located atop the indicated vertical support, in this case, a pilaster. Here triglyphs recede behind inscribed plaques. Library, Mundelein Seminary, Illinois.

Sacrificial architecture: one theory suggests that triglyphs (Latin, *femores*) represent the chopped thigh bone of a sacrificed animal and the drops below (Greek, *guttae*), the marrow and fat dripping from the bone.

Comparative orders from *Cyclopaedia: or, A Universal Dictionary of Arts and Sciences*, Ephraim Chambers. London, 1728.

This sort of intentional change can be understood as an optical correction. When humans look at things, the effects of optics are at work, and we experience things as distorted. One might call this the nature of optics, or one might call it a result of the Fall: we perceive things imperfectly. The rails of train tracks, for example, give the appearance of rising toward the sky and getting closer together as they go off into the distance. We know that they don't actually do this, but their appearance tells us something that we know is not accurate. Intentional distortions to reverse this false appearance, called optical corrections, can alleviate the apparent imperfections in a building, where its vertical members appear to get closer together and lean out toward the viewer as they rise in height, like the train tracks. At the Parthenon, the Athenians actually tilted their columns inward slightly, bowed their steps, and curved their floors to counter this effect.

Irregular structural members form the starting point for poetic representation on modillions. Garage, Libertyville, Illinois.

Modillions revealing poetic and regularized structural logic. Chapel, Naval Academy, Annapolis, Maryland.

At the heart of this concern for optical correction is the desire for the earthly object, imperfect as it is, to appear to be perfect. The building allows the viewer to not only participate visually in something that has earthly richness and is expressive of high ideas, but also to experience a perfection that is beyond the facts of earthly material. Inert matter becomes the revealer of something higher than itself. Decoration, then, is not merely antiquarianism. *Proper decoration makes the natural forces of the fallen world created by God more evident, and it can be raised through the application of discovered knowledge in the intellect and the desire of the will to reveal the nature of things as they appear in a restored, perfected, redeemed world.* Properly applied, one might claim that decoration can be a vehicle for "undoing the Fall" in architecture, just as the intentionality of making icons bearers of divinity requires departing from the literal facts of portraiture.

In Classical architecture, the architect makes an architectural icon, not the portrait of an engineering solution. Understanding this concept requires an imagination that values poetry and can see how departures from the literal reveal the transcendent without negating the specificity of inherited tradition and the material itself. Needless to say, a mind that dismisses the possibility of transcendence will not be convinced by this line of reasoning. Perhaps the practically minded might see this as some sort of high-brow fluff. The hard realities of engineering might appear at first as more satisfying. But Classical architecture is indeed the engineer's friend: it makes the realities of structure *more* evident, not less. But the engineer must value tradition and appreciate poetry.

Any number of elements in what we call "Classical" architecture share in this process of revelation and idealization. The shaft of a column generally meets a base. This base is most often wider than the shaft of the column, suggesting that the greater surface area helps transfer the downward force of the column to the horizontal of the ground, just as a foot transfers a body's weight more gradually than simply

having a leg terminate at the ankle. This is a common process found in nature: trees widen as they reach the ground, for example. But a close look at a column shows that where the shaft meets the base, it widens dramatically and curves in a shape called an *apophysis*, again revealing the transfer of compressive weight, and indicating its shift in direction. Then, when the shaft meets the base, a series of pieces makes the transition from vertical to horizontal.

In one of the standard column base arrangements, for instance, an upper torus, lower torus, and scotia make an appearance. Each cushion-like torus has a convex shape, reaching outward as if it were soft and bulged outward as the weight of the column pressed down upon it, like a marshmallow between two squeezing fingers. This sense of compression not only receives the weight in a graceful manner, but gives the impression of a coiled spring, pushing back and giving the column a sense of dynamism and equilibrium. The molding between the upper and lower torus, known as a scotia, has a concave shape and acts in a similar manner as something that separates. These moldings can be even more subtly modulated. A scotia, for instance, can be very tall, suggesting that the column's downward force is rather minimal, or it can be very low, given the impression that a great weight is pushing the concave shape almost flat. This subtlety of expression shares much in common with the spoken word in poetry. Certain words carry more expressive force than others; a person can be merely "appealing" or one can be "stunning," for instance. Subtlety of expression is at the heart of poetry and is always concerned with the clarity of the revelation of meaning or idea. This is always done intentionally, however, so that the author of the usage is not to be thought ignorant or incapable of beautiful revelation.

Revelation of structural forces is not the only thing that Classical architecture does, but whatever else it does, Classical architecture is always designed with structural clarity in mind. Nearly every part of the Classical vocabulary reveals how

Classical elements used inappropriately. Left, top: Pilasters appear structurally inadequate, improper entablature. Left, bottom: Gothic elements meet catalogue-ordered Doric columns, no entablature. Above: Overly large and heavy overhang appears to be inadequately supported.

forces act and how pieces come together. The tops of columns, known as capitals, always make a transition from vertical to horizontal, whether it be the curved shape of the bowl-like Doric capital, the spirals of the Ionic, or the top of a Corinthian capital, whose upper leaves can curl into coils that bend as if bearing the weight of the beam above. The basic premise of all architecture—that verticals hold up horizontals—forms the basis for the expression of Classicism. The **entablature** of any one of **the orders** forms the poetic representation of the horizontal beam that spans the distance between columns. This entablature consists of many parts, much the way that a book is divided into chapters and chapters into sections, then sections into sentences, and so on. The complexity of a book is not an intentional obfuscation of its content. It provides the organizing principle which reveals its meaning. So it is with Classical architecture. An entablature is divided into a *cornice*, a *frieze*, and an *architrave*, and the architrave is often divided

---

entablature: superstructure of moldings that lie horizontally atop a row of columns, divided into many smaller parts, which are given canonic arrangements according to different column types.

the orders: the standard term for the canonic modes of arrangement of columns and moldings, the best known of which are Tuscan, Doric, Ionic, Corinthian, and Composite.

into three *fascia*. These parts all have a structural logic as poetic representations of the structural origins of architecture. They are more than mere reminders of structure, however, because they do not simply represent the post and beam construction of the primitive hut. They are designed with proportional relationships based on geometric harmonies that please the eye, much in the way that the proportionality of notes on a piano keyboard mean that some sound harmonic together while others are dissonant. Moldings also provide texture and cast shadows, like the surface of a hilly landscape or the musculature of the human body. Without this texture, the building literally falls flat.

The basic structure of a building, however, usually requires more than two poles and a beam. All sorts of secondary structural elements prove necessary, like diagonal roof rafters, beams that span the walls to make a ceiling, and yet smaller members that serve as lath for plaster and so on. Classical architecture expresses these secondary elements poetically as well. The triglyph, one of the most well-known parts of the Doric entablature, marks the poetic representation of the end of a beam that spans the walls. This structural clarity can be virtual or *fictive*, since there may be steel doing the literal work of holding up the building. Even when fictive representation of structure, decoration still must follow the rules of structure so that it appears to do what it would be doing if it were actual structure. A triglyph, for instance, should logically be placed atop a column, since the basic structural system of column-supporting-beam is to be maintained in much the same way that rules of grammar are followed so that the content of the sentence is clear.

In a similar fashion, *modillions* and *dentils* reveal structural clarity. Modillions are large ornamented blocks that appear near the top of many entablatures. These blocks signify

Differing signifiers of structural logic. Left, top: Simple iron brackets. Left: Ornamented arch lands on the end of a beam. Left, bottom: Classical stone moldings indicate compression beneath the iron of the Eiffel Tower, Paris. Above: Modernism's insistence on the industrial aesthetic and literal rather than poetic expression of structure. Below: Gradation of the strength of materials from bottom to top reveals and echoes the nature of the natural order.

Architectural exuberance indicates the festive nature of a place without losing structural clarity.

the ends of the roof beams that come down from the ridge of the roofline and are supported by the horizontal of the entablature. As modillions, these blocks are not literally the ends of beams. They are fictive, but they reveal the nature of the structural forces at work as if they were literal. Dentils work in a similar way, but signify the ends of many smaller structural units. All are given proportion, number, shape, and enrichment to beautify the building and establish a legible marker of the building's importance. Just as the maker of the primitive hut tied ropes of complex patterns on the house of the tribal leader, so using a richer, embellished form of decoration begins to speak of the hierarchical relationship between buildings. Buildings are then legible not only in their own structural logic, but also when compared with one another, and an entirely new level of signification begins to emerge.[5]

Learning to "read" Classical architecture requires, first of all, recognition that there is, in fact, something to read. This means that buildings are not merely neutral skins for human action, but bearers of meaning even in the very materiality of their structural logic. Then follows familiarity with the basic "alphabet" and grammar of the language. Specialists in Classical architecture will no doubt have great knowledge of these rules, and they can serve a parish well in new design. Perhaps this short introduction can help a pastor or building committee choose an architect and examine his or her work more intelligently. A person does not need to be a poet to commission a poem, but he or she should know something of

poetry in order to know why a poet is needed and what distinguishes good poetry from bad.

The concept of decoration dovetails nicely with an architectural theology for the time of image in the Age of the Church. Since liturgical architecture itself is to be sacramental, even seemingly mundane features like structure can be elevated to a sort of sacramental revelation. Christ's divinity on Mount Tabor at the Transfiguration did not destroy his human nature; rather, it showed it glorified and radiant. We can think of structure in a similar way: the poetic overlay of decoration is not foreign to the earthly qualities of engineering; they are its *glory*. Engineering is good, a high calling for the application of will and intellect to material. But decoration reveals more about the nature of structure in a way that is beautiful, not because "it has always been done that way," or because a group of scholars have said so, or because it is associated with political power or ideology, but because it adds to *claritas* by adding something necessary to full understanding (*integritas*).

In our age that privileges novelty and creativity, this inherited Classical system might seem to chafe at the spirit of artistic freedom. In one sense, it does. It asks artists and architects to forgo the notion of absolute license to do whatever they want and to learn the rules of the Classical grammar and syntax. Most of life is like this. Poets are "constricted" by the use of the letters of an alphabet, by the rules of grammar, and the conventions of societal understanding. This is not the same as copying the past. One can write *West Side Story* after seeing *Romeo and Juliet,* and one can invent a poem with greater insight in a way never done before. One can add new words like "all mimsy were the borogoves" to the English language, as did Lewis Carroll in his famous poem *Jabberwocky.* But if the additions depart too far from recognizable conventions, they will move farther from conveying meaning. When people look at architecture and don't know what to make of it, either intuitively or intellectually, it no longer speaks to them, and it fails to convey its message. Christian architecture should *always* convey its message, undoubtedly with greater or lesser participation according to the knowledge brought by the perceiver. But no one should ever see a church building, no matter how simple, with the thought that Catholicism is something unimportant, shabby, irrelevant, merely earthbound, or mechanistic. Nor should anyone leave a church building thinking that Catholicism stopped advancing in 1570 or 1920. Classical architecture is always primarily about ideas, and secondarily about forms. So as new insights come in the realm of ideas, new architectural expressions emerge. However, the forms must always correspond to the ideas and never contradict them, just as the insights gleaned from Aristotle by Thomas Aquinas did no violence to the teachings of Jesus Christ.

Decoration reveals the inner logic of structure by joyfully celebrating it. It may seem odd at first blush to celebrate physics. But the order of the world provided by God who gave everything number, measure, and weight reveals to us the beauty of the divine mind. A Corinthian capital doesn't highlight where forces change direction in the same way as a bolt at an intersection of steel beams does. It reveals structure by giving festive *delight:* delight in the harmonies of mathematics, nature, physics, craft; a delight in being freed from the drudgery of mediocrity. Decoration makes the strain of pushing and pulling in physics look easy, graceful, and balanced. Similarly, the movements of an accomplished ballet dancer are far removed from everyday walking and gesturing. They are an elevated type of movement, always giving a sense of ease and grace to very strenuous activity. Decoration does the same for architecture. It is indeed fictive, but not for the sake of falsity. Its fiction makes the Truth more evident, and the Truth is that we affirm the goodness of creation and recognize that materiality is not an end in itself. A perfectly solved engineering solution indeed has a beauty proper to itself, but a structural solution that then has an overlay of Beauty proper to a higher end enters the realm of decoration.

If an architect could invent a way of designing buildings that has greater subtlety, articulateness, specificity, historical association, and conventional clarity than a living, inherited Classical tradition, then by all means, it should be done! If it expresses the Catholic faith's embrace and fulfillment of history better than has been done before, its Truth will be radiant, its completeness will be obvious, and its clarity will ring true. It will be obvious and inevitable, and it will, no doubt, use decoration, because decoration tells us the Truth about the nature of things. But because legibility depends upon conventions of the inherited tradition, replacing Classical architecture proves exceedingly difficult.

When we know the innermost ontological nature of things, we experience the joy of a beautiful thing. And in that Beauty we rest in anticipation of the heavenly rest of the beatific vision. So architecture becomes a vehicle for eschatological anticipation, a time when all is radiant in its nobility, that is, its know-ability. Again we are reminded of the Second Vatican Council's call for liturgical art and architecture to have a "noble beauty" (SC, 124), a knowable, legible, radiant, properly oriented completeness. Decoration is critical to this task.

---

1. Carroll William Westfall, *Architectural Principles in the Age of Historicism* (New Haven: Yale University Press, 1991, pp. 270–273. I choose here to use Westfall's definition of decoration as an enrichment related primarily to structure. There are others who argue differently for good reasons, which I respectfully acknowledge. Many of the fundamental points made in this chapter about the nature of decoration and its characteristics are drawn from Westfall's important contribution in the book named above, even where not cited specifically in the text, and I acknowledge my great debt to his work.

2. Demetri Porphyrios, *Classicism is Not a Style* (London: Architectural Design and Academy Editions, 1982), 57.

3. Vitruvius, *Ten Books on Architecture*, Book I, ch. 1, par. 3.

4. Westfall, *Architectural Principles in the Age of Historicism,* 273.

5. For more on the structural logic of Classicism, see Demetri Porphyrios, *Classical Architecture: The Living Tradition* (New York: McGraw-Hill, 1991).

Chapter 7

Ornament: Clarity through Revelation of Use and Purpose

Another method of enriching architecture is called *ornament*. Despite the common understanding of the term, ornament is not to be understood as something pleasant but unnecessary, to be purchased at the import store and forgotten until a guest uses it as a conversation starter. Ornament is intricately related to Beauty, because like decoration, it clarifies the Truth about a building. *Ornament is an enrichment of a building in order to reveal a building's use or purpose.*[1] Furthermore, the nature of the ornament reveals the status of a building in relation to other buildings. Since buildings take their status from the use to which they are put, ornament adds to *claritas* by allowing the building to express the importance of the activities that happen within. In the case of a church, it speaks of the nature and importance of Christianity as well as the nature of the liturgy itself.

The utilitarian components of a building, those primitive basics needed to make a building stand up, are common to all buildings. However, not all buildings are of equal dignity, because not all human activities are of equal dignity. Some buildings are used to worship God, for instance, and therefore deal with things public, sacred, and eternal. Since the things of eternity are of greater import than private, secular, and temporal things, the activity of worship is of higher inherent dignity. Therefore the church building takes a higher dignity as well. We understand intuitively that a church is a more important building than, say, an electricity-generating plant. Both are important, and we might even say necessary, for proper human living. But the one has a higher inherent dignity than the other because worship of God has a higher dignity than electric generation.

ORNAMENT AND ONTOLOGICAL REALITY

Properly designed ornament clarifies a knowable but otherwise invisible reality. A building of higher status receives more and better ornament than one of lesser status, just as it

Legible building types, ornament, and siting indicate the use and therefore the hierarchical relationships between buildings. Gaming, Austria.

Ornament reveals a home's occupant: a bishop's coat of arms.

receives more precious materials, higher levels of craft, and a more important site. Ornament is closely tied to decorum, the property of being fitting. When architecture is appropriately ornamented, we know that it neither lacks the amount of embellishment needed to make its inherent dignity clear to the viewer, nor does it have more than it needs. A small parish church should not be more elaborately ornamented than the diocesan cathedral, for instance. If it were, it would be improperly ornamented since its architecture would claim a dignity higher than the building actually deserved. This mismatch between ontological reality and external expression reduces the beauty of the building. The reverse is also true: if the cathedral, in the name of ideology or ignorance, lacks the ornament that speaks of its inherent dignity, it fails to represent what it is and therefore lacks beauty because it lacks completeness (*integritas*) and therefore *claritas*. Of course, within all rules, exceptions occur (such as a cathedral dedicated to Saint Francis, which may seek to imitate his poverty), but these should always be intentional and clearly evident. Simplicity should be noble, not shabby.

Swags, inscriptions, color, and beads indicate ritual festivity.

Ornament provides one of the important tools in this clarification. Just as decoration helps to make the processes of nature evident in structure, so ornament clarifies the importance and ontological reality of human activities through the architecture that serves them. Ornament is something *added* to a building and, like decoration, is not necessary in the utilitarian sense. It has no structural function, literal or fictive. A building will still stand up even if it lacks the clarity brought by decoration, and so it is with ornament. But ornament makes the ontological reality of a building more clear, and therefore contributes to Beauty.

The cross on the top of a church steeple is ornament, telling the purpose and use of a building. To put a cross on any other non-church-related building would seem decidedly inappropriate even without much deep thought, because this ornamental convention remains strong in our culture. A coat of arms with the insignia of a bishop placed over the entry to a residence tells the viewer that a bishop lives there. If the viewer is schooled in ecclesiastical symbolism, he or she might even know who the bishop is, what the characteristics of the diocese are, and what this bishop emphasizes in his ministry. With the simple addition of a small ornamental device, the building comes alive with expressive knowledge about itself, becomes more legible, and increases in *claritas* by no longer lacking that which it needed to speak of its reality. When *integritas* was reached, clarity resulted.

An extreme example of the power of ornament is a typical McDonald's restaurant. The "golden arches" of McDonald's are perhaps one of the most recognizable pieces of ornament ever designed. They do not hold up the building, but they instantly let the viewer understand the use of the building, and therefore its purpose and inherent dignity. Think of the confusion that would arise should a person go into a building with the golden arches on its roof and find a fried chicken restaurant inside, or more troubling yet, a chapel

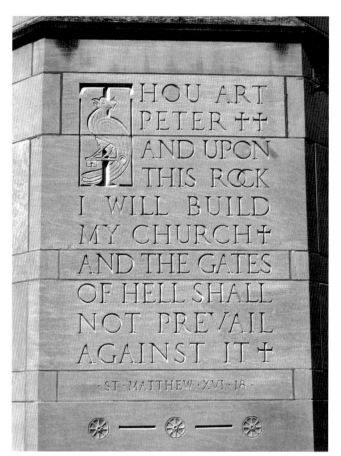

Inscriptions serve as ornament and reveal the nature and purpose of a building.

Even recognizably modern buildings can use ornament to increase *claritas* and therefore Beauty.

Crosses as revelatory ornament.

with an altar and tabernacle and no hamburgers at all. Ornament clarifies the use of a building for us, and when the ornament fails to match the building's purpose, we become confused and even angry that the building misled us. The *claritas* of Beauty allows us to rest in the knowledge that what we perceive is true, and when architecture sends the wrong signal in either ornament or decoration, we are not freed from the rest of abstraction, and therefore not freed from our condition as beings with fallen intellects. Therefore we do not rejoice in knowing, and we are denied an anticipation of the *eschaton* when God is all in all. A church that does not "look like" a church fails in a similar way, even though churchliness can come in an infinite number of expressions.

If every building in the world looked the same, there would be no way to distinguish church from bank from school from home from outhouse. *Claritas* would be quite low, and therefore so would Beauty. Beauty and hierarchy, then, are related. This is not hierarchy as the world often thinks of it, characterized by the arbitrary whims of unjust hereditary rulers in pre–Revolutionary France. This is hierarchy that results from the nature of things. Some activities simply are of higher dignity than others, and therefore buildings, as markers of that dignity, show characteristics matching that hierarchy. Beauty is experienced as the clear revelation of the ontological reality of a thing

that lacks nothing, has nothing in excess, and is oriented to its proper end. Carefully considered variety, which includes hierarchical difference, is essential to knowing a thing, and therefore experiencing Beauty.

Ornament clarifies hierarchical relationships. Clothing, for instance, ornaments the body. A certain type of uniform clarifies who is a police officer, nurse, janitor, or judge. Brides wear long white dresses and veils, carry flowers, and walk extra slowly down church aisles. All of these behaviors would be absurd on any other day, but because a wedding day is hierarchically more important than other days, ritualized ornament and behavior become clarifying signifiers of this otherwise invisible reality. This echoes the writings in the book of Isaiah, where the author speaks of rejoicing in God

People ornament their bodies to indicate festivity, and buildings do the same.

Ionic column "wears" a necklace and indicates festivity.

"like a bride bedecked with her jewels" (Isaiah 61:10). In another example, a simple button would hold a man's collar closed, and a silk cravat or Texan string tie provides more than is necessary to complete this utilitarian task. But the tie does several things. It connects to the time before buttons were invented and, as an artifact, keeps alive the memory of things past. Second, it brings a bit of glory to the clothing in a way that is sacrificial since it is not "necessary" in a utilitarian sense. Because of this connection to the past and its sacrificial nature, the tie becomes a marker of the importance of the person's role in society or the event he is attending. Men wear ties on important occasions, not for a day on the beach. The tie reveals to the world that the wearer believes that what he does is important. This works in a similar way with jewelry. Adorning the body with a necklace or earrings makes the body more expressive of its higher ambitions and potential for glory. Gold and gems are radiant and reflective, as is nearly every biblical image of divinized glory. People wear jewelry and flowers, and so do buildings!

Our recovery of the proper place of ornament is critical. In many respects, the Modern age in architecture was hostile to ornament, seeing it as some sort of holdover from another age for devotees to the past. The great manifestoes seeking a "modern" architecture almost universally sought to disconnect the inherited conventions of both decoration and ornament from current practice.[2] But as C. W. Westfall has written, neither decoration nor ornament is "an option that can be left off according to the whim, 'taste' or ideology of the architect or builder. Decoration and ornament are necessary parts of the design . . . and provide its completion in the way that the nose completes the nostrils and therefore the face."[3] Noses are not really necessary for breathing since a simple set of holes would do. But the nose adds beauty and completes the face and lets the viewer know whether a creature is a human being or

a dog. When Hollywood wants to portray an alien or monster, often a face is shown without a nose or a human with an animal face, making a monster. Architecture has its equivalents.

As with decoration, ornament aids in the sacramental fulfillment of architecture. A thing that is a sacrament, in the broadest sense of the word, reveals a reality that the senses could not otherwise perceive. Ornament is part of the way in which the mere material stuff of the earth takes on the garment of otherworldly beauty. The book of Exodus relates how God tells Moses: "I am going to come to you in a dense cloud, in order that the people may hear when I speak with you and so trust you ever after" (Exodus 19:9). While one would think that hearing the voice of God alone would certainly suffice, God chooses to "ornament" himself visually, appearing in the form of a cloud, clarifying the reality of his presence. When God gave the instructions for the building of the Tabernacle of Moses and later the Temple of Solomon, specific ornaments were required to reveal to human eyes and minds the pattern of heaven. The letter to the Hebrews reiterated this notion, writing: "They serve at a sanctuary that is a copy and shadow of what is in heaven. This is why Moses was warned when he was about to build the tabernacle: 'See to it that you make everything according to the pattern shown you on the mountain'" (Hebrews 8:5).

Part of this temple pattern was a rich palette of ornament. Carved palm trees, flowers, gourds, and angels indicated that the large room, or *hekal*, of the temple was a sacramental evocation of the Garden of Eden, signaling

The classical palmetto ornament serves the Christian message in a proper inculturation as a symbol of paradise, the temple, and the Passion.

Ornamental angels take on a sacramental role by indicating the otherwise invisible angelic beings who praise God in the Sacred Liturgy.

Palmetto plant.

loves him greatly, and Joseph's brothers rip it off of him in jealousy (Genesis 37:3). When the Lord punishes the Israelites for worshipping the golden calf, he signified their lack of glory by telling them: "Now take off your ornaments and I will decide what to do with you" (Exodus 33:5). Solomon's Song of Songs speaks of the beauty of the bride with the words "Your cheeks are comely with ornaments, your neck with strings of jewels. We will make you ornaments of gold, studded with silver" (Song of Songs, 1:11–12). In the story of Moses, we read that the Egyptians lost their glory when God freed the Israelites, who then took the Egyptians' ornaments of gold and fabrics before they left and crossed the Red Sea. The Israelites then offered their ornaments for the construction of the tabernacle.[4] Moreover, the book of Isaiah relates that when the prophet comes to relate a year of favor from the Lord and proclaim liberty for captives, God gives them "a garland instead of ashes" (Isaiah 61:3) and clothes them in the "garments of salvation," just "as a bridegroom decks himself with a garland, and as a bride adorns herself with her jewels" (Isaiah 61:10). The fresh radiance of a flower garland

humanity's return to right relationship with creation. Through the medium of carved cedar—that is, through ornament—the reality of restored creation was made present. Similarly, the Holy of Holies contained images of two large angels, and the ark itself was topped by two more angels that marked the seat of God's very presence. The veil of the temple as well as the priest's garments contained ornament, both in pictorial image and pattern, as did the bronze columns outside the building, which were covered in an ornamental pattern called "almond work," with capitals composed of pomegranates. Never was this ornament meant as an end in itself. It was not "a style." It was a vehicle for revelation, and therefore served a sacramental purpose. One might argue that God himself sanctioned the proper use of ornament because art and architecture were the vehicles for his self-revelation.

The scriptures, of course, are full of the language of ornament. The Old Testament uses the term as a clarifying marker of status, glory, or favor with God. Israel gives his son Joseph the richly ornamented robe of many colors because he

The scriptures often use gem-like color and radiance to indicate a person filled with grace, and an architecture of the Sabbath does the same.

is a symbol of festivity, life, and offering, while ashes speak of dullness, lifelessness, and dust.

Ezekiel 28:11–13 speaks of a beautiful being walking in Eden, who, when in God's favor, was ornamented with rubies, topazes, emeralds, and other gems with gold mountings prepared for him at his creation. Later, when he disobeyed God in the pride of his beauty, he was "turned to ashes on the earth." This passage recalls the famous breastplate of the high priest in the temple containing 12 similar gems engraved with the names of the 12 tribes of Israel, suggesting their restoration of creation back to a gem-like, radiant state of God's grace. The walls and streets of the heavenly Jerusalem itself are described as being composed with precious gems and gold for this same reason. In heaven, God is all in all so everything is described as gem-like and radiant with light. The earthly liturgy partakes in the same reality as the heavenly liturgy, but still celebrates the liturgy of heaven through earthly signs and symbols. But they are signs and symbols of *heavenly* realities (SC, 122). *So to make a church building that best participates in those realities, ornament is necessary because it is the established convention that marks a heavenly condition and friendship with God, something which becomes possible after the redemption wrought by Christ.*

All of this language, of course, is not to be taken too literally because gold and gems are things that we recognize and value in our earthly nature, and serve as symbols of the radiance of God's presence and blessing. But the word *symbolic* does not mean "dispensable" or "fake." Rather, quite the opposite is true. Theologically understood, a symbol mediates presence to us and should be thought of in terms of the sacramentality of earthly material. It is the vehicle through which our earthly senses come to know invisible realities.

Ornament, then, is something consonant with our nature. At times, it is a sign of God's favor and the glory given to humanity. At other times, when humans use it badly, it becomes a sign of humanity's desire for glory which does not belong to it, as was the case with Adam and Eve grasping in the Garden for what was not yet properly theirs. When God laments that his people have forgotten him, he asks: "Does a maiden forget her jewelry, a bride her wedding ornaments? Yet my people have forgotten me, days without number" (Jeremiah 2:32, *Holy Bible: New International Version*). Psalm 73:6 describes the wicked as wearing their pride like a necklace. The prophets who call Israel back to the Lord repeatedly speak of ornament as a misused tool, comparing Israel to a prostitute who flaunts her glory for the wrong reasons. Ornamental richness is always meant to signify what is true, and not, like the biblical language of the harlot, be a false attraction to something not of God. The challenge today is as it always has been: to use ornament theologically and responsibly, not negate its value because it has been abused.

Ornament and decoration combine to reveal the nature of the church building. Church of St. Andrew, New York City.

FESTIVITY AND SACRIFICE

The origins of architectural ornament are, of course, subject to many theories, and our challenge is to see how this inherited ornamental tradition can be put to our sacramental use today. When speaking of some of the ornamental details of the Classical tradition, art historian George Hersey again poses a good question: "Why at great expense do we have stone carvers make replicas of beads, reels, eggs, darts, claws, and a type of prickly plant (the acanthus) that grows only in certain parts of the Peloponnese? Why wrap a courthouse in what an ancient Greek would interpret as the garlands or streamers used to decorate sacrificial oxen?"[5]

These questions are indeed worth asking, not just as a look to the past, but as a way to support today's practice. The poetic expression of structure seems to answer its own questions since structure remains a constant in our world. But what of the ornamental legacy of the past, which seems to have its origin in pagan sacrificial ritual? Is using ornament from the pagan past akin to acceptance that we sacrifice bulls and goats? The answer, of course, is no. The Christian revelation absorbs and fulfills the inheritance of the pre–Christian world, either Jewish or pagan. Von Balthasar's challenge remains: How do we develop a theory of aesthetics in which "the total aspiration of worldly and pagan beauty is fulfilled while all the glory is at the same time given to God in Jesus Christ"? In proper inculturation, Christianity certainly does require the purging of elements contradictory to Christianity. However, when something from a non–Christian culture contributes to the Christian mission, it is welcomed. Saint Augustine himself wrote that whatever was "rightly said" by non–Christian cultures must be appropriated for Christian use.[6]

Here the important point emerges: *the ornament of Western Classical architecture finds its origins in ritual sacrifice. Catholicism is rooted in the festive ritual sacrifice of the Eucharist.*

Ornament as trope of ritual sacrifice. Temple of Vespasian, Rome, 79 AD.

Ornament is therefore a potent sign of the meaning of the liturgy. It is unlikely that the beads, flowers, and leaves of the Classical vocabulary are going to cause wholesale reversions to pagan religious practice; the premises that underlie architectural ornamentation have been so deeply ingrained and fulfilled in the Judeo–Christian tradition that we can easily see them now as expressions of Christian festivity. Psalm 68 reminds us, "in festive gatherings, bless the Lord," and so we do. When a bride adorns her hair with flowers, we recognize that she is ornamenting herself because of the Christian importance of the sacrament of Marriage. When we give out Easter eggs, we recognize the symbolism of the blessing of new life signified by the egg without fear of reverting to a pagan tradition. Our culture still recognizes the continuity: Christian ritual and festivity are signified by doing festive things, and these always include ornament. Speaking of Easter, Saint Athanasius writes: "God now gives us the joy of salvation that shines out from this feast, . . . allowing us to pray together and to offer common thanksgiving, as is our duty on the feast." However, because the victory of Christ is complete and eternal, all things are festive and every Sunday celebrates the Resurrection of Easter. Athanasius adds: "The grace of the feast is not restricted to one occasion. Its rays of glory never set. It is always at hand to enlighten the mind of those who desire it."[7] Proper church architecture is therefore festive architecture,

showing signs of its festivity even when the church is not filled with people. The wedding feast of heaven continues eternally even when we do not specifically reveal it liturgically, and the church building keeps that continuous witness in its architectural ornament.

It is worth noting what characterizes festivity. Festivity connotes celebration, a freedom from work and a pure enjoyment of something because it is good in itself.[8] Festivity always has the character of being something exceptional, and festive events are "something special, unusual, an interruption in the ordinary passage of time."[9] Festivity and hierarchy are related then, because festivity is by definition extraordinary, just as a wedding day is extraordinary compared to other days. On earth, festivity is understood in relation to freedom from servile work. One would hardly expect a bride to go to work on the day of her wedding; the wedding itself is meaningful enough to take the day off. The sabbath is always festive for a similar reason. The freedom from work allows for the contemplation of the Good, and it brings joy because it is an experience of possessing what one loves; in this case, right relationship with God.

Liturgy is also always festive because it is a participation in the things of heaven, a time of freedom from servile work and freedom for praise and contemplation of God who sanctifies us. On earth we celebrate this festivity through the vehicle of material signs and symbols. However, we join the heavenly beings, "those who even now celebrate it without signs . . . in the heavenly liturgy, where celebration is wholly communion and feast" (CCC, 1136). Heaven is festive and a place of rest because it is a condition of complete freedom from the effects of the Fall, free from work—either intellectual or physical—where complete Beauty reveals itself to all. A church building is therefore a refuge to "rest in the Lord and see his joy is like a banquet, and full of gladness and tranquility."[10] A true banquet is joyful and yet tranquil, fully engaging the delight of the senses, but without excessive indulgence. Yet it requires something to mark it as festive, to distinguish a meal from a feast and a heavenly banquet table from a galley kitchen. Ornament is one of the most important ways that the human race makes that reality knowable.

Liturgy, as an anticipation of heaven, is festive. Church architecture is liturgical architecture, and as such, is a festive architecture. Composed of signs and symbols in order to reveal its ontological reality (and therefore be beautiful), it uses the architectural conventions of festivity inherited from God's providential preparation now fulfilled in Christ. This requires ornament.

George Hersey's invaluable contribution to understanding the place of Classical ornament, the provocative little book called *The Lost Meaning of Classical Architecture*, has revealed that most Classical ornament has its origin in ritual sacrifice. He calls these architectural devices "tropes" of sacrifice; that is, architectural turns of phrase that serve as "records

State Capitol, Lincoln, Nebraska

City wall, Jerusalem

Radio City Music Hall, New York City

Lord & Taylor, New York City

Lincoln Park Zoo, Chicago

High School, Topeka, Kansas

Church of the Beatitudes, Galilee

Courthouse, Evansville, Indiana

Mosaic, Church of the Holy Sepulcher, Jerusalem

Volta Building, Washington, DC

Pilgrim Congregational Church, Lincoln, Nebraska

Ornamental plaster detail after Michelangelo

Chapel, Mundelein Seminary, Illinois

Library, University of Cincinnati

University of Notre Dame, South Bend, Indiana

State House, Topeka, Kansas

Chapel, Mundelein Seminary, Illinois

Volta Building, Washington, DC

University of Notre Dame, South Bend, Indiana

Church of All Nations, Jerusalem

Hotel, Washington, DC

Gotham Hall, New York City

Lyric Opera, Chicago

Bridge tower, Chicago

University of Notre Dame, South Bend, Indiana

Post office, Newton, Illinois

Lincoln Park Zoo, Chicago

War memorial, Nashville, Tennessee

Pantheon, Paris

St. Thomas Church, Fort Thomas, Kentucky

Hotel, Washington, DC

Georgetown University, Washington, DC

Pantheon, Paris

Electricity substation, Chicago

School gymnasium, Topeka, Kansas

Triglyphs with ornamented metopes.

Current-day festive ornament. Georgetown, Washington, DC.

of sacrifice." This concept is not all that difficult to understand in modern life. If one were to visit a church on a
Saturday afternoon, finding a white runner down the center
aisle with swags of flowers, ribbons, and beads tied to the pew
ends, we would see the record of the sacrifice of a wedding
Mass. The demands of festivity required the "sacrifice" of
flowers, which could otherwise be growing happily in a field,
as well as the sacrifice of the money used to pay for them.
This enrichment of the architecture, this *something added*,
clarified the festivity and importance of the occasion. Carving
flowers into the stone, wood, or plaster simply makes those
signs of festivity permanent.

This way of marking festivity did not appear in a vacuum. As one might expect, early groups of sacred trees in
Greece were "often decorated with the gear and materials
used in sacrifice. . . : bones, urns, horns, lamps, fruit and vege-
table relics, flowers, and weapons."[11] Israel itself had regulations
determining the sacrificial offering of fruits to God even as
early as the time of Cain (Genesis 4:3), and the Festival of
First Fruits developed into an elaborate system of bringing
agricultural offerings to the temple (Leviticus 23:9). In the
pagan world, the remains of animals were often attached to
the temple buildings. Certain parts of an animal were considered more sacred than others: heads, horns, and thigh bones
were particularly associated with the life-giving fluids of the
animal.[12] Hanging pieces of the animal on the building signified that the sacrifice had been completed. Tropes of the
remains of sacrifice and festivity eventually found their way
into the permanency of architecture. Flowers and swags, once
literally attached to buildings, become conventionalized and
are made part of ritual architecture. Even today, traditional
architecture is full of carved images of swags, flowers, and
fruit. Just as we hang boughs of holly or pine on our stair rails
at Christmas to mark festivity, our buildings do it in a more
permanent sense. A courthouse or public library, for instance,
might seem at first to be an odd place for carved ornament.

Egg and dart molding with bead and reel motif. Church of All
Nations, Jerusalem.

But the administration of justice and the proliferation of
learning are indeed worth celebrating; they are among humanity's noblest and most God-like activities. Even a private house
deserves ornament, celebrating the life of the family within and
its relationship to the political order of the city.

The number of possible ornamental motifs is as endless
as the human imagination. Benjamin Henry Latrobe used
tobacco leaves and corn cobs as ornamental motifs in the
United States Capitol building, signifying his inculturation of
the Classical language to the flora of the New World. Bertram
Goodhue used corn and cattle in his Nebraska State Capitol
(ca. 1924) to speak of the locality. The YMCA in Jerusalem
used biblical plants and animals to make a truly remarkable
set of individual capitals. Chicago's Lincoln Park Zoo even
put lizards, snakes, and snails in the Corinthian capitals of its
reptile house. Classical buildings are covered with all sorts of
beads, leaves, flowers, vines, baskets, animals, tools, ribbons,
fruit, berries, scrolls, geometric patterns, angels, saints, crosses,
chalices, and just about anything else that has meaning in
civilized culture.

Certain motifs have maintained a place in modern culture, as evidenced by the fact that egg-and-dart molding is

Bucrania at the Art Institute of Chicago. Daniel Burnham, architect, 1893.

Leaves and flowers as ornament, American College of Surgeons, Chicago.

still available in local home centers today. Eggs remain potent symbols of new life, and in the ancient world they were often offered as sacrifices, with the eggs laid by birds at temples sold as souvenirs.[13] Of course, birds are featured throughout scripture, from the dove that returned with an olive branch to the dove as image of the Holy Spirit. Moreover, the nesting of birds, and presumably the laying of eggs, appears as a sign of favor or blessing in several biblical passages. Ezekiel speaks of the Lord planting a branch of Israel on the mountain, where birds will nest and find shelter (Ezekiel 17:23). Before it disobeyed God, Assyria was compared to a beautiful tree in which birds nested (Ezekiel 31:6). Psalm 84 speaks of the sparrow laying her young by God's altars. So the egg as ornament speaks volumes about nature, blessing, new life, and the temple in both Judaism and pagan religions. But the eggs of the egg-and-dart molding are not literal. As usual, they are

fictive because they are actually shown as if their shell has been cut away, revealing the yolk inside, revealing the life within. Does this molding deserve a place in Christian architecture? Certainly. Is it simply a meaningless holdover from the ancient world? Certainly not. At the very least, the extra craft required to produce them signifies a building of high status. At its highest reading, this simple inherited molding speaks of God's blessings, new life, continuity with history and tradition, and ritual sacrifice. The Bible tells of these things in words, icons do it with pictures, ritual does it with actions, and architecture does it with ornament.

Other architectural artifacts from the pagan world remain with us still, and more closely than we might expect. A walk down Michigan Avenue in Chicago to see the Christian paintings at the Art Institute requires walking past the carved images of bull skulls (called *bucrania*) to this day. The origin of the triglyph speaks again to the inherited sacrificial associations of Classical architecture. Triglyphs are made up of three vertical rods, as the name suggests (*tri* = three; *glyph* = line, thing chopped). So a triglyph is made of a thing chopped into three. One theory suggests that in pagan ritual sacrifice, the thighbone of an animal was chopped into three (as confirmed by the Latin terms for the parts: *femores*, akin to our modern word *femur* or *thighbone*) to prove that the god had descended upon an altar. The pieces of thighbone were wrapped in fat and attached to a building at the ends of beams. The triglyph shows this as well, with small droplet-like devices called *guttae* at the bottom (Gk, *guttae* = drop). So the life-giving marrow and fat symbolically drip from the bones, signifying the presence of the god.[14] Eventually this sacrificial convention became geometricized and decorative, added directly into the architecture. This architectural "ghost" carries the memory of pre–Christian religion into our own times. Triglyphs, and the spaces between them, called *metopes*, are everywhere in Classical architecture, old and new, waiting to be read.

Top and above: Christian adaptation of classical triglyphs and metopes with symbols of Christian sacrifice of the Passion. Chapel of the Flagellation, Via Dolorosa, Jerusalem, rebuilt 1929.

The language of the bloody sacrifice of animals no doubt sounds foreign to Christian ears glad to live in the time of the unbloody sacrifice of the Mass. Once modern eyes and minds get past the gruesome details of these architectural origins, what is today's Christian supposed to make of them? Important to remember is that the Catholic liturgy is, in its supreme way, a **trope**. The very fact that we offer an *unbloody* representation of the very same Passion and death of Jesus Christ that occurred on Calvary means that our sacramental experience comes under another form, notably the offering of bread and wine, which are then returned to us as the Body and Blood of Christ. After all, what is the Eucharistic liturgy but the supreme offering of the Body and Blood of a Victim

trope: from the Greek word *tropos*, meaning "a turn," as in a turn of phrase or the use of an expression in a figurative sense.

who becomes present on our altars. What did the Greeks and Romans give us but the architecture that symbolizes ritual sacrifice. A Christian seeking to give all of the beauty of the world to God, including the glory of the pagan world as von Balthasar asked, sees this providential gift as something that Christianity can embrace, purify, and make its own. Now, in the time of image, we experience the offering of the blood of a Victim in sacramental form in the Eucharist. The *Logos incarnatus*, as Cardinal Ratzinger called it, is offered as a sacrifice of praise, just as its Doric entablature and triglyphs offer a silent, visible architectural praise drawn from the history of sacrifice. This, again, requires ornament.

Architect Donato Bramante's church of San Pietro in Montorio in Rome (ca. 1502), better known as the Tempietto, for example, uses a rich Doric entablature with the full sequence of triglyphs and metopes. But here we see a brilliant Christianization of the inherited tradition. In the otherwise blank metopes, Bramante inserted carved implements of the ritual sacrifice of the Mass: chalice, paten, candlesticks, and incense boat, among others. Here, troping ornament reveals the clarity of the purpose of the building by using a "baptized" pagan system, which not only serves as decoration (the triglyphs mark the ends of beams and therefore clarify structure), but also absorbs an ornamental system that signifies the presence of God through ritual sacrifice. The notion of sacrifice is only heightened here, since the chapel marks the spot of the martyrdom of Saint Peter, who, in imitation of Christ, sacrificed his own life. Amid it all, the high level of craft and the continuity with tradition speak of a building of a high level of importance proper to this place and its history. This is the architecture of *claritas* because its ornament is the marker not only of utilitarian facts, but now also the glory of the Truth. Without this ornament, the building would be and tell less than it does now, revealing less of its ontological reality. It would lack *integritas* and therefore *claritas*; it would therefore be less beautiful. Similarly, a chapel commemorating the sacrifice of Christ on the Via Dolorosa (Way of the Cross) in

Above and right: Christian adaptation of the Classical markers of structure and ritual sacrifice with symbols of vessels from the Mass. "Tempietto," Rome. Donato Bramante, architect, 1502.

Jerusalem places images of the Passion in the equivalent, metope-like areas.

Important to remember, though, is that the necessity of ornament is not a license to use it inappropriately or in excess. Ornament is always meant to clarify the meaning of a building by enhancing the clarity of its meaning. If the ornament becomes the dominant feature of a building—that is, if ornament becomes about ornament and not revelation of ontological realities—it becomes a murky dead end closed in on itself. Here one can think of Christ's words in Luke 21:5 to the apostles who were remarking about how the temple was "adorned with beautiful stones and with gifts dedicated to God." Christ admonished them not to be overly interested in those stones since they were merely a *shadow* of the new temple of his body. In our own day, we use stones to anticipate in the *image* the *reality* of our heavenly future, so they are ordered not to themselves, but reveals what we hope to be: glorified. These architectural signifiers should never be con-

Troping ornament in a Catholic setting.

fused with the reality that is signified, but neither should that which is signified be denied signification out of a fear of being misread. "Gilding the lily" is indeed problematic; it obscures the beauty of the lily itself by covering it in gold leaf, denying the lily's power to reveal itself. But denying the value of the lily is a puritanical approach unbecoming of a sacramental worldview. Beauty is always found in the proper mean between excess and deficiency.

Worth noting here is that the revelation of reality in architecture does not come at the expense of the world's history or the specificity of the inherited tradition. In contrast, it radiates *through* them, fulfilling them and reminding us that *God works in history, the present, and also anticipated eschatology.* This approach to the Classical tradition is not a "pagan revival." So, in a very contemporary-sounding sense of inculturation, Christianity can fulfill the pagan architectural traditions it was born into in Roman Jerusalem, where it would be nurtured in its early years. Classical architecture has served as the basis for Christian architecture ever since.

This is not to say that every builder through history knew what these ornaments meant. Perhaps they accepted the inherited tradition, knowing it was good without knowing its

Leaves adorn the elaborated keystone, combining decoration and ornament.

Swags of fruit and beads upon shield as emblem of victory.

Ornament makes the invisible visible, Our Lord Christ the King Church, Cincinnati, Ohio. Edward Schulte, architect, 1957.

architectural **etymology**. But the cultures that used it often knew it came from the time of the apostles and that it provided the way of making "high" architecture. When the cultural revivals that we call "renaissances" occurred, people understood more accurately the proper syntax of Classicism. Classicism as understood here does not epitomize any one period of architecture, whether it be ancient Rome, Greece, Byzantium, or medieval France. It allows for an infinite variety of manifestations as known in different times and places.

---

etymology: the study of the history and origins of words.

Just as we can still see the Latin and Greek roots of the English language, we can still see the Classical roots of our architecture today. What it always requires, however, is the desire to speak of the pre-history, history, nature, and importance of Christianity. There may someday be an inspired genius who develops a language of architecture that expresses Christianity perfectly without using the Classical sources. However, developing a new language of architecture from zero would be like developing a new language for speaking from zero—organic growth aids in legibility. Classicism is not

Exuberant ornament establishes the importance of the church building. St. Paul–St. Louis Church, Paris.

a "style," it is a method;[15] it is a way of doing things that clearly manifests the realities of Christianity.

Good liturgical architecture, like good preaching, should do something for everyone who hears it. It should attract and please the uneducated, it should edify and educate those who bring a greater knowledge, and it should delight the specialists whose knowledge demands the possibility of deep contemplation. Saint Irenaeus reminds us that God doesn't need the service given by humans, even as he commands obedience.[16] Similarly, God doesn't need ornament. It is humanity that needs to serve and praise God, and it is humanity that benefits from the sacramental revelation through material things by the application of will and intellect in imitation of the creator. A sense of awe at the architecture of Christianity is the beginning of a sense of awe at Christianity itself. It is for this reason that the Renaissance architect Leon Battista Alberti (1404–1472) wrote that a church which "delights the mind wonderfully, captivates it with grace and admiration, will greatly encourage piety." Therefore, he wrote: "I would wish the [church] so beautiful that nothing more decorous could ever be devised; I would deck it out in every part so that anyone who entered it would start with awe for his admiration at all the beautiful things, and could scarcely restrain himself from exclaiming that what he saw was a place undoubtedly worthy of God."[17]

The language of ornament forms a critical tool in meeting these demands.

1. Carroll William Westfall, *Architectural Principles in the Age of Historicism* (New Haven: Yale University Press, 1991), 273.

2. Adolf Loos's famous 1908 essay "Ornament and Crime" associated ornament with criminality, claiming it was erotic in origin, even going so far as to write: "The evolution of culture is synonymous with the removal of ornament from utilitarian objects. . . . therein lies the greatness of our age, that it is incapable of producing a new ornament. We have outgrown ornament. We have fought our way through to freedom from ornament. . . . Soon the streets of the city will glisten like white walls. Like Zion, the holy city, the capital of heaven. The fulfillment will come." Here we see a theology of architecture that denies materiality, thinking instead that the heavenly future, which will be without mediation of matter, can be done in the earthly realm. See Ulrich Conrads, *Programs and Manifestoes on 20th-Century Architecture* (Cambridge, MA: MIT Press: 1997), 19–24.

3. Westfall, *Architectural Principles in the Age of Historicism*, 272.

4. Exodus 35:20–29: "Then all the congregation of the Israelites withdrew from the presence of Moses. And they came, everyone whose heart was stirred, and everyone whose spirit was willing, and brought the Lord's offering to be used for the tent of meeting, and for all its service, and for the sacred vestments. So they came, both men and women; all who were of a willing heart brought brooches and earrings and signet rings and pendants, all sorts of gold objects, everyone bringing an offering of gold to the Lord. And everyone who possessed blue or purple or crimson yarn or fine linen or goats' hair or tanned rams' skins or fine leather, brought them. Everyone who could make an offering of silver or bronze brought it as the Lord's offering; and everyone who possessed acacia wood of any use in the work, brought it. All the skillful women spun with their hands, and brought what they had spun in blue and purple and crimson yarns and fine linen; all the women whose hearts moved them to use their skill spun the goats' hair. And the leaders brought onyx stones and gems to be set in the ephod and the breastpiece, and spices and oil for the light, and for the anointing oil, and for the fragrant incense. All the Israelite men and women whose hearts made them willing to bring anything for the work that the Lord had commanded by Moses to be done, brought it as a freewill offering to the Lord." See also Exodus 10:21—11:10.

5. George Hersey, *The Lost Meaning of Classical Architecture* (New Haven: Yale University Press, 1988), 1.

6. Saint Augustine, *On Christian Doctrine*, Book II, ch. 40.

7. Saint Athanasius, *Easter Letter* (Ep. 5, 1–2: PG 26, 1370–1380) as given in the Liturgy of the Hours, Office of Readings, Friday of the Fourth Week of Lent.

8. For more on a Catholic and highly liturgical view of festivity, see Joseph Pieper, *In Tune With the World: A Theory of Festivity* (South Bend, IN: St. Augustine's Press, 1999), originally published in 1963. Unless otherwise specified, the major ideas on festivity presented here are drawn from this work.

9. Pieper, *In Tune With the World*, 3.

10. Saint Ambrose, *Treatise on Flight from the World*, in the Office of Readings, Saturday of the Second Week of Lent.

11. Hersey, *The Lost Meaning of Classical Architecture*, 13.

12. Hersey, *The Lost Meaning of Classical Architecture*, 31.

13. Hersey, *The Lost Meaning of Classical Architecture*, 34.

14. Hersey, *The Lost Meaning of Classical Architecture*, 30–31.

15. See Demetri Porphyrios, ed., *Classicism Is Not a Style* (London: Academy Editions, 1982).

16. Saint Irenaeus, *Treatise Against Heresies* (Lib. 4, 13, 4–14, 1: SC 100, 534–540) as given in the Liturgy of the Hours, Office of Readings, Saturday After Ash Wednesday.

17. Leon Battista Alberti, *On the Art of Building in Ten Books*, VII: 2, 113–114, Joseph Rykwert, Neil Leach and Robert Tavernor, trans., (Cambridge, MA: MIT Press, 1994), 194.

Chapter 8

Columns and Pillars of the Church

The discussion of the column has so far centered on its role in decoration and ornament. But columns are multivalent, signifying many things at once. Some theorize that Classical architecture is primarily a clarification of structure; others, that it is primarily about expressive content. Good Classical architecture really does both, just as a poem has structured meter and rhythm even as it expresses important ideas. Structure, decoration, ornament, allusion, hierarchy, anthropomorphism, and sacramentality all coexist in the column. Some columns are larger than others, display more ornament, are made of materials more or less precious, and appear in the species we call Tuscan, Doric, Ionic, Corinthian, or Composite, just to make a start. Columns are also symbols of *people*, and people are the living stones of the Church, who in turn are symbols of the tribes of Israel, who are themselves symbols of all of humanity. So the potential for the Christian use of columns is quite rich.

Unlike an egg-and-dart molding, which requires a certain amount of inculturation to be understood in the Christian context, columns get much of their symbolic meaning from scripture itself. Just before receiving the tablets of the Ten Commandments and just after hearing from the Lord, Moses sets up an altar and sacrificed bulls *after setting up 12 columns representing the 12 tribes of Israel* (Exodus 24:4). Already in Exodus, then, columns represented something other than themselves and something other than mere structural support. They represented people and groups of people. And the inspiration for this action was God himself.

Columns always represent something other than themselves and always have certain characteristics: they are squat, elongated, elegant, or abrupt. They look like Laurel or they look like

Anthropomorphic columns, Curacao.

Saints as "pillars of the Church." Church of the Nativity, Bethlehem.

Hollow bronze columns at St. Peter's Basilica evoke those of the Temple of Solomon.

Hardy, like Audrey Hepburn or Ethel Merman, like the delicate goddess Diana or Mars, the god of war. The author of Psalms recognized this. When praying that God might lower the heavens and come down, he also asks that God bless Israel's daughters by making them "graceful as columns, adorned as though for a palace" (Psalm 144:12).[1] These are not only righteous daughters who "uphold" the covenant, but ones who also display a certain glory in their ornamentation. They are not ornamented as for some small house, but for a *palace*, the palace of the king.

Columns are also metaphors representing God's support and blessing, things which do God's work. In the book of Judges, Samson destroys the temple of the Philistines who were about to offer sacrifice to their god Dagon by asking God for supernatural strength to topple its two primary columns (Judges 16:25–30). Perhaps the most famous columns of the Old Testament are the two great hollow bronze columns of Solomon's Temple, mentioned in 2 Chronicles 3:17 as being given the human names Jakin and Boaz. The meaning of hollow bronze columns would not be lost throughout history, with the great bronze baldachino in St. Peter's Basilica making this link quite explicit.

In the New Testament's many comparisons of the Church to architecture, the Christians are called living stones. But in Galatians 2:9, Cephas, James, and John are specifically called pillars of the church. This metaphorical language indeed gives the architect many possibilities. The Church is composed of the earthly people united with the heavenly citizens, all with Christ as their head. These beings "support" the Church (*ekklesia*) as a holy enterprise. But the church building is a symbol of the Church, not merely as the earthly gathering, but the Church's participation in the glory of heaven through an anticipated eschatology. So if the building represents the glorified people in union with heaven, and in scripture people are called pillars, why not use the column as the architecture symbol of the saints? Here we see Providence at work, as history has provided a glorified expression of structural necessity and poetic overlay as conventions developed in time and place. Columns were already understood as representing people even before the birth of Christ. In this providential preparation we find an important architectural-sacramental element.

COLUMN AS HUMAN BEING

The primary development of the Classical orders happened before the Incarnation, so by definition they are pre–Christian in origin. John Onians's insightful book, *Bearers of Meaning*, provides ample evidence that columns were highly articulate markers as early as the sixth century BC, where different columns were very clearly associated with different Greek city-states, and their use made important political statements.[2] But the very terminology of the column is also anthropomorphic in its origins. The top of a column is called a capital, from the Latin word for head, *caput*. Columns also have bases, from the Greek word *basis*, meaning "foot" or "dance." Beneath columns one often finds pedestals, deriving from the word *pes*, Latin for foot, which also gives us the words *pedal* and *pedestrian*.

In his treatise, Vitruvius relays his well-known version of the origin of the three major columnar orders, Doric, Ionic, and Corinthian, all of which took their inspiration from the human body. The Doric column, he writes, was developed by the Athenians who wanted to build a temple but did not have an established proportional system to use, which would be strong enough to bear the load and also be "of satisfactory beauty of appearance" (IV.1.vi). So they measured the foot of a man and found that this foot was about one-sixth of his height, and they made a column that was six times as tall as it was wide at its base, setting up the proportional system of 1:6 in ratio of diameter to height. The Doric column, then, had a particular character because of its particular proportions: it displayed the "proportions, strength and beauty of the body of a man" (IV.1.vi). Later, the proportions would be thought more elegant at 1:7, but the Doric has been understood ever since as representing a male person because it would be considered in the nature of things for men to have certain proportions. The aforementioned Church of San Pietro in Montorio (chapter 7, p. 119) rightly used the Doric order not only because it was associated with sacrifice, but also with Saint Peter as a male saint, receiving the columns that speak of his nature.

Ionic columns literalized as caryatids. Macy's, New York City.

The Ionic order, Vitruvius writes, arose from the desire to build a temple to the goddess Diana, one that would be proper to her nature as a feminine deity. Vitruvius claimed the 1:8 diameter-to-height ratio suggested the "characteristic slenderness of women" (later revised to 1:9), which was further emphasized by suggesting ornamental

Decorated Ionic capital. Church of the Annunciation, Nazareth.

hair-like ringlets decorated with fruit, which we now understand as the spiraling volutes of the Ionic capital. The shaft of the column was given a series of carved channels known as fluting, representing the folds of a woman's dress. So in the two types of columns, Doric and Ionic, he writes, "they borrowed manly beauty, naked and unadorned, for the one, and for the other, the delicacy, adornment and proportions characteristic of women" (IV.1.vii).

The Ionic women, moreover, were not just any women, but *married* women, and presumably, mothers. Vitruvius writes that *caryatids*, as columns in the shape of women that are known, were named for the women of the Greek town Caryae, involved in the Persian wars of the fifth century BC. Caryae proved traitorous, and as punishment was sacked by all of Greece. As the rules of engagement were set at the time, the men of the town were put to death, but the women were taken into slavery and forced to maintain their dress and

Corinthian column as woman. Louvre, Paris.

ornaments as married women (I.1.v). Their proportions, then, were not those of the teenage girl, but the motherly woman, and their status as slaves of the state is suggested by the slave-like work of holding up the entablature of a building. It also gives new meaning to the *torus* molding found at the base of columns. George Hersey argues that "the cavetto molding, common in column bases, gets its name from heavy rope, and a torus . . . is also a rope. . . ."[3] Traces of the origin of the torus as a rope can be found throughout Classical architecture.

The astragal of the column base is depicted as a rope, suggesting the bound feet of captives.

The young, unmarried girl or virgin was represented by the Corinthian order. Vitruvius relates that a young maiden from Corinth had died just before her marriage. Her loved ones laid a basket full of offerings at her grave, putting a large square tile atop it to keep things in place. The basket had unwittingly been placed atop the roots of an acanthus plant, which sent up it shoots along the

Callimachus discovers the funerary basket and develops the Corinthian capital. Thomas Gordon Smith, painter.

face of the basket with its vine-like tendrils curling under the corners of the tile. The architect Callimachus stumbled upon this arrangement and discovered in it the starting point for a column capital and regularized its characteristics and proportions. Traces of this basket can be found in the Corinthian capital to this day. Since the basket is placed atop the column, it gives the Corinthian an even greater height in relation to its diameter, giving it the "slenderness of a maiden," which admits "prettier effects in the way of adornment" (IV.1.9).

Though Vitruvius's writings are considered historically inaccurate in places, even as myth they still hold weight because the ideas they

The basket origin of the Corinthian capital on display. Church of the Holy Sepulcher, Jerusalem.

present carried meaning through the ages as if they *were* accurate, and the conventional signs became paradigmatic and recognizable. More importantly, Vitruvius verbalizes a kind of humanism that Christians could adopt quite easily.[4] Columns are abstracted people. People are the living stones of the Church, with each having a certain symbolism according to their gifts. Since the Church is made of many members, some people, like the evangelists and canonized saints, are "pillars of the Church," and columns make this knowable in architecture. This explains the common symbolism of the use of 12 columns in churches, representing the apostles, but as Exodus shows, also representing the 12 tribes of Israel for whom the apostles are a Christian fulfillment. We remember that even as early as the fourth century, Eusebius reports that the Emperor Constantine built the Church of the Holy Sepulcher with 12 columns to represent the 12 apostles, calling the columns a "splendid offering to his God."[5]

Thistle Corinthian, YMCA, Jerusalem

Tulip Corinthian, YMCA, Jerusalem

Fish and nets Corinthian, YMCA, Jerusalem

Daffodil Composite, YMCA, Jerusalem

Isaac and ram Corinthian, YMCA, Jerusalem

Isaiah 11:6 Corinthian, YMCA, Jerusalem

Basket Corinthian, Church of the Holy Sepulcher, Jerusalem

Jerusalem cross Corinthian, Church of All Nations, Jerusalem

Corinthian with birds drinking, Cathedral, Wheeling, West Virginia

Sacred Heart Corinthian, Marytown, Libertyville, Illinois

Oxen Composite, YMCA, Jerusalem

Borochoff House, Jerusalem

Church of the Holy Sepulcher, Jerusalem

Church of the Holy Sepulcher, Jerusalem

Buddha Corinthian, Gandhara (now Pakistan), 3rd–4th century

Bird Corinthian, St. Germain des Pres, Paris

Church of the Loaves and Fishes, Tabgha, Galilee

Getty Villa, Los Angeles, based on Temple of Vesta, Tivoli

Getty Villa, Los Angeles

Getty Villa, Los Angeles, after Vitruvius

Greek Patriarchate, Jerusalem

Leaf and fruit Ionic, YMCA, Jerusalem

Decorated Doric, Macy's, New York

Proto Doric, Getty Villa, Los Angeles

Ionic Capital, Getty Villa, Los Angeles

Wheat Corinthian, YMCA, Jerusalem

Florentine Corinthian, St. Giles Church, Oak Park, Illinois

The elements of classical architecture are known for conserving traditional forms, but this need not lead to rigid uniformity. Like language, a way of designing which respects a stable lexicon can arrange and rearrange its constituent parts to remain legible while saying something completely new. In this form of "pious skepticism," the wisdom of past ages is respected while addressing the needs of the current age.

Harp Corinthian, Lyric Opera, Chicago

Corinthian caryatid, Louvre, Paris

Archaic Ionic railing, State Capitol, Nashville, Tennessee

Hunting-themed Corinthian, Louvre, Paris

Turtle Corinthian, YMCA, Jerusalem

Public library, Nashville, Tennessee

Milk Grotto, Bethlehem

St. Boniface Church, Evansville, Indiana

Banana Republic, Chicago

Reptile Composite, Lincoln Park Zoo, Chicago

Iris Corinthian, YMCA, Jerusalem

Maritime Doric, Naval Academy, Annapolis, Maryland

Art Deco Corinthian, Chicago

Victorian Gothic Corinthian, St. James Church, Chicago

Church of the Visitation, Jerusalem

Our Lady of Guadalupe Seminary, Denton, Nebraska

Cathedral of St. Joseph, Wheeling, West Virginia

Eagle Corinthian, U.S. Supreme Court, Washington, DC

Modernized Ionic, school, South Bend, Indiana

Christian Corinthian, Chapel, Mundelein Seminary, Chicago

Cherubic Corinthian, St. Hyacinth Church, Chicago

Simplified Corinthian, bank, Huntington, New York

Medieval Corinthian, Sainte-Chapelle, Paris

Corn and wheat Corinthian, State Capitol, Lincoln, Nebraska

Ionic with hanging ornament, apartment building, New York City

Corinthian, Getty Villa, Los Angeles

Art Deco Corinthian with logo, Packard dealer, Winnetka, Illinois

Corporate Corinthian, office tower, New York City

Newberry Library, Chicago

Eagle Composite, Annapolis, Maryland

HIERARCHY OF COLUMNS

Columns have also been understood as belonging to a hierarchy of status. Though the particular arrangement has varied some over the centuries, the historical convention has emerged as follows from low to high: Tuscan (a simplified Doric), Doric, Ionic, Corinthian, and Composite. This last column type, the Composite, is not mentioned by Vitruvius because it was unknown to him, having been developed in the Roman imperial period. But the Composite provided a synthesis of the Ionic and the Corinthian, displaying both the spiraled volutes of the Ionic and the leafy acanthus of the Corinthian.

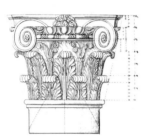

Composite capital showing volutes of the Ionic combined with the acanthus leaves of the Corinthian.

Its proportions were even more slender, and it stands at the top of the architectural hierarchy. For this reason, St. Peter's basilica, as rebuilt in the Renaissance, used the largest Corinthian columns in Rome to establish its place at the top of the city's architectural hierarchy, but then used the Composite order for the bronze baldachino over the altar and tomb of Peter on the inside, marking the highest status spot within the highest status church. Moreover, these hollow bronze columns clearly established a connection with the similar bronze columns of the Temple of Solomon. Solomon, the builder of the Temple of Jerusalem, was David's son, and for this reason, Christ is called the "Son of David" as the builder of the new Temple of his Body, the Church (Matthew 22:42, Luke 20:41, Matthew 1:1, Luke 18:38). Associating oneself with the Temple of Solomon was to imitate Christ's building up of the Church, the goal of any sincere pastor of souls as well as every church architect.

Intriguing theories have emerged in recent years about the Composite order and its use under the Emperor Constantine, widely hailed as the first Christian emperor. Until Constantine, the Composite was the order used by Roman emperors as a symbol of military victory, and it appeared on their triumphal arches. In a great exception, Constantine's triumphal arch takes the Corinthian instead of the Composite, a move that has been called "a transfer of the Composite, emblem of Roman superiority, to the new religion" of Christianity.[6] It therefore became a symbol of a new kind of victory, not the military victory of the empire, but the conquering of sin and death by Christ. This architectural element becomes, then, a sign of otherwise invisible spiritual realities. One also finds Composite columns at the east end of the original St. Peter's, built by Constantine, and in his daughter's mausoleum chapel, now known as the Church of Santa Costanza in Rome.

Constantinian Basilica of St. Peter in Rome with "Solomonic" Composite columns.

In other cases, columnar hierarchy worked together with anthropomorphic symbolism. The Church of Santa Maria Maggiore in Rome, for instance, dates to the 440s AD and was the first church in Rome dedicated to the Virgin Mary, finished shortly after the Council of Ephesus had declared her the Mother of God. It is also singular in its day in its exclusive use of Ionic colonnades in its nave, especially when compared to Corinthian and Composite in Rome's other great Christian basilicas. Here we see a diminishing of

Corinthian columns on the Arch of Constantine, supporting the claim that Constantine "donated" the Composite to the Church.

Saints identified as columns, Notre Dame, Paris.

Ambulatory, Abbey Church of St- Denis, Paris.

Columns "become" saints at St. Ita Church, Chicago. Henry Schlacks, architect, 1927.

the architectural hierarchy in a church dedicated to the Virgin, and some have proposed that it sought "to imitate but not equal the three great basilicas of the Lateran, St. Peter and St. Paul."[7] One might add as well the notion that the Ionic, as reminder of the widows of Caryae, was the column not just of women, but of mothers, giving the choice of the Ionic a particularly Marian dimension as Mother of God.

History provides countless examples of the intentional use of columns to make theological points. Abbot Suger's 1144 text called *De consecratione*, for instance, wrote that the 12 inner columns of his famous ambulatory of St- Denis near Paris represented the 12 apostles, while the outer ones represented prophets, all of which rose up to support the building just as the apostles formed pillars of the Church.[8] One finds a pun here since the Latin verb *aedificare*, "to build," is the word used to build a building as well as "build up" the Church as a spiritual body. The column-as-person motif appears widely in Gothic architecture, seen at the famous reliquary chapel of Sainte-Chapelle, where a saint is fixed to each of

the building's 12 columns, and in many triumphal arch portals of the great Gothic cathedrals, where columns alternate with elongated figures, many of whom appear to grow out of the columns themselves. This motif was even used in Chicago as late as the 1920s at the Church of St. Ita by Henry Schlacks, where the ceiling ribs land on Corinthian capitals and small segments of columns, which then symbolically transform into statues of the saints, the pillars of the Church.

Hierarchy of building purpose elucidated by columns: embedded Doric pilasters, freestanding Ionic columns, smaller partially embedded Corinthian columns.

When columns become *saints*, rather than slaves of the ancient world, we see transformation of slaves into friends (John 15:15). Even medieval columns still have the torus molding, symbolizing the bound feet of slaves, but this slavery is transformed into keeping the commandments of Christ in love and not fear (John 15:10). A column now supports the church in a way that symbolizes what *friends* do: sacrifice for others out of love. The book of Revelation expresses this idea when heaven is described as a fulfillment of the Temple of Solomon, the "temple of God" which contains his throne (Revelation 7:15). The angel instructs John to write: "He who conquers and perseveres, I will make him a pillar in the temple of my God; never shall he go out of it" (Revelation 3:12). Christians who persevere through the great trials become like columns, those who are happy never to leave the temple and therefore never leave the presence of God.

Understanding the meaning of the column unlocks the ideas behind their use. Several notable examples can help establish the place of this continuous language in our own day. The campus of the University of Saint Mary of the Lake, the home of the major seminary of the Archdiocese of Chicago, was built between 1917 and 1934, and provides one of the most nuanced uses of the orders in the United States. The university's gymnasium makes use of Doric **pilasters**, not only using the low-status Doric, but embedding them into

the walls as "flat columns," using the traditional architectural hierarchy, which sees things embedded as lower status than things freestanding. The university's dormitories use larger Ionic columns, establishing their middle status as small residential and therefore political units. The classroom buildings, places of learning, move upward to the Corinthian, but with columns only three-quarters visible, suggesting that though the high status order is used, it is used in one of its lower manifestations. The orders then move on to large Corinthian pilasters on the library, using an important order on a large scale, but still remaining embedded. Eventually, the interior of the chapel, the highest building in the university's hierarchy, receives 12 of the university's largest, round, freestanding columns, picked out with color and gold leaf. At the University of Saint Mary of the Lake, each building speaks of its own inherent place in an ontological hierarchy, while at the same time the entire campus can be "read" as one essay by comparing one building to another. It is the use of the Classical orders that makes this legibility possible. If the sup-

---

pilaster: popularly known as a "flat column," an upright architectural member that is technically a pier because it is rectangular in plan, but is treated as a column. Pilasters typically extend only a third of their width or less from a wall, suggesting that they are embedded in that wall.

Hierarchical arrangement continues: large embedded Corinthian pilasters, and large, freestanding Corinthian columns reserved for the chapel. Joseph W. McCarthy, architect. Mundelein Seminary, Chicago, 1917–1934.

ports were all steel I-beams, or even all Doric columns, the theological reality inherent in these buildings would not be made knowable to the eye by architecture and therefore be less available to the mind.

In the more theologically sophisticated buildings of today's New Classical movement, this understanding of the language of the orders continues a legible tradition. The church of St. Michael the Archangel in Leawood, Kansas (2009), uses the orders in light of their structural and anthropomorphic meanings to make a theologically derived and readable whole.[9] The parish asked for a church that in general recalled Rome and the connectedness of their parish to

the eternal city. Doric is the primary column type in the church's exterior and interior, a reference to the masculine, warrior-like quality of the patron, Saint Michael the Archangel. The Ionic appears on the nave interior clerestory, referring to the Church's many female saints in the conventional location above the Doric. Here the lower, wider (and therefore stronger) proportions of the Doric visually support the more slender Ionic above. The Corinthian appears in the sanctuary, marking the increased importance of the primary location of the ritual action. In a very subtle fine-tuning, the marble altar alone receives the Composite order. Here the highest status object in the building—the altar as image of Christ and heavenly

Articulate use of the orders continues in current work. St. Michael the Archangel Church, Leawood, Kansas. David Meleca, design architect, 2009.

banqueting table brought to Earth—receives the marker of highest status. Moreover, the altar's Composite capitals are of a completely new version of the conventional type, which we might call the "St. Michael Composite." Here the scrolls of the Ionic and the leaves of the Corinthian find themselves ornamented with a sword, the symbol of Saint Michael's victory over Satan. Just as the sacred trees in the pagan world were bedecked with trophies; just as humans ornament their hair, bodies, and homes for ritually festive occasions; just as the history of the column from ancient Greece to today has developed conventions that are still legible to those who are architecturally catechized; so the Composite pilasters of new the altar of St. Michael's Church in Kansas fulfill von Balthasar's challenge that today's aesthetic absorbs the beauty of the pagan world while giving all the glory to Jesus Christ. Imitation need never be copying; a preacher can read the same scripture as every other preacher in history and still make a new sermon. The tradition is alive and should show the evidence of the inspiration of the Holy Spirit in our times as well as every other, bringing due honor and reverence to the rites in a way wholly new yet intimately familiar.

So the Classical inheritance in architecture is more than a set of forms from a past age. Some have argued that Classicism is not "of our time," seeing history as formed by a series of discontinuous epochs each having its own distinct identity. To a certain extent this is true, and every great epoch develops an art that people later look back on and begin to characterize as belonging to one period or another. But what makes church architecture appropriately "churchly," even in differing generations, is what is *continuous* about it. These continuities occur most importantly in the realm of theological ideas, and to a certain extent, the architectural forms of each period are secondary. But secondary does not mean unimportant. The continuity of forms makes ideas legible to the next generation. So new architecture, at least until the twentieth century, has always had a profound respect for traditional ideas and inherited forms. Although many have tried, no one has come up with a substitute for the articulate language of Classicism and its poetry, allusion, anthropomorphism, clarity of hierarchy, recognizable conventions, structural logic, and Biblical connotations. The claim that a steel I-beam is simply the column done in twentieth- or twenty-first century garb (or as a Classicist would note, lack of garb) simply cannot be supported. A well-welded steel beam or poured concrete post will never be what a well-designed and crafted column is.

Classicism belongs in our time as much as any other because the ideas it represents so effectively still remain in our culture. God still lives. The Church still thrives. The Holy Spirit still inspires new songs, poetry, paintings, sculpture, and architecture. Earthly matter still becomes the vehicle for revelation in God's divine pedagogy of salvation. People are still "pillars of the Church," and the angels and saints still stand at the throne of God, singing, "Holy, Holy, Holy." The laws of physics still operate, and we still use our gifts of creativity to make structure poetic and sacramentally glorified. We still

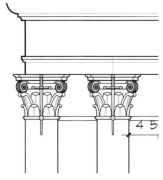

St. Michael Composite.

Interior, St. Michael the Archangel Church, Leawood, Kansas, 2009.

understand that Christianity's roots are deep even as we discover new things about God's revelation. So we take the tradition and embrace it warmly, seeing it as a treasure that we guard and from which we learn. While we make churches that address the particular needs of our place and time, architectural continuity allows us to realize that we are united with all Christians who have gone before us, building a visual hymn to the Lord's glory by imitating the order and radiance of heaven, making visible the warriors of the heavenly army and venerating the memory of the saints as we eagerly await the Savior (SC, 8). Then we can rightly say that we have added our architectural voice to "that wonderful chorus of praise in honor of the Catholic faith sung by great men in times gone by" (SC, 123).

4. In addition to the anthropomorphic qualities of columns as individual units, Vitruvius argues that the proportions of the many and varied pieces are based on modular systems drawn from the proportions of the human body (Book 3, ch. 1), as the famous Vitruvian man has kept alive in cultural memory to the present day. A Christian, of course, would understand the human body as a source of revelation about the God in whose image it is made, and would see Vitruvius as ripe for inculturation, especially since he claimed that temples should be based on these proportional systems. In our own day, we understand that the church building is a sacramental building that represents the Temple of Christ, which is the Mystical *Body*. Since we have to choose a proportional system from somewhere, the human body, pinnacle of creation, serves as a starting point.

5. Eusebius, *Life of Constantine*, Book 3, ch. 38.

6. Onians, *Bearers of Meaning*, 59.

7. Onians, *Bearers of Meaning*, 67–68.

8. Abbot Suger, *De Consecratione*, ch. 5, in Erwin Panofsky, *Abbot Suger On the Abbey Church of St- Denis and Its Art Treasures* (Princeton: Princeton University Press, 1967), 105: "The midst of the edifice, however, was suddenly raised aloft by columns representing the number of the Twelve Apostles and, secondarily, by as many columns in the side-aisles signifying the number of the [minor] Prophets, according to the Apostle who buildeth spiritually."

9. Designed by David Meleca of Meleca Architects in Columbus, Ohio, in association with David Livingood of GLPM Architects of Lawrence, Kansas. Denis McNamara of the Liturgical Institute in Mundelein, Illinois, architectural and theological consultant. Father William Porter, pastor. EverGreene Studios provided the sanctuary's mural.

1. It is worthy to note that though several different translations use the term *column*, the Latin of Psalm 144 does not include the term *columna/ columnae* specifically: "*Quorum filii sicut novella plantationis in iuventute sua filiae eorum conpositae circumornatae ut similitudo templi*," somewhat literally translated as "Whose sons are as new plants in their youth: Their daughters decked out, adorned round about after the similitude of a temple." The Hebrew root word *zaviyth* used here signifies either a corner or a corner pillar, which is most likely the definition on which the translation as *column* is based.

2. John Onians, *Bearers of Meaning: The Classical Orders in Antiquity, the Middle Ages, and the Renaissance* (Princeton, NJ: Princeton University Press, 1988), 15–18.

3. George Hersey, *The Lost Meaning of Classcal Architecture* (New Haven: Yale University Press, 1988), 21.

Part IV

Iconic Imagery as Eschatological Flash

Since the Mass includes the heavenly liturgy, full, conscious, and active participation requires knowing that reality.

The question of liturgical imagery has remained thorny since the earliest days of Christianity. The fear that images would become idols has dogged Christian thinkers as early as the post-apostolic era when images were spare and highly symbolic so as to be distinguished from the statues of pagan religions. As the centuries progressed, images became understood as less dangerous, and the theology of the icon eventually reached great heights. Over time, though, certain superstitious excesses sometimes appeared in religious imagery, with icons sometimes thought to be "magic" or efficacious in themselves. The famous iconoclastic controversies of the eighth and ninth centuries in Byzantium brought this question into high relief, even to point of legal disruption and violence, until Saint John Damascene's defense of icons, *On Images* (ca. 730 AD), became the great answer to the question. The medievals gloried in their images in stone, paint, metal, and stained glass, but even they had their excesses, as chronicled by Saint Bernard of Clairvaux's well-known letters and writings. The new era of iconoclasm that occurred in the Reformation sent shockwaves throughout Christianity, evoking a dramatic and corrective response from the post–Trent Catholicism characterized by rich layering of polyvalent imagery. The Tridentine principles, though rather vague, held their own until their occasionally unruly climax in the late nineteenth century. What we see here is a recognition of the power of the image, even, and perhaps especially, by the iconoclasts who feared their influence. The sacred image holds its place in the world of Christianity now as ever.

But even as images have been used in churches for centuries, the Western Church gives very little official teaching on liturgical art other than general notions that images should be provided for the veneration of the faithful and should be without error. Though the Second Vatican Council states strongly that sacred images should be retained, it also asks bishops to "exclude from the house of God and from other sacred places those works of artists which are repugnant to faith, morals, and Christian piety, and which offend religious sense either by their distortion of forms or by lack of artistic worth" (SC, 124). While this is good advice, it is hardly a ringing endorsement or rich theology of sacred imagery, especially when compared to the developed theology of the icon in Eastern Catholic or Orthodox Churches. Orthodox author Leonid Ouspensky hit the nail on the head when he wrote that the Roman Catholic Church seems to have no operative theology of what liturgical art *is*, only what it should *not* be.[1] The reason is largely the Church's position of reaction to the Reformation, attempting to root out the excesses that led in part to the Reformation's rejection of imagery.

Iconic imagery allows us to "see" the souls in purgatory who also participate in the liturgy.

Station 13, Cathedral of Christ the King, Lexington, Kentucky.

Perhaps it should not surprise us that a certain confusion about liturgical imagery appeared in the Catholic Church in the years immediately after the Second Vatican Council, causing many parishes to strip away their statues and murals, often to the dismay of the faithful. Because the Western Church did not supply a positive definition of the liturgical image, many people simply didn't know how images were to be used in the liturgical context, a condition which remains widespread today. An anomalous interpretation of the "spirit" of Vatican II led some to think that the banishing of imagery was in order, only perhaps tolerating of one or two devotional statues for those so inclined.

The text of *Sacrosanctum Concilium* itself made no such iconoclastic suggestions, stating quite frankly that "the practice of placing sacred images in churches so that they may be venerated by the faithful is to be maintained" (SC, 125). Vatican II did not come without its caveat, however, adding in the same paragraph: "Nevertheless their number should be moderate and their relative positions should reflect right order. For otherwise they may create confusion among the Christian people and foster devotion of doubtful orthodoxy." This "both/and" language is typical of the two-part rhythm of Council texts, first urging strongly the general philosophical position, then warning against exaggerations of that position. One can translate this line in everyday speech as: "Keep your sacred images, but make sure they don't become understood as idols or take prominence over the liturgy itself." Again, this hardly proves to be a positive theology.

While presuming the goodwill of all involved, it is reasonable to claim that the immediate post-conciliar liturgical

Iconography serves as a locus where the heavenly and the earthly overlap.

and artistic implementations have manifested an exaggerated **iconoclastic** position. Not unexpectedly, this has sometimes bred a reactionary counter-position of uncritical **iconodulia**. Simply arguing that a church full of paintings and statues is "too pre–Vatican II" hardly defines a proper intellectual engagement with the Church's teaching and tradition on imagery. On the other hand, simply collecting the plaster Victorian statues from the ecclesial antique dealers and arranging them willy-nilly as part of the nostalgic accouterments of "the old days" fails for similar reasons. The large, unadorned churches so common to the 1980s have earned the unflattering (and often justifiable) title of "empty barns" by some more interested in polemical bomb throwing than rational discourse. On the other hand, I recall a few years ago showing a mural of the Trinity, the angels, and saints in the heavenly Jerusalem from the Cathedral of the Madeleine in Salt Lake City to a parish building committee, causing a member of the committee to give the shocking response: "I don't want all that *garbage* in my church." Exaggerated positions indeed still hold sway. One liturgical artist wrote recently that today's people are "taught to read" and therefore "no longer need pictorial representations."[2] This lack of understanding of the liturgical role of iconography demands a response for our times, one rooted in the teachings of Vatican II and which can be nourished by the iconic traditions of the Eastern Churches.

If church builders and their allied artists are going to move forward into a future based not on uncritical reactions to iconophobes, **iconodules**, iconoclasts, the Reformation,

---

iconoclastic: from the Greek, literally "icon breaker," one who destroys images.

iconodulia: veneration given to icons.

iconodules: those who venerate icons.

Ionic images must always retain legibility even as they depart from established conventions. Saint John Berchmans Church, Chicago.

the Council of Trent, or a hermeneutic of discontinuity, it is worth asking the question anew about the purpose of the sacred image and its liturgical use. In a time when architectural and artistic theology has been worked and reworked according to the polemics of reformation, counter-reformation, and downright revolt, it is useful to "breathe with both lungs" of the Eastern and Western Churches and return to the sources to rethink our modern application. The broad principle is this: *Liturgical imagery, properly speaking, is fundamentally sacramental. Because it is part of the rite and not extrinsic to it, it is proper to the liturgy itself.*

An architect uses stone, wood, and glass to make a building that sacramentally recalls the temple, expresses the

Iconic imagery departs from photorealistic conventions to make the Truth more evident.

sacrificial realities of Christ's Mystical Body, and anticipates the glory of the heavenly Jerusalem. In a similar fashion, a maker of liturgical images uses the very materiality of wood, stone, gold, and pigments to *reveal* preexisting spiritual realities that would be otherwise unknowable. The liturgical artist helps to reveal that the entire liturgical assembly, the *Christus totus*, celebrates the liturgy (CCC, 1136–1144). This assembly includes not only the earthly beings who participate through sign and symbol, but also those who celebrate without signs in the heavenly liturgy: the Trinity, the angels, the saints, even the souls in purgatory who exist on the edge of glory. "It is in this eternal liturgy that the Spirit and the Church enable us to participate whenever we celebrate the mystery of salvation in the sacraments" (CCC, 1139).

sensate beings: beings, like humans and unlike angels, who acquire information via bodily senses.

But unless any of us is a mystic given unusual graces to see these heavenly realities, how are they to be made knowable to us? The answer lies in the *image*, not merely as an earthly picture, but as a revealer of otherwise invisible realities. These beings who participate in the heavenly reality of the liturgy are made known to us through the image, a sacramental sign which makes present to our senses the realities that would have no other way of being known. An icon of Saint Peter is not simply a reminder that Peter is "up there" in heaven; it is instead a locus where the heavenly reality and the earthly image overlap and the presence of the saint is sacramentally mediated to us in ways suitable to our nature as **sensate beings**. Therefore, the making of liturgical imagery is a theological act, and *liturgical images are theology in pictorial form*. That which we know to be true is presented to our eyes and imprinted in our minds.

So image making requires not only technical skill, but also careful knowledge of theological premises understood not only as textbook propositions, but as knowledge that comes from revelation through prayer and the reception of the sacraments. Moreover, it requires submission to the will of the Holy Spirit, who uses the artist as a vehicle of revelation to others. Noted theologian Paul Evdokimov reminds us of the passage from 1 Corinthians, saying that "no one can say 'Jesus is Lord' unless he is under the influence of the Holy Spirit" (1 Corinthians 12:3). Similarly, he writes, "no one can represent the image of the Lord unless he is under the influence of the Holy Spirit who is the divine iconographer."[3] Architect Ralph Adams Cram called the liturgical artist a "minister in minor orders" for this very reason;[4] the artist's calling is indeed lofty. Hans Urs von Balthasar called the process of making revelatory things as one "where the image (*das Bild*), in the Spirit, becomes transparent of him who made the image (*der Bildende*), and this maker of images is God and man in unity."[5] So artistic skill is a gift, as John Paul II wrote in his *Letter to Artists*, and proper artistic execution requires a joining of nature to grace. The more we know about images, the more we bring to them and the more they can nourish us and dispose us for proper worship. The intention here, then, is to begin again at the beginning, laying down principles for sacred art, which can help renew our fundamental understanding of their nature, types, and use.

1. Leonid Ouspensky, *The Theology of the Icon* (Crestwood, NY: St. Vladimir's Seminary Press, 1978), 12–13.

2. Linda McCray, "Passing on the Faith through Contemporary Visual Language," *Liturgical Art Today* 9 (Spring 2008), unnumbered page.

3. Paul Evdokimov, *The Art of the Icon: A Theology of Beauty* (Redondo Beach, CA: Oakwood Publications, 1990), 3.

4. Ralph Adams Cram, "The Ministry of Art," *The Ministry of Art* (Boston: Houghton Mifflin, Co., 1914), 237.

5. Hans Urs von Balthasar, *Glory of the Lord*, v. 1 (San Francisco: Ignatius Press, 1985), 85.

Chapter 9

Sacred Image and Iconic Revelation

Following the divinely inspired teaching of our holy Fathers and the tradition of the Catholic Church (for we know that this tradition comes from the Holy Spirit who dwells in her) we rightly define with full certainty and correctness that, like the figure of the precious and life-giving cross, venerable and holy images of our Lord and God and Savior, Jesus Christ, our inviolate Lady, the holy Mother of God, and the venerated angels, all the saints and the just, whether painted or made of mosaic or another suitable material, are to be exhibited in the holy churches of God, on sacred vessels and vestments, walls and panels, in houses and on streets. . . .

—Second Council of Nicea, 787 AD

The declaration made by the Second Council of Nicea establishing the propriety of displaying holy images came after long debates about the nature of liturgical art. The particular questions surrounding their use, which the Council addressed, arose from centuries of haggling over the place of images in Christian worship and life. Certainly, the Old Testament prohibition against graven images in Exodus 20 and Psalm 97 seemed clear enough, as did the danger of idolatry associated with the golden calf (Exodus 32). Yet the Old Testament was not as singularly opposed to images as might be assumed, as the directions given by God for the fashioning of the bronze serpent attests (Numbers 21:4–9), as does the ornament of the temple with its carved angels, flowers, oxen, pomegranates, and palm trees (1 Kings 6:18–20). Surviving artwork in the catacombs reveals that the Christian church made use of imagery as early as the second century and perhaps earlier. With imperial patronage and freedom to worship under the Emperor Constantine, Christianity flowered with a great belief in the ritually public expressions of the faith, something not foreign to Christianity, but deeply intertwined with an incarnational theology.

Eusebius's mention that the Church of Tyre was built with doors wide enough so that non-Christian passersby could see in and be attracted by the artistic beauty reinforces

Christians can represent Christ because Christ chose to represent himself. Church of Multiplication of the Loaves and Fishes, Galilee.

139

Carvings from post-temple synagogues reveal the presence of figural ornament in the time of the early Church. Capernaum, Galilee.

the idea that art and architecture were part of the Christian evangelization process even in the early fourth century.[1] Moreover, the ruins of late synagogues in Palestine show that figural imagery was a fairly standard part of their architectural designs. The synagogue in Dura Europos, rediscovered in 1932, showed an enthusiastic embrace of figural imagery in its large murals in the third century. But the theological basis of the development of the theology of the holy image in Christianity grows directly from its rootedness in sacramental theology, which is itself rooted in the Incarnation. As such, imagery is not an accessory to the liturgy or merely a concession to the uneducated, but something proper to the sacred liturgy itself.[2]

Today, congregations building new churches often fail to consider the integral role of Christian imagery in the liturgy and therefore in the church design and budget. I've seen art and furnishings budgets that allow a six-figure sum for pews and then hope there is money left over for some statues. Architects are often so interested in getting the accessibility and zoning problems solved that imagery becomes a sort of afterthought for a statue or two when the pastor asks the architect where the devotional areas will be. But if we take the words of the *Catechism of the Catholic Church* seriously, and realize that "Christian iconography expresses in images the same Gospel message that scripture communicates by words" (CCC, 1160), then we must give at least as much attention to the role of images in a church as we do to the reading of scripture.

Scripture tells us of heavenly realities. Images show them to us.

THE RELATIONSHIP BETWEEN IMAGES AND THE LITURGY

The discussion of liturgical imagery is not a question of nostalgia. Rather, it centers on the very nature of the Incarnation and the means by which the goodness of material creation becomes, in the Spirit, the bearer of revelation and the divine life that God desires to communicate to his creatures. Since *Sacrosanctum Concilium* tells us that "in the earthly liturgy we take part in a foretaste of that heavenly liturgy which is celebrated in the holy city of Jerusalem toward which we journey as pilgrims" (SC, 8), one of the most important vehicles for perceiving that foretaste is the sacred image. As such, images are not extrinsic to the liturgy, but integral to it. Through images we *see* the Mass, just as through proclamation we hear the Mass. The challenge today, as ever, is to understand the true nature of liturgical images and use them most effectively

Icons show beings that have been fully divinized and show no trace of the effects of the Fall.

to bring about the full, conscious, and active participation of the faithful.

We can still learn about the nature of images by reading the works of Saint John Damascene. Though written in the eighth century, his *On Images* has remained a standard work on the topic to the present day, evidenced by its citation in the 1997 *Catechism of the Catholic Church*. In response to claims that the veneration of icons was a form of idolatry, John Damascene laid a foundational theology of icons rooted in the concept of the Incarnation. Though God the Father remained unrepresentable, he claimed, the Son chose to take on human form, and therefore became circumscribed, literally, had a "line written around him." In the Incarnation, Christ took on materiality and therefore established a precedent that could be followed by later generations: *Christians could represent Christ because Christ chose to represent himself.* Since it was clearly God's will that Christ's human body, made from the dust of the earth, be seen by human eyes, it followed logically that Christ's image could continue for the eyes of succeeding generations in similar materiality. Moreover, in the Transfiguration, Christ showed his heavenly glory, intending that human beings see and understand his divinity and power. So the precedent was set for iconography that revealed a divinized human body.

John Damascene makes a crucial distinction in order to answer charges that images were idols. He defines an image as a "likeness of the original with a certain difference," not an exact reproduction. Again establishing a Godly precedent for his claims, he argues that the Son was in fact an image of the Father, sharing and making present the Father's reality, distinguished only be being begotten. In sending his Son, God established a precedent by which humans could act in imitation of the creator. When properly made, an icon could participate in this sacramental "**economy** of images." Damascene found confirmation of the ability of material things to reveal the invisible things of heaven in Romans 1:20, where Paul writes: "Ever since the creation of the world his invisible nature, namely, his eternal power and deity, has been clearly perceived in the things that have been made." Moreover, argues Damascene, images serve the mission of the Church, because "the image speaks to the sight as words to the ear; it brings us understanding."

Perhaps Saint John Damascene's most valuable insight into the nature of images was his distinction between *latreia* and *proskenesis*. *Latreia* is the absolute worship due to God

---

economy: from the Greek word meaning "household management," economy refers to the arrangement or mode of operation of something.

Iconic imagery is also proper to the Western Church. Church of the Dormition, Jerusalem.

Facing page: Perspective is often intentionally distorted in icons to indicate a supernatural existence. Church of Multiplication of the Loaves and Fishes, Galilee.

alone, which was decidedly *not* the honor given to images. An icon instead received dulia, or veneration, an honor that was transferred to its heavenly prototype (hence the term *proskinesis*; *pro* = toward, and *kinesis* = movement). When a person kisses a book of the scriptures, he is not worshiping the paper and ink of the book itself but using that kiss as a sign of the reverence held for the Word of God, so an image is not venerated for its own sake but as a means to show the esteem held for the subject of its depiction. To think an image as something that has a power in itself is to succumb to *idolatry* (idol + *latreia*, worship).

In our days, however, fear of idolatry is not a major concern. We simply do not find Catholics arguing against images out of worry that the faithful will confuse *latreia* with *proskinesis*. More often we miss the connection between the sacred image and the liturgy itself as bearer of **anamnetic** remembrance and eschatological anticipation. Before his election to the papacy, Pope Benedict XVI taught that the "point of images is not to tell a story about something in the past, but to incor-

porate the events of history into the sacrament."[3] We see the eternal Christ of past events in images, he says, and we are taken into those events in the "liturgical transmission of history," a new way of understanding time, in which "past, present and future make contact because they have been inserted into the presence of the Risen Lord."[4]

In other words, anamnetic remembrance means making things real and present once again, and this is possible because in Christ many seemingly disparate realities coexist. When Christ is present, he is present in all of his facets as priest, prophet, and king, as fulfilled typology presented in the Old Testament, as Head of the Mystical Body, and as the one seated on the throne of heaven. Icons become the bearer of this reality and show more than historical scenes from the "Bible as literature"; they make present the spiritual realities contained in that sacred history. Here iconic sacred images are sacramental. Christ and the Spirit allow for participation in the very reality of the being depicted. In that sense, icons always represent some facet of the risen Christ, whether it be his typological precursors or members of his Mystical Body. Proper liturgical imagery, then, is always characterized by a union of creation, Christology, and eschatology.[5]

In using the word *icon* or *iconic*, the Western ear is likely to think exclusively of the painted, two-dimensional images on board and gold leaf common to the Eastern Churches. But to speak of something as "iconic" includes a much broader category, as evident in the word's origin. The word icon comes from the Greek *eikōn*, from the verb *eikenai*, meaning "to

anamnetic: from *anamnesis*, a calling to mind, but which in the Jewish tradition inferred not simple recall, but a making present that which was remembered.

A golden background indicates a saint's heavenly location. Serbian Orthodox Monastery, Third Lake, Illinois.

resemble." But other types of icons or images exist. The Bible is an image in words, for example. Christ, of course, is the most perfect icon of the Father, like him in all things except that he is begotten. The primary consideration here is that the image be sacramental, a participation in and revealer of otherwise invisible divine realities. Some iconographers (literally "icon writers") claim that the three-dimensional sculptural image is not sufficiently removed from the fallen earthly reality, and therefore not nearly iconic enough. In the West, more naturalistic sculpture and painting have been understood as being iconic despite its departure from the Eastern formal conventions.

No matter what form the liturgical image takes, any proper iconic image shows certain characteristics. *Most importantly, an iconic image is not an earthly portrait, but one that represents a being restored with divine life.* No longer is the earthly person shown as a fallen human being subject to the effects of original sin, but instead is divinized and glorified. (Images of angels and the persons of the Trinity, of course, reveal divine perfection as well.) By definition, then, a saintly person represented in an icon cannot be a living being still in the process of divinization. Rather, *an iconic image shows a completed process of divinization, the glory that things will have after Christ comes again.* Therefore, iconic representations always embody an eschatological perfection, a divinization which is not based on earthly notions of faddish attractiveness, but on the theological notion of restoration as foreshadowed in the **"Taboric light"** of the Transfiguration.

Otherworldly expressions: three-dimensional images can also take on iconic qualities. Mundelein Seminary, Chicago.

For this reason, John Paul II could write that icons are, by way of analogy, sacraments, because they make "present the mystery of the Incarnation in one or other of its aspects."[6] Pope Paul VI had used similarly strong language in 1963 when he said that he honored "the artist who fulfills an almost priestly ministry close to our own." The artist, he said, made the mysterious treasures of the Faith sensible "in the manner of sacrament; that is, by the sacred and sensible sign of art." He went on to chastise artists who had "renounced the creation of intelligible work," making the realm of art one of "suffering and confusion. . . ." "One cannot escape the realization," he said, "that the current artistic idiom is today an irrational and

Taboric light: the dazzling glory of revelation in divinized nature, as evidenced in the Transfiguration on Mount Tabor.

Stained glass shows saints appearing gem-like and radiant with light, signaling their heavenly condition. St. Thomas Episcopal Church, New York City.

tribalistic abstraction that does not make sense."[7] Excessive abstraction and "symbolism" have been recognized as one of the great problems of the twentieth century precisely because it placed earthly artistic theories ahead of spiritual realities and pastoral necessities. Liturgical art often failed to become a revealer of spiritual realities, and therefore failed to be either beautiful or sacramental. It was also not iconic.

Here we find two points to address: because it reveals heavenly realities, an iconic sacred image by definition must be rooted in Truth to make present its own ontological reality. Second, and more importantly, every icon, no matter the subject of the representation, primarily represents Christ in his Mystical Body. The Virgin, the saints, even the angels "truly signify Christ, who is glorified in them. They make manifest the 'cloud of witnesses' who continue to participate in the salvation of the world and to whom we are united, above all in sacramental celebrations" (CCC, 1159). In these sacred images, the inability of human beings in their current fallen state to "see" heavenly perfection is partly healed, just as Christ's Transfiguration "healed" the inability of Peter, James, and John to see his divinity. So the power of the icon derives from the power of Christ, whose Incarnation, Passion, death, and Resurrection made possible the tearing of the veil and the wide distribution of God's presence and access to divine life. The iconic image, whether mural, sculpture, or traditional Eastern icon, participates in mediating the reality of Christ in one facet or another.

But in all cases, iconic images are glorious representations of God's holy deeds with their fulfillment in Christ, past, present, or yet to come. They are always perfected, beautiful, contemplative, revelatory, luminous, and conformed to a divine model because "a saint is not a superman, but one who lives out his truth as a liturgical being."[8] In sum, in an iconic image "it is man 'in the image of God,' finally transfigured 'into his likeness,' who is revealed to our faith" (CCC, 1161). The popular nomenclature of an icon as a "window into heaven" is accurate, though one might say heaven's reality comes to the window sill as much as we look in.

An icon is more than a scientific expounding of the latest theory of biblical studies, just as the naming of a sacred image as "Baroque" or "Byzantine" relies on art history instead of theology. Here again Beauty should become the compelling power of the Truth, that which en-thuses us to engage in the work of prayer. The Beauty of the image moves the will to approach that which is True and Good. As Saint John Damascene wrote: "the beauty of images moves me to contemplation . . . and infuses the soul with the glory of God." In this contemplation, the reality of the mystery is not only brought to the mind as with a history painting, but "imprinted in the heart's memory" (CCC, 1162), and a person then goes forth into the world slightly more conformed to the divine likeness. In the writings of Pope John Paul II and the *Catechism* we see the Church

"breathing with both lungs," East and West, with the Eastern tradition teaching the Latin rite once again, that images are not expendable afterthoughts or concessions to personal piety. Rather, they are rich sources of theological knowledge that attract people in order to draw them to the mysteries of faith and, ultimately, have them become more like God by becoming accustomed to the things of heaven.

Based on these theological principles, a number of practical rules follow. Because they show the *reality* of a being's divinization, and not merely the hope, the subjects for icons should be the persons of the Trinity, angels, or canonized saints; that is, those that the Church has determined to be in heaven. Memorializing worthy pastors, civil leaders, or even popes and patriarchs with a portrait is a venerable activity; however, it should be noted that unless they are canonized, strictly speaking, they should not appear as iconic, liturgical imagery. Similarly, iconic images always present persons who are

Combining Eastern and Western conventions. St. Monica–St. George Church, Cincinnati.

deceased, because only those who have passed beyond the veil can fully participate in this sharing of divine life.

Saints in icons do not look photorealistic. They are always recognizably human, showing a human nature. But at the same time, they seem to shed many of the literal signs of everyday existence. Their large heads, oversized eyes, unusual skin tones, dry gaze, impossible poses, and lack of typical three-dimensional perspectival representation make them look recognizably iconic. These are breaks from the conventional representations of realistic imagery; one might call them distortions of literal reality. But as in all poetic representation, the facts are distorted to make the Truth more evident. This intentional distortion separates the subject of the icon from everyday

Saint Dominic's earthly life depicted in idealized terms. *Saint Dominic and the Eighth Way of Prayer.* Leonard Porter, painter, 2005.

Facing page: Mosaic, statuary, marble, and metalwork combine to give a revelatory flash of the heavenly Jerusalem. Christ wears the breastplate of the High Priest. Eucharistic Chapel, Cathedral of Saint Louis the King, St. Louis, Missouri.

existence, emphasizing that this person is no longer in the natural, fallen realm but in a place of divine glory, where death and decay cannot reach. The historical Peter, for instance, did not walk around Palestine with hair always in place, a perfectly wavy beard, and keys in his hand. Nor did he wear a wrinkle-free toga of yellow and blue and stand in a landscape of gold leaf. An iconic representation distorts these facts for increased legibility and clarity of meaning. The keys give the viewer information on the identity of the saint, and the perfection of his outward appearance and radiance of golden background speak of Peter's

An iconic, heavenly treatment in three dimensions.

Even the landscape shows its divinization in iconic imagery. Ascension Church, Oak Park, Illinois.

and lay lights and darks simultaneously, iconographers lay the darkest color down first in large patches, then layer lighter colors one atop of another until the lightest colors are used last. In this process, an image is brought forth from darkness into light, just as God brought light from the darkness in the first chapter of Genesis. One could also see the process of writing an icon as a microcosm of the experience of the soul that moves from darkness to light as it grows more and more into the likeness of God (2 Corinthians 3:18).

ABSTRACTION, UNIVERSALITY, AND IDEALIZATION

This language about the nature of the Eastern icon and its particular genius does not mean that there are not lessons here for the Latin rite. Many iconographic purists argue that sculptural three dimensionality or images painted with three-dimensional perspective are inherently foreign to the iconic image. But given that the Western churches have an established sculptural and perspectival tradition, the challenge is to learn what the foundational theology of the icon can teach. The current state of liturgical art in most Western countries suggests that two extremes are in play: one finds either overly abstracted or **expressionistic** forms suspicious of traditional representation, or conversely, sentimental neo–Victorian realism. Those favoring abstract or expressionist art decry the "empty" formalism or mere sentimentalism of "holy card art," while others claim that mere splotches of color or monstrous elongations hardly convey the glory of a saint. To top it off, many liturgical goods catalogues are ready and eager to provide people on both sides with low quality versions of whatever they desire.

current spiritual and bodily wholeness and heavenly "location" or state.

Because they show the Fall undone, iconic images show no signs of the Fall's effects: vice, bodily decline, or spiritual disorder. True liturgical art is not without zeal, even though a saint's expression might seem at first to make the figures appear tired or blasé and their gestures overly languid or effortless. But this is precisely the point: these beings represent human nature reunited with divine life, and their gaze is always beyond the viewer. They contemplate God in a perfect rest that comes from the effortless comprehension of divine beauty. Even rocks, trees, and animals depart from highly realistic representation in icons because God's divine life has restored nature as well. Furthermore, the figures in icons are never shown in raking light, which casts deep shadows across their features. Instead, light appears to glow from within them, establishing that in the joy and peace of full communion, God's life radiates from within, because in heaven there is no sun or moon, and "the glory of God is its light, and its lamp is the Lamb" (Revelation 21:23). Even the very process of writing an icon imitates the process of creation. Rather than mix paint colors

In order to bridge this aesthetic divide, a summarizing theological principle can be stated as follows: *Liturgical art should be naturalistic enough to be legible, abstracted enough to be universal, and divinely idealized enough to be eschatological.*

Realism and naturalism are not the same thing, and each has its own place. In most dictionaries, their definitions are nearly interchangeable, and in the fields of philosophy and theology, definitions vary widely. For the current study, it is helpful to distinguish between the two. *Realism* as used here presents the factual reality of an object as closely as possible to its perceived earthly externals. A realistic image in an extreme form might be called *photorealism*, in which an otherwise purely earthly photographic scene is reproduced in some other medium, intentionally avoiding artistic interpretation. *Naturalism*, however, we might say reveals the nature of things

---

expressionistic: related to expressionism, a movement in the art in which the artist chooses not to depict objective reality, but his or her subjective expression of inner understanding of the object.

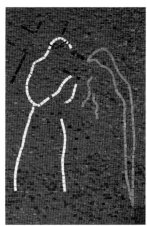

Expressionistic or "excessive symbolism" in sacred art.

so that they are legible as being members of a certain category. Though no one has ever seen a person in real life that looks like an icon, we nonetheless see enough human features to recognize a human face, male or female, old or young. Naturalism removes traces of earthly detail, and therefore, without denying the value of legible form, allows for the primacy of meaning by removing external distraction and "quieting" the image.[9] At the same time, recognizable iconography remains essential so that the viewer can know the content of the image. While it may seem trite to a world that values novelty over continuity to show Saint Peter with his keys for centuries on end, this legibility ensures that the worshipper knows what the image represents. The primary job of an iconic image is revelation of spiritual and intellectual content, not primarily acquiescence to the art theories of the day.

But the term *realism* can be used in a much deeper way as well. In the great tradition, human beings are understood as still subject to the effects of the Fall. Because of that, we suffer illness and decay. We are weak and often choose vice over virtue. But this fallen nature is not what we *really* are; our *reality* is God-like, virtuous, glorious, and supernatural. It happens that at present, we still groan toward perfection, we are still a pilgrim people moving toward the time when God will be all in all and we will be restored to our real nature. In this sense, the iconic image is *more real* than the photorealistic

image. But in order to show the most real depiction of the Truth of our existence, certain details about our individual, fallen, daily life need to be abstracted away.

The Virgin Mary, for instance, is rarely represented as an average woman of the eastern Mediterranean around the year zero. Though this, indeed, was her veiled earthly identity, the Truth about her is much greater: she was conceived without sin, she is Queen of the apostles, she reigns as Queen of heaven, and so on. So artists leave certain details of her earthly reality behind in order to reveal her transhistorical Truth. This approach again finds its authority in the Transfiguration of Christ, where the expression of his divinity did not mean that Christ took on a new state; he simply showed that he really was the Son of God by letting his body become the vehicle for the revelation of his glory.[10] While this approach has not been popular among those who privilege factual accuracy over transcendent Truth, it nonetheless is the proper avenue for making an iconic image. Rather than diminishing the power of intellectual content, proper abstraction actually reveals more than it conceals, just as Christ's evident glorious divinity at the Transfiguration did not abolish his human form, but glorified and elevated it. The universality of his Christ-ness became evident beyond his previously veiled appearance. The clever bumper sticker that reads "My boss is a Jewish carpenter" really should read: "My boss is the Second Person of the

Excessive realism limits expression to earthly realities.

Trinity, the Word Made Flesh who reigns in glory and is present in his Church and the Eucharist, though he took the veiled form of an earthly Jewish carpenter for about 33 years." Sadly, we have no bumpers that long.

Abstraction and *universality* are terms that carry multi-valent meanings today. In common parlance, the term *abstraction* usually indicates a lack of pictorial representation or narrative content, and reminds most people of the abstract painters of the twentieth century and their canvases filled with crude-looking figures or simple bands of color. These abstract painters sought to go beyond the mere externals, trying to simmer down to the concentrated inner essence of the subject by minimizing the details of its pictorial reality. In the case of Expressionism, striking and distorted forms were intended to dazzle and disturb the viewer by disrupting the formal perfection of the exterior of the object represented. In Abstract Expressionism, any traces of representational imagery were completely removed, leaving only swaths of color. In each case, an attempt was made to reach the representation of some sort of universal essence by removing the so-called secondary details of its earthly representation.

Since liturgical imagery is *theology in pictorial form*, the particular theological understanding an artist chooses will usually determine the outcome of the form. Those who distrust the material world will minimize, break, or distort pictorial form. Those who believe creation to be good will trust pictorial form to convey spiritual realities.[11] The extremes of

Modernist abstraction are often not suitable for iconic representation because they lose *claritas*, the power of a thing to convey itself to the mind. Beauty radiates *through* the form, not in spite of it, just as Christ's divinity radiated through his human body at the Transfiguration. The Transfiguration "took place not in such a way that the Word left the human image, but rather in the illumination of this human image by His glory."[12] So it is with the clay, wood, stone, or paint we use to make our liturgical art.

Just as knowledge of God is made present through the very words of the proclamation of the Gospel and not despite those words, so the form of the image itself is not a distraction from its content, but the very vehicle for its expression.

However, if the earthly details of an image overwhelm the invisible spiritual reality it is intended to convey, then the form becomes a dead end because of its very lack of abstraction. Instead it becomes a natural history diorama or historical image. In his masterful encyclical *Mediator Dei* (1947), Pope Pius XII exhorted Catholic artists to avoid the excesses of "symbolism" and "realism" because the spiritual needs of the faithful were to be given greater consideration than any particular contemporary school of art. Abiding by this principle, he argued, would keep even modern liturgical art rooted in a healthy approach to tradition and make it worthy to be counted with the sacred art of all time.[13]

However, in either case, some abstraction is required. In the theological sense, abstraction is the process by which defi-

Instead of being shown transformed by divine life, excessive realism merely shows saints bound to the effects of the fall. Cathedral of Our Lady of the Angels, Los Angeles.

nite universal concepts are pulled from the experience of many examples. A person who has seen only one woman, for example, has no reason to think that other women might look different. After seeing a thousand or a million different women, however, that same person could be able to distill out the essence of woman-ness. In this process, the mind sees what is common to all women, realizing that the secondary details that distinguish one from another are not of primary import. Medieval paintings of the Madonna and Child look different from Byzantine

Virgin Mary statue, Cathedral of Our Lady of the Angels, Los Angeles. Robert Graham, sculptor.

versions, but in either case, the essence of the subject manages to come through despite sometimes radically different external appearances. The challenge, then, is for the artist to make an image that captures the essence not only of the individual subject, but the universality of the ontological category to which the subject belongs. Normally this comes through the

Saint Therese of Lisieux revealed as a human radiant with divine life. Leonard Porter, painter, 2008.

Liturgical art should be naturalistic enough to be legible, abstracted enough to be universal, and divinely idealized enough to be eschatological. Marytown, Libertyville, Illinois.

process of abstraction combined with the developed skill of the artist.

When an iconic image is made, however, something more than mere human abstraction is necessary. The job of the liturgical artist is to paint Christ or the saints not as they might appear in a history book, but as fully liturgical beings, that is, as they *appear in their heavenly glory*. This indeed requires abstraction to reveal the highest qualities possessed by human beings, but must also add heavenly perfection of form, thereby showing the being as filled with divine life. This does not mean simply combining the attributes of a number of different women and then putting a halo, strange clothes, or a meditative facial expression on an otherwise fallen-looking person, as is the case in the image of the Virgin over the entry to the Cathedral of Our Lady of the Angels in Los Angeles. The now much-beloved tapestries inside the cathedral, which are intended to represent the communion of saints, are not what they could be for the same reason. Rather than serving as images of beings in heaven transformed by divine life, they read instead as everyday people wearing costumes. Importantly, they were intended to be so, as "the faces are life-like, and were modeled after actual people." The artist

wanted the saints to look like "people we would see walking down the street."[14]

The artist who reveals spiritual realities must know what a soul radiant with divine life is, what it might look like, and what characterizes it. This requires knowledge of what divine life itself is. And this requires a revelation, that is, grace, whose source is God. However, to know God means to have a prayer life that seeks the grace and inspiration found in reception of the sacraments, fasting, and personal prayer.

An unheavenly expression on an otherwise well-crafted image.

It means letting the body and the mind become instruments of the Holy Spirit, submitting the human will to the will of God. Anything that is merely human, poorly executed, or absurd does not become a vehicle for revelation.

Here the labor of acquiring artistic skill finds its sacramental elevation which imitates the creative process of God himself. While God creates from nothing, the human artist uses material of this earth, and because artists possess the spiritual gift to imitate the creator, they give form and meaning to otherwise inert material.[15] To do this badly is within the possibility of most people who are motivated to attempt it. Doing it reasonably well requires a certain amount of motivation, training, and practice. An artist who excels will recognize a "gift" for the vocation, something that came from without, yet still depends on human cooperation. A good liturgical artist rises above even these elevated heights, abstracting all the virtue of humanity at its best, "sees" the glory of God through a gift of the Holy Spirit, and then finds a way to make the inexpressible glory of heaven in some way knowable to the senses of others.

Divine idealization is also a necessity in iconic liturgical art, and its purpose is to show participation now in the eschatological realities of the time when God is all in all. Idealization here does not refer to conforming to some earthly ideal or secular artistic movement. In fact, just the opposite is the case.[16] "The icon's role is not to bring us closer to what we see in nature, but to show us a body which perceives . . . the spiritual world."[17] The secular world may have some ideal that it chooses, whether it be the physique of a bodybuilder or supermodel, but the iconic ideal always represents the unity of person and the fullness of divine life. An iconic image is therefore always eschatological in orientation, participating by way of foretaste in the time mentioned in the book of Revelation when creation is renewed and when man's participation in the divine life is complete.

The guidelines for liturgical artists, then, are clear without being overly restrictive. Because people need to know in what reality they are participating, naturalistic legibility remains critical. Yet in order to avoid making a liturgical image that looks only like the model or the person next door, a certain abstraction is required to make the image universal even in its very local expression. Finally, the divine idealization of the image portrays a perfection brought about by grace, which nonetheless does not obliterate the real human characteristics of the subject. It reveals its heavenly realities, yet, properly speaking, becomes sacramental. It rises to the request of the Second Vatican Council to partake of the signs and symbols of the heavenly realities and is therefore suitable for Catholic worship.

the citation given in Pope John Paul II's *Letter to Artists*, ff. 7: Saint Gregory the Great in a letter of 599 to Serenus, Bishop of Marseilles: "Painting is employed in churches so that those who cannot read or write may at least read on the walls what they cannot decipher on the page," *Epistulae*, IX, 209: CCL 140A, 1714.

3. Joseph Ratzinger, *The Spirit of the Liturgy* (San Francisco: Ignatius Press, 2000), 117.

4. Ratzinger, *The Spirit of the Liturgy*, 117.

5. Ratzinger, *The Spirit of the Liturgy*, 125.

6. Pope John Paul II, *Letter to Artists* (1999), no. 8. The phrase "by way of analogy" here is critically important. Images that are sacramental reveal something of God, but are not of the same order of the seven sacraments, which are instituted by Christ and confer grace. Iconic images, like icons, have a similarity to sacraments, but with a certain difference.

7. Pope Paul VI, "Impromptu Discourse at the Opening of the Fourth National Congress of Catholic Union of Italian Artists," February 2, 1963, collected in Ruth Nanda Anshen, ed., *Paul VI Dialogues Reflections on God and Man* (New York: Trident Press, 1965), 165–167.

8. Paul Evdokimov, *The Art of the Icon: A Theology of Beauty* (Redondo Beach, CA: Oakwood Publications, 1990), 15.

9. I know of one monastic chapel in which a new, life-size crucifix was made in bronze which shows Christ's underarm hair and other bodily literalities in a supposed quest for the expression of the humanity of Christ. What it does instead, however, is fail to quiet the image sufficiently so as to allow the reality of Christ's divinity to radiate forth. As such, it is not an iconic image, but merely a representation of a dead man on a cross, subject to the effects of death and not animated by the glory of the Resurrection. It unwittingly contains, then, a denial of Christ's victory over death.

10. Leonid Ouspensky, *Theology of the Icon* (Crestwood, NY: St. Vladimir's Seminary Press, 1978), 189.

11. For more on the theological implications of Expressionism, see Denis McNamara, "Reflections on Tillch's 'Protestant Principle' in Sacred Art," *Communio* 33 (Winter 2006), 597–613.

12. Sixth Session of the Seventh Ecumenical Council, as cited in Ouspensky, 189.

13. "Modern art should be given free scope in the due and reverent service of the church and the sacred rites, provided that they preserve a correct balance between styles tending neither to extreme realism nor to excessive 'symbolism,' and that the needs of the Christian community are taken into consideration rather than the particular taste or talent of the individual artist. Thus modern art will be able to join its voice to that wonderful choir of praise to which have contributed, in honor of the Catholic faith, the greatest artists throughout the centuries." Pope Pius XII, *Mediator Dei* (1947), par. 195.

14. Francis J. Weber, *Cathedral of Our Lady of the Angels* (Los Angeles: St. Francis Historical Society, 2004), 281.

15. John Paul II, *Letter to Artists*, 1999, par. 1.

16. The term *idealization*, like so many other artistic terms, can bring a variety of meanings. Leonid Ouspensky vigorously rejects the use of the word in relation to icons, thinking it a substitution of an earthly system of representation for the heavenly divinization. The iconic image, by contrast, begins with the spiritual reality of the conformity of the divine likeness. I use the term *idealized* as referring to conforming to the ideal of the divine rather than some human ideal of representation.

17. Ouspensky, *Theology of the Icon*, 208.

---

1. Eusebius, *Church History,* X.4.38.

2. The long tradition of using images as the textbooks of the illiterate certainly has its value. However, this functional approach to imagery does not exhaust their purpose. A merely pragmatic approach to sacred imagery reduces the sacramental nature of the icon to a mere illustration of sacred history. For an early reference to the place of images for the illiterate, see

Chapter 10

Historical, Devotional, and Liturgical Images: Principles for Contemporary Church Builders and Renovators

The "both/and" nature of things Catholic supports many types of images, and each has its own ontological character and proper beauty. The problem in many parishes from the nineteenth century to today, however, is that different types of images were and are used in a way foreign to their nature. Devotional images sometimes crowded out tabernacles and dominated sanctuaries. This confusion led to the great call for the twentieth-century liturgical movement to reevaluate the place of images in Catholic churches. In the early decades of the twentieth century, many liturgical leaders called for a de-cluttering of church sanctuaries; not to leave them bare, but to clarify the liturgical nature of the altar by giving it due prominence as well as giving churches separate areas for devotional prayer. Sometimes, however, people only heard the former admonition and forgot the latter, leading to many cases of abusive over-reactions against ecclesial images in the years following the Second Vatican Council. The iconoclastic tendencies that appeared after the Council were indeed often disproportionate and extreme, and the ecclesial culture has yet to establish a clear understanding of the role of images in the liturgy. For this reason, a proper understanding of images can help current-day builders and renovators make proper choices.

TYPES OF ECCLESIAL IMAGES

Ecclesial images come in three basic types: *historical, devotional,* and *liturgical. Historical* images show scenes from history—either secular, sacred, or something in between. Though this type of image is relatively uncommon in new churches in the West today, a long tradition of showing scenes from history has filled the walls of its great Catholic churches. Common to many Polish churches in Chicago, for example, is the tradition of painting scenes from the history of a parish, representing the pastor, the sisters, and even school children. Images of Cardinal George Mundelein, who reigned as Archbishop of Chicago from 1915 to 1939, were placed in several murals

Devotional image that reveals otherworldliness. Saint Thomas Church, Fort Thomas, Kentucky.

The intersection of history and eternity in mosaic. Marytown, Libertyville, Illinois.

and mosaics in the archdiocese, even in his own lifetime. Much more common in both the east and the west, however, are images of sacred or ecclesiastical history. Many large murals common to Catholic churches in the nineteenth century showed paintings of Christ in the carpenter shop, for example, as an image of domestic bliss. Other images might show the martyrdom of a saint, the baptism of Augustine, or the commemoration of a particularly important event in Christian history. Historical images are important, recalling the history of Christianity, which is summed up in Christ, and keeping alive the memory of the saints and biblical events.

The intersection of historical, devotional, and liturgical imagery in a Crucifixion from the Stations of the Cross. Cathedral, Lexington, Kentucky.

A second type is the *devotional* image. Images of this type are generally understood to be used for personal devotion, either paraliturgically or outside of the liturgy. Typically, the figures are shown alone with their poses and glances directed toward the devotee, and their human characteristics are often emphasized. In this way, the Christian has a place for individual piety, a strong engagement of the emotions, and a wider range of expressive possibilities. As a rule, devotional usage of any of the arts—from sculpture to music to written prayer—allows for much greater flexibility and individual personality than does liturgical usage. Devotions by their nature are largely personal, even when prayed in groups. Examples of devotional art might

include the head of Christ surrounded with thorns, a patron saint associated with a certain disease or locality, or even the Stations of the Cross. In the latter case, sacred history and devotion overlap, as people recall Christ's life and express their devotion for the suffering of Christ at the same time.

Lastly, a type of representation much forgotten is the *liturgical* image, which presents the *liturgy itself*. Just as liturgical music, properly speaking, uses the *texts* of the liturgy (the Kyrie, the Gloria, the Creed, etc.), liturgical imagery shows the activity of the liturgy itself. Typically, the parts of the liturgy represented in imagery are those that are not otherwise visible, notably its cosmic and heavenly dimensions. Liturgical art reveals the nature of heaven itself, and is intensely theocentric, revealing the glory of the heavenly realm and showing the heavenly beings filled with divine life. All is radiant, orderly, and restored. The expressions of these heavenly beings are not focused on the emotional and personal agonies of their earthly life, but completely transfixed by the glory of God. Their gaze is fixed on God and they act as

Historical, Devotional, and Liturgical Images

Through the ages, Catholic churches have been enriched with images of many kinds, recalling sacred history, supporting devotional practice, and providing a foretaste of heavenly realities. Each is important and useful in the life of a Christian, yet each is distinct, and proper usage clarifies their theological and liturgical foundations.

Historical images recall the history of Christianity and keeps alive the memory of the saints and biblical events. Examples might include the martyrdom of a Saint Peter, Christ in the carpenter shop, or the baptism of Augustine. Historical images are, properly speaking, subordinated to the liturgical elements of a church.

Devotional images are used for personal devotion, either paraliturgically or outside of the liturgy. The humanity of a saint is typically emphasized in devotional art, and figures are typically shown with their poses and glances directed toward the devotee. Here the Christian finds a place for individual piety, a strong engagement of the emotions, and a wider range of expressive possibilities. Devotional images properly belong in a distinct area suitable for private prayer, and should not be confused with liturgical art.

Liturgical images reveal the liturgy itself, particularly in its heavenly and cosmic dimensions. Intensely theocentric, liturgical images reveal the glory of the heavenly realm and show the heavenly beings filled with divine life where all is radiant, orderly, and restored. This sort of image is most proper in the sanctuary of a church, though it might flow out to the nave, and *belongs to the liturgy itself* because it provides "signs and symbols of heavenly realities."

The heavenly liturgy on display in liturgical art. St. Monica–St. George Church, Cincinnati.

Events of Christian history portrayed in historical art. Serbian Orthodox Monastery, Third Lake, Illinois.

one body praising and contemplating the Lord. The setting, typically, is the heavenly Jerusalem described in the book of Revelation.

The apse mural of the Cincinnati Church of St. Monica–St. George shows liturgical art on a grand scale. The Trinity is central, and the beings in the mural have their gaze directed to God, with the only exceptions being those saints whose role it is to make eye contact with the earthly worshipper and direct their gaze to God. Here the angels and saints sing their constant praise to God in a paradise symbolized by the palm trees and colorful birds. The water of grace flows from the cross supported by the Father and the Son on their thrones, and then flows down to the world. This image is neither merely historical nor devotional, even though it has some areas of overlap with these two categories. Here the heavenly and cosmic liturgy are made visible, so that as the documents of Vatican II exhorted us, the earthly worshipper may more fully, actively, consciously, and fruitfully participate "in the earthly liturgy" where "we take part in a foretaste of that heavenly liturgy which is celebrated in the holy city of Jerusalem toward which we journey as pilgrims, where Christ is sitting at the right hand of God, . . . we sing a hymn to the Lord's glory with all the warriors of the heavenly army. . ." (SC, 8).

It may come as a surprise to some that great iconographic programs are not only tolerated, but actually supported by the

A devotional image given its own chapel and angelic evidence of heavenly realities. Saint Thomas Church, Fort Thomas, Kentucky.

Facing page: Historical, devotional, and liturgical images frequently intersect in the Eastern tradition.

theological premises expressed in the Second Vatican Council. When the Council texts are seen according to Pope Benedict's **hermeneutic** of reform rather than the hermeneutic of discontinuity, the liturgical reform of the Second Vatican Council does not emerge as a break with the received liturgical tradition. Instead, one realizes that the Council was conceived from the beginning to help the faithful understand the liturgy as the union of heaven and earth where the People of God, who form the Mystical Body with Christ as its Head, are united with the heavenly beings in praise of the creator for God's glorification and the sanctification of humanity. The liturgy says as much: "May the Lord accept the sacrifice at your hands, for the praise and glory of His Name, for our good, and the good of all his Church." Our prayers unite with those of the heavenly beings in order to praise God's name and receive divine life from him. Seeing this reality is indeed in accord with Vatican II. What is decidedly not welcomed by the Council, however, was a misuse of imagery, confusing devotional with liturgical and letting devotional imagery overwhelm the liturgy itself.

Each type of image is good in itself and welcome in a church. The important point, however, is that the different types should not be confused with each other or used incorrectly. If one had to arrange the different types of images hierarchically, liturgical imagery, unsurprisingly, would be most proper to the liturgy, and therefore most suitable for visibility during the liturgy itself. It is relatively stable in its iconographic content because it always relates to the eternal liturgy, which is itself stable and eternal. The liturgy, and therefore liturgical art, provides relatively little room for personal expression because it belongs to the many members of the Mystical Body. Liturgical art, therefore, must remain broadly universal even in its localized and ecstatic heights and properly belongs to the area of the sanctuary and altar.

The Church's devotional life flows from and returns to the liturgy, yet it is a step away from the liturgical action properly understood. As such, devotional imagery ranks lower than liturgical art and belongs in areas dedicated to devotional activity. These might be side chapels, niches, or outdoor grottoes. In its personal nature, devotional art and devotional activities allow for much wider ranges of emotional expression. Its proper place is some distance from the altar and sanctuary, yet with a sense of an intimate link to the liturgy itself.

Historical images, while still good, are yet farther from the liturgy theologically, and rightly belong farther from the sanctuary, in the rear of the church or on side walls. Sometimes different images overlap several categories. A crucifix or Crucifixion scene, for instance, could fall into all three: it shows sacred history, can be used for devotion to the Passion

Living beings receive a more earthly, naturalistic treatment in the iconic tradition. Serbian Orthodox Monastery, Third Lake, Illinois.

Facing page: Mater Dolorosa Chapel, Marytown, Libertyville, Illinois.

of Christ, and remains at the heart of the Sacred Liturgy's re-presentation of the sacrifice of Christ to the Father. Categorization of ecclesial imagery, then, takes some careful consideration and shows considerable variety.

Many liturgical scholars in the twentieth century looked to the Victorian church interiors and quite correctly perceived the problem of devotional imagery overwhelming the altar and sanctuary itself. Very often a large image of the church's patron saint or some non-liturgical biblical scene garnered a prominent position on the church's rear walls. Elaborate reredoses or statues of saints often overwhelmed the tabernacle or altar itself. The response of many theologians of the time was to establish a situation in which first things were put first again, second things second, and peripheral things on the periphery.[1] This meant moving devotional images to proper locations, replacing devotional murals in sanctuaries with liturgical ones, and re-establishing the primacy of the altar and tabernacle. This interest, of course, was central to the Liturgical Movement's concern that people in the pews participate in the liturgy itself and do not substitute devotional activities, as good as they might have been, for the Mass itself.

---

hermeneutic: *a method or principle of interpretation.*

Angels, saints, and the movement of the stars indicate the heavenly and cosmic dimensions of the liturgy. St. Clement Church, Chicago. Father Gleb Werchovsky, iconographer.

ICONOGRAPHY AFTER VATICAN II

This fine-tuning of the use of imagery was not at all a condemnation of the importance of figural representation in a liturgical setting, despite what happened during many renovations after the Second Vatican Council. Proper fine-tuning sought to make the main altar, tabernacle, and crucifix primary. Devotional images were reduced in scale and moved to proper chapels or shrines; they were never meant to be banished. Despite the call of the Council documents themselves, which stated that devotional images were to be retained (SC, 125), an understandable but regrettable confusion rose among some liturgical specialists, who often confused this re-ordering of devotional imagery as a call to remove all or nearly all imagery from a church. Moreover, liturgical imagery, where it existed, was sometimes confused with devotional imagery and discarded. Murals, color, and pattern, thought to be mere Victorian excess instead of the signifiers of the golden, jewel-covered walls of the heavenly Jerusalem, were often painted over in neutral beiges and grays. The "beigeification" of our Catholic churches happened for many reasons, not the least

of which was the attempt to undo the confusion of devotional imagery with liturgical imagery, that occurred in the nineteenth century.

As post-Modernism has arisen in the last decades, congregations have chosen to return imagery to their churches. A common response to the denuding of churches in the 1970s is the pulling of saccharine plaster statues out of the basement or ordering new ones from the church furnishings companies. These images very often support the piety of the people, so they are not to be dismissed too lightly. However, it would be best to not repeat the mistakes of the nineteenth century and make them crowd the sanctuary once again, or simply recreate from old molds the hyper-realistic images which lack proper abstraction or eschatological revelation. Furthermore, simply tucking a Saint Joseph in one side, a Virgin Mary on the other, and a life-size crucifix in the center does not really make a proper liturgical iconographic plan.

Jacques Maritain laid an outline for liturgical art in 1935 from which we might learn today.[2] He wrote that artistic merit and talent of the artist were a given. But several elements must be added to that talent to make art suitable for

Devotional images, while good in themselves, should not overwhelm the altar and tabernacle.

Devotional image.

liturgical use. First, the art must possess *orthodoxy*, conforming to doctrinal truths. Second, it needs to be primarily *liturgical*, that is, conforming to the proprieties of the liturgy itself. To this we might add today that it be a liturgical subject, that is, an image of the worship of God rather than a devout scene from sacred history. Third, he argued that its inspiration be "authentically religious," not the outgrowth of non-theological art theories or formulas. Nor should its inspiration be sentimental or "archaic," he argued, succumbing either to shallow emotion or to the notion that older always equals better, whether the first century or the thirteenth. In all of this, he said, the orthodoxy and liturgical qualities should be legibly knowable to the viewer. The image was meant to be an analog of some other reality, letting the earthly material become a bearer of the divine. It should come as no surprise that Maritain, a Thomist scholar of the theology of beauty, would speak of images this way. His call for orthodoxy implied *integritas*, his call for a liturgical orientation in art speaks of *consonantia*, and legibility and knowability refer to *claritas*. Since liturgical art reveals the liturgy, and the liturgy includes all of heaven, earth, and purgatory, *claritas* requires an eschatological rooting and the inclusion of many things the purveyors of church art have often forgotten in recent years.

In our own day, a response to the call for a new evangelization might be learning anew how liturgical imagery relates to the deep theology of beauty. We owe it to our parishioners to offer them an artistic plan that addresses imagery properly. In a time when the heavenly and cosmic dimensions of the liturgy are unknown by large percentages of the Catholic clergy and faithful, a renewal of liturgical art is urgently needed. In the name of full, conscious, active, and fruitful participation, liturgical imagery deserves a great comeback. How can we participate fully in the liturgy when we don't understand the full extent of its reality, both earthly and heavenly? Effective liturgical architecture uses highly specific and articulate forms, revealing, in the Spirit, the heavenly realities. In fact, one cannot separate four phrases from the Council's commentary on sacred art and architecture: "active participation" (SC, 14), "noble beauty" (SC, 122), "signs and symbols of heavenly

Angelic liturgical participant.

Liturgical imagery: Christ reigns in priestly vestments among angels and saints in a golden, heavenly background with Father and Spirit above. Saint Thomas Church, Fort Thomas, Kentucky, 1939.

realities" (SC, 122), and "turn men's thoughts to God persuasively and devoutly" (SC, 122). Active participation requires a perception of the reality in which one participates, in this case, the glory of the Heavenly Banquet joined to earth in sacramental form. To understand the banquet as *heavenly*, signs and symbols of heavenly realities are required, which in turn requires noble beauty (from the Latin, *nobilis*, knowable), a beauty that reveals the ontological reality of the liturgy itself. Here we find again the new foundation for the place of figural art in the liturgy, one completely consistent with the Council's call for active and conscious participation, and consistent as well with the long tradition of the Church.

1. The Rev. H. A. Reinhold, "The Liturgical Church," *Church Property Administration* 5 (June–July 1941), 7.

2. Jacques Maritain, "Reflections on Sacred Art," *Liturgical Arts* 4 (1935), 131–132.

Part V

Introduction to the Twentieth Century

The twentieth century brought a renewed interest in the liturgical nature of the Mystical Body of Christ. Saint Joseph Cathedral, Wheeling, West Virginia. Felix Lieftuchter, muralist.

In our day, the Catholic Church manifests the hope, expectation, and occasional disappointment of legitimate growing pains. The twentieth century was for the Church and the world a time of change and optimistic expectation, something which proved that the Holy Spirit was still active in the world. People often dismiss the last one hundred years as a time of unprecedented murder and cultural decline, and if one looks at the period's history of war and genocide, one might be tempted to agree. But the twentieth century also gave us a new, fresh look at the world, theology,

and the Church. The brittle shell of Romanticism and the simplified and condensed theological manuals, as attractive and safe as they might have been in a time of turmoil and challenge to the Faith, needed to be cracked open in order to reveal something greater and better, like an animal that needed to shed its old shell to grow bigger and stronger. The problem, however, is that before a new shell can grow again, the animal is highly vulnerable. Cardinal Ratzinger made a similar point about the Church's liturgy before the Council, claiming that it was like a fresco that had been covered with

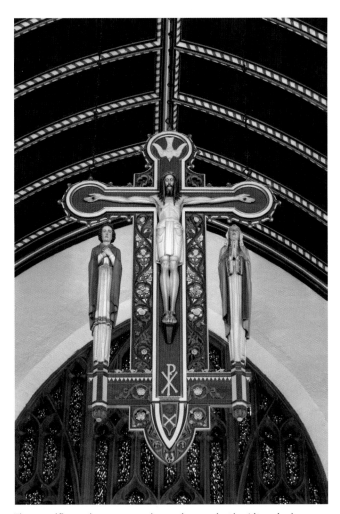

The crucifix took on renewed prominence in the Liturgical Movement.

so many layers of whitewash that its pristine purity was diminished.[1] Stripping off the layers lets one see the fresh colors again, but leaving it exposed—or even worse, continuing to scrape even into the painting itself—runs the risk of losing some of the original material. The twentieth-century Liturgical Movement, which has its roots as far back as the eighteenth century, convincingly made the case for scraping off the whitewash, and popes from Pius X to John XXIII depended on its research to authorize the work. The texts of *Sacrosanctum Concilium* provided the "work order," so to speak, for this restoration.

Since the time of the Council, the Church has been like this exposed fresco. The scraping away of the surface is sometimes painful to watch; many people had become accus-

tomed to the pale colors they remember from their childhood, but they trusted that the Church knew what it was doing. But the optimism of joyful rediscovery in the twentieth century was indeed real: understanding the readings at Mass, singing the Kyrie and the Gloria, understanding the liturgy as something they prayed *with* the priest as members of the Mystical Body of Christ, recognizing that the Mass was central to a Christian's life, singing the hours of the Divine Office at their proper times, and rooting out lingering strains of **Jansenism**. These were indeed great things.

But for many, something seemed to go wrong to subdue this optimism. A "neo-conservative" is sometimes humorously called "a liberal who has been mugged," that is, someone whose original genuine optimism has met the face of reality and had to be called back to original principles. It is worth remembering that both John Paul II and Benedict XVI were considered "liberals" at the time of the Council, both were fully committed to the heart of the Liturgical Movement's concerns as approved by the Church since Pius X's *motu proprio Tra le sollecitudini* in 1903. Yet somehow things started appearing in liturgical life, which seemed to go beyond the texts of the Council, and both John Paul II and Benedict XVI have repeatedly asked the faithful to return to the Council's *texts* for inspiration and proper implementation. One could safely bet his or her life on the fact that no serious, authoritative document on liturgical reform leading up to the Council—or the documents of the Council themselves—ever called for the abuses that occurred in the heady days after

Modern, yet traditional. Cathedral of St. Peter in Chains, Cincinnati.

Jansenism: an austere movement named for Dutch theologian Cornelius Otto Jansen, which sprang up within the Catholic Church after the Council of Trent, possibly derived from Calvinism. The movement's theology was complex, and many of its tenets were condemned by different popes through the centuries. The word as popularly used today refers to an overly severe, scrupulous approach to sin and reception of the sacraments.

the Council, and which still linger in certain places today: clown Masses, the consecration of raisin bread, or the re-definition of the church building as a large secular house. Here, many well-meaning people have scraped into the fresco of the liturgy, potentially causing the loss of some of its original content.

A better analogy perhaps here is misguided restoration. Imagine repainting Christ in Leonardo da Vinci's *Last Supper* by dressing him as a clown! The absurdity here is obvious and the art world would be up in arms. But the liturgy is in some ways like a painting, a living image of the realities of heaven and earth joined together. The priest, acting *in persona Christi*, is a sacrament of the cosmic, heavenly, liturgical Christ (SC, 33), and dressing him as a clown for a "clown Mass" is a failure of understanding of the highest order. Whatever a priest does liturgically should be a symbol of what Christ would do at the right hand of the Father in heaven. Similarly, the words the Church uses in liturgy are the words said to Christ, the Bridegroom of the Bride, and this Bride is the Mystical Body, which is itself the People of God united to their Head. So the words of the Bride, the Church, are the words both inspired by and offered to Christ, the Groom. Liturgical changes, then, reach deep into theological realities, and can only be made with the utmost trepidation.

Understanding fully the sociology of the liturgical reform since the Council will take many years. But enough time has passed that we can investigate and analyze the twentieth century and figure out how to go forward. Though we are still feeling the effects of the great shattering of the old brittle shell, the shape of the liturgy is returning once again. As Pope John Paul II stated, the liturgical reform is done. The books are revised, the Council closed. "We are not in the same situation as 1963," he wrote. "One has to speak of an ever deeper grasp of the Liturgy of the Church, celebrated according to the current books and lived above all as a reality in the spiritual order."[2] This is indeed quite true today as it was when he wrote it two decades ago.

Sacrosanctum Concilium was promulgated nearly fifty years ago, and many of the things done in its name on the local level were addressing needs particular to its time. But fifty years is a long time. Would someone in 1963 have said that the conditions then were still the same as in 1913? Why do we then often act as if the liturgical needs of the People of God are the same today as they were in 1969? Are too many of us guilty of a certain conservativeness even in our self-perceived "spirit of the council"?

Ask any 25-year-old today if the liturgical standards of 1970 meet their needs. The year 1970 means their parents' coming of age, a decade and a half before they were born. Their parents (or more likely their grandparents) chafed under a rigid system that sometimes undervalued the active participation of the people. Today's 25-year-old (and even up to today's 40-year-old) has sometimes chafed under liturgical instability, disarray, excess creativity, liturgical casualness, and even in some cases open rebellion in matters of faith and praxis. Their desires are no more reactionary than those of their grandparents, and probably less so. Stability and certainty are virtues to be sought, even as licit flexibility keeps the Tradition supple and open.

If an architect or liturgical consultant hasn't modified his or her architectural or liturgical assumptions since, say, 1978 when the Bishops' Committee on the Liturgy document *Environment and Art in Catholic Worship* was released, then they are doing a disservice to the Church. On the other hand, if the growing pains of the immediate post-conciliar era caused anyone to retreat into a static pre-conciliar past like Moses' Israelites who wanted to return to the security of slavery in Egypt, it is time to see the limitations of this position as well. This is not about "liberal" or "conservative" or "restorationist" or "progressive." It is about Truth and the pastoral needs of people in the pews. It is about Christ's revelation to his people and the salvation of the world being made legible to the people of this time and place. Ultimately, it is about a faithful reception of the Second Vatican Council.

So the questions that arise today are indeed still about what the Second Vatican Council intended. But what the Council intended is knowable by its *texts*. The "spirit" of the Council is only as reliable as the texts that support it, since there is no promise that the Holy Spirit will guide any ordinary individual's interpretation of its meaning. For people over 60, Vatican II was an event. For anyone born after 1960, Vatican II is a text. So the meaning of the text requires careful examination. This suggests not only that the words of *Sacrosanctum Concilium* are expected to be authoritative and mean something, but that the Council texts are to be understood in relation *to the ideas that gave rise to them as well as those that came after them*. *Reform* is an official action of the Church, which formalizes the ideas presented in the scholarship, publications, and discussions of a *movement* that precedes it. *Sacrosanctum Concilium* did not grow from what happened in 1970; it grew from what happened in 1903, 1947, and 1963.

So the question remains as to how we interpret Vatican II, and how we then evaluate whether what happens today (or happened in 1973) is in line with the Council's intentions, which were themselves drawn from the Liturgical Movement and its leaders. But in its liturgical *reform*, the Church sifted out those things from the movement which it thought detrimental. One of the clearest characteristics of the modern Liturgical Movement, though, was loyalty to the Pope and compliance with the notion that the authority to reform the liturgy belongs to the Holy See. In that spirit, Pope Benedict XVI's guidelines for understanding the meaning of the Council provides us with a useful tool to understand

Church of the Holy Sepulcher, Jerusalem.

a rejection of the Tradition nor as a failure to go far enough away from it. They represent the Spirit guiding the Church, just as the Spirit guided the election of John Paul II and Benedict XVI. The texts of the Council crashed headlong into the culture of Modernity, with its characteristic features of skepticism, methodological doubt, scientific rationalism, and radical dualism.[4] Of course, the Spirit will draw the Truth out of the culture's chaos, but this happens slowly with a certain anxiety and uncertainty. As always, well-meaning people did their best in understanding the intent of the Council, and some fell a bit short or went too far. This is not occasion for anger or vitriol, but for compassion and charity. It should make us zealous to clarify the Truth as we stay near the barque of Peter.

Architecture is the built form of ideas, and church architecture is the built form of theology. When we misunderstand theology, we build an architecture that proclaims that misunderstanding. So we look for a genuine liturgical theology, one that clarifies and fulfills all that the Church has taught. This requires an attitude of loving respect for the Tradition, one that does no violence to the past even as it makes new contributions. It takes all that was True and Good and Beautiful before 1963 and fulfills it in a way that becomes obvious and inevitable because it is right. When we understand our theology properly and act on its principles, we will then build beautiful churches.

our own times. Benedict has brilliantly outlined the issues at hand with his characterization of two fundamental approaches to understanding the Council. In his now famous Christmas address of 2005, Benedict reminded us that the document *Redemptionis Sacramentum* (2004) acted in continuity with the Holy See's role as guardian of the liturgy to provide "a practical guide to the correct implementation" of the Council's documents on liturgy.[3] The same Vatican office that had the authority in 1965 to begin the liturgical reform process has also given us the instruction on how to understand it several decades later. More importantly, Benedict has given us the concepts of the *hermeneutic of reform* and the *hermeneutic of discontinuity*. This teaching provides a new way to understand the late twentieth century and our own times.

Vatican II cannot be understood as a break with the legitimate Tradition, Benedict argues. It followed upon decades of hard work and careful consideration of the ideas of some of the best theological minds in the Church's history. The Council texts themselves are to be seen neither as

1. Cardinal Joseph Ratzinger, *The Spirit of the Liturgy* (San Francisco: Ignatius Press, 2000,) 7–8: "We might say that in 1918 . . . the liturgy was rather like a fresco. It had been preserved from damage, but it had been almost completely overlaid with whitewash by later generations. In the Missal from which the priest celebrated, the form of the liturgy that had grown from its earliest beginnings was still present, but, as far as the faithful were concerned, it was largely concealed beneath instructions for and forms of private prayer. The fresco was laid bare by the Liturgical Movement and, in a definitive way, by the Second Vatican Council. For a moment its colors and figures fascinated us. But since then the fresco has been endangered by climatic conditions as well as by various restorations and reconstructions. In fact, it is threatened with destruction, if the necessary steps are not taken to stop these damaging influences. Of course, there must be no question of its being covered with whitewash again, but what is imperative is a new reverence in the way we treat it, a new understanding of its message and its reality, so that rediscovery does not become the first stage of irreparable loss."

2. John Paul II, *Vicesimus Quintus Annus: Apostolic Letter on the 25th Anniversary of the Constitution Sacrosanctum Concilium*, December 4, 1988, no. 14.

3. *Address of His Holiness Pope Benedict XVI to the Roman Curia Offering Them His Christmas Greetings*, December 22, 2005, reprinted as "Interpreting Vatican II," *Origins* 35 (January 26, 2006), 534–539.

4. See Robert Barron, "Beyond Beige Churches," *Antiphon* 6 (2001), 14–22.

Chapter 11

The Liturgical Movement and Church Building

The church building is not simply a place for the convenient exercise of prayer and instruction and for the enactment of the liturgy. The church edifice is itself a part of the liturgy, a sacred thing, made holy by a divine presence through solemn consecration, it is a sacramental object, an outward sign of invisible spiritual reality. . . . The space is enclosed and made to be a holy place, and the structure itself is made holy in an elaborate ceremony of consecration. . . . The chief function of a church edifice is to express and promote relationship between God and men, the greatness and goodness of God and the homage and love and gratitude of men.

—Rev. William Busch, pioneer of the American
Liturgical Renewal Movement, 1955[1]

Dialogue of Modernity with tradition in figural carving. Our Lord Christ the King Church, Cincinnati. Edward Schulte, architect, 1957.

The twentieth-century Liturgical Movement found its apex in *Sacrosanctum Concilium*. About this there is no question. After more than one hundred years of examining, researching, proposing, questioning, licitly and even illicitly experimenting, the Church was ready in 1962 to make official reform in its liturgical books. This reform did in fact grow from a liturgical "spirit," because a "spirit" always characterizes a *movement*. By contrast, *reform* occurs when the Church tests the spirits and acts prudently by virtue of its history and office as guardian. The spirit of the Liturgical Movement was characterized by optimistic hope that the riches of the liturgy could be opened up more completely for more people and that the people could be properly disposed to receive them. The goal of the twentieth-century Liturgical Movement was the goal of the liturgy itself: the glorification of God and the sanctification of God's people.

The term *Liturgical Movement* refers here to the great outpouring of ideas and holy desire for the renewal of the liturgy in the years before the Second Vatican Council. Conferences were held, books were written, papers were delivered at scholarly conferences and published in journals. People in the pews were asked to learn about and then pray the liturgy more closely and actively. Latin–English hand missals appeared in pews, and Gregorian chant was revived because it allowed people to sing the texts of the Mass. A closer following of liturgical laws was promoted, and the importance of the Liturgy of the Hours, liturgical reading of scripture, and the liturgical year was emphasized. People were asked to draw from the sacramental life of the Church more often and more fully by preparing themselves to receive the sacraments and to take the liturgical parts proper to them. The goal was to help people drink more deeply from the springs of divine life found in the Church and her sacraments by sharing in the exercise of the priestly office of Jesus Christ: offering the self to God as a sacrifice and in turn receiving the divine life of sanctification. This participation would be done *actively* to the greatest degree possible, and also *fully* by taking the liturgical parts properly belonging to each participant. It would be prayed by Catholics educated as to what they were *consciously* doing in order to be *fruitfully* transformed into the likeness of Christ. Transformed by divine life, they would then bring received grace to the world and make disciples of all nations and reform the culture. Here in a nutshell is the great mission of Christ in the Church, and that great hope of Vatican II: that the Church would change the world so recently wounded by two world wars and a depression.

The leaders of the Liturgical Movement knew that to be even partially denied the source of divine life in the sacraments because of ignorance, mistaken notions of piety, or obsolete social conventions was a tragedy and a missed opportunity. Without divine life, human nature remained in its fallen condition; with divine life it would grow in conformity to Christ and manifest Christ-likeness in peace, justice, and love. People who love God and one another because of God's grace do not make war on their neighbors, do not look past the plight of the poor, or seek their own good at the expense of another. The Second Vatican Council was convened within living memory of the world wars, the use of nuclear weapons, and the Great Depression, not to mention in the shadow of aggressive atheistic communism. The sharing of God's divine life was the answer, and the Sacred Liturgy was the means for receiving it. The imperative tone in the Council's documents is certainly understandable.

The leaders of the Liturgical Movement knew that the sacraments were valid. They knew that sacramental power came from Christ and that the sacraments were effected *ex opera operato*, from the power of God by virtue of the work itself being done. But liturgical scholars of the time agreed that for many reasons, people were not receiving the grace of the sacraments as fully and fruitfully as they might. They were not able to participate as deeply, consciously, fully, and as actively as they should because they were not always properly disposed to receive this grace most fully. The Church calls this kind of efficacy *ex opere operantis*, literally "from the work of the worker," meaning that the fruits of the sacraments also depend in part on the disposition of the one who receives

Altar dedicated to Saint Joseph in its own chapel. Cathedral Wheeling, West Virginia.

them. The Liturgical Movement therefore sought to help people participate in the liturgy by more clearly opening the mysteries of the Church to the people and then helping people be rightly disposed to receive them.

And so a move to make God's dispensation of divine life in the sacraments more effective emerged in the Church. The movement was encouraged by Pope Pius X in his 1903 *motu proprio Tra le sollecitudini*, formally recognized by Pius XII in his 1947 encyclical *Mediator Dei*, and found its apex in *Sacrosanctum Concilium*. Importantly, "reform" was not the goal of the Liturgical Movement, nor was it the goal of *Sacrosanctum Concilium*. Reform was always a means to an end. The goal was the glorification of God and the sanctification of humanity. The goal was "divinization," the transformation of humanity to be like God through grace. The great scholar of the Liturgical Movement, Godfrey Diekmann, OSB, claimed shortly before his death that divinization was one of the great forgotten ideas of the liturgical discussions after the Council.[2] The human hope for any liturgical event is exactly this: that God be glorified and that we be restored in Christ,

Devotional image given a proper setting. Cathedral, Wheeling, West Virginia.

filled with divine life. Many changes to the liturgical life followed from these principles, including those affecting liturgical art and architecture.

The history of the Liturgical Movement has been chronicled many times over by competent scholars, most recently by Alcuin Reid in his noteworthy book *The Organic Development of the Liturgy*.[3] There is no need or possibility to give an exhaustive history of its main protagonists here.[4] Like any similar endeavor, different figures of the Liturgical Movement advocated different things in differing ways and to differing degrees. But the essential methods and goals had a common core. A short pamphlet published in 1930 as part of the "Popular Liturgical Library" series explained the movement in everyday language. The Liturgical Movement, it said, sought "a change in the spiritual orientation of the faithful," which would result in a "strong, virile Christianity."[5] It went further to summarize the movement's fundamental premise:

> Liturgy is the official divine service of the Church for the glory of God and the sanctification of the faithful. It is the re-enactment, the re-presentation of the work of redemption. The liturgy is the principal manifestation of the vital expression of the inner life of the Church, the life of Christ Himself. When the liturgy is celebrated the Church glorifies God and dispenses Christ-life to her children, so that from "*quasi modo geniti infantes*" (as newborn babes) they may attain "to the perfect man, to the full measure of the stature of Christ." (Ephesians 4:13)

From this defining starting point, the following claim could be made:

From this we can readily see what the Liturgical Movement means . . . a movement towards the liturgy, a movement towards the Christ-life giving mysteries: The Holy Sacrifice of the Sacraments, the Sacramentals, the Solemn Prayer of the Church and the Liturgical Year; but also toward those external things which are so necessary for the . . . pious, attentive [and] devout celebration of these mysteries.[6]

So the movement was primarily concerned with the transformation of the human soul, but recognized that proper externals remained important and necessary for this transformation to happen. Though the movement was not primarily about vestments, candlesticks, and rubrics, they were given the essential supporting role in sacramentalizing the liturgy of the Church. Later the notion of the full liturgical assembly as image of the Mystical Body of Christ would add the notion of corporate worship to the mix, especially after Pope Pius XII wrote his encyclical *Mystici Corporis* in 1943. The worshipping assembly would then be understood as one body acting in unity with Christ as its head, signified by the priest as head of the body constituted by people. Here was the full exercise of the priestly office of Jesus Christ, a theme that would be a return in the texts of Vatican II.

This renewed emphasis meant that certain things began to change quite organically. Liturgical pioneer H. A. Reinhold summed up the liturgical movement pithily in 1941 when he wrote that it "put first things first again, second things in the second place, and peripheral things on the periphery."[7] This meant that the Mass was primary and devotional life secondary. Secondary did not mean unimportant, just that it did not overshadow the centrality of the Church's sacraments.[8] This meant that devotional prayers should not replace the prayers of the Mass itself, for instance. Though the fervor against the Rosary and other devotions sometimes reached an exaggerated pitch after the Council, it started out quite innocently. Devotions were welcomed and indeed considered necessary, just not as a substitute for the liturgy.[9] This also meant that devotional imagery should find its proper place, not crowding the altar and sanctuary, but at home in a dignified chapel or niche. This notion was sometimes exaggerated after the Council to such a degree that in many parishes all statues and images were removed from churches altogether.

ARCHITECTURAL RESPONSE

The principles of the Liturgical Movement had a direct effect on liturgical art and architecture. Since the fundamental goal of the Liturgical Movement was that people understand and participate in the Sacred Liturgy, any architectural decisions that hindered this participation were open for reconsideration. The Liturgical Movement was born into the waning days of the Romantic Movement in architecture, evidenced

A freestanding altar, spacious sanctuary, eschatological orientation, and tester reveal the influence of the Liturgical Movement. Cathedral of St. Peter in Chains, Cincinnati.

by the style revivals of the nineteenth century. Today, many people love the glory and solemnity of their Victorian churches, and for many good reasons. The Romantic mind is generally understood by art historians to be reacting against the rationality of the Enlightenment, the destruction of medieval monuments in the French Revolution, and the more puritan strains of the Reformation. But even as early as the mid eighteenth century, concepts of picturesque (emotionally pleasing painterly arrangement) and the sublime (the subjective reaction to "delightful horror," as Burke put it in 1757) had made their appearance in art and architecture, as evidenced by countless country scenes of pastoral Italian countrysides, often filled with foreboding ruins from ancient times.

A romantic fascination with the supposed shadowy, mysterious, medieval world appeared in certain secular buildings. Later, the fiercely Catholic apologist and famed Gothicist Augustus Welby Northmore Pugin (1812–1852), working with the English **ecclesiologists**, developed a huge international movement to restore Gothic architecture to its

supposed rightful place as *the* true Christian (and therefore Roman Catholic) architecture. His famous 1843 treatise, *True Principles of Pointed or Christian Architecture* spawned thousands of churches and other buildings on the medieval model throughout Europe, the United States, and colonial territories. John Ruskin (1819–1900) promoted the Venetian Gothic in his widely read *Stones of Venice* (1851), causing a flurry of **polychromed** Gothic buildings in what has now become known as High Victorian Gothic.

The architecture of the nineteenth century brought a lot to the table. At its best, it was deeply rooted in the tradition, offered high levels of craft, plentiful devotional imagery, rich materials, and proclaimed the semiotics of "churchliness"

---

ecclesiologists: a movement in the Anglican Church centered in Cambridge, England, which proposed a return to high church ritual, particularly as developed in the Middle Ages.

polychromed: literally "many colored," an architectural term signifying the juxtaposition of contrasting colors in building materials.

Heroic Modernism, low *claritas*. Saint John's Abbey Church, Minnesota. Marcel Breuer, architect, 1961.

after an era of Enlightenment rationalism which sometimes denied these very things. These churches are finding favor today for the same reasons. Quite often, though, Victorian churches are rooted in the realm of the emotion, because in Romanticism, "art is understood as the expression of an interior feeling of infiniteness and as the exteriorization of the experience of God in the affections."[10] The churches of Romanticism were often architectural and artistic externalizations of emotional responses. Again, for this very reason they often brought with them much that was good; a church that "feels like" a church will probably "look like" a church, and this is an important part of *claritas*.

Theologian Hans Urs von Balthasar, a critic of Romanticism in general, admitted that the Romantics often preserved "a sense of the unity of beauty and religion, art and religion, when they had almost no support from theology."[11] In other words, the architectural forms themselves were carrying a theology with them rather than the theology providing the foundation for the architecture. One simply does not find many architects or theologians in the nineteenth century speaking of liturgical art and architecture as vehicles for divinization. Pugin speaks of Gothic architecture as Christian because it developed in the Middle Ages, which he considered an age of faith. The Classical he understood as pagan. This either/or distinction between Gothic and Classical is a product of concentrating on the external facts of "style" rather than the internal logic of theological idea. For Pugin, association with a "feeling" of medieval piety was enough to build an argument for Gothic architecture as the *only* Christian architecture.

Where this left all the great Classical buildings from the time of Constantine to Michelangelo to Pugin's own day was not his concern.

Emotion belongs in the liturgy. But when sentiment instead of theology becomes the dominant determining factor of liturgical art and architecture, things are set up for a fall. The Modernist architects could then come some decades later, as they did, and say something like this: "Emotionalism was a particular response in 1890, and that time is over. *My* response is that we need something that speaks of our time. Our time is defined by technology and the machine. So church architecture should partake of the industrial aesthetic." So architects built large concrete structures, the most famous of which, perhaps, is the church of St. John's Abbey in Collegeville, Minnesota. Later, in the time after the Second Vatican Council, another Romantic streak ran through the Catholic Church, which said, "The emotional needs for grandeur and solemnity in the pre-conciliar Church no longer apply. The *new* emotional needs demand up-to-date authenticity and commonness. So church buildings should be modeled on the house: a welcoming, hospitable, domestic space with *feelings* of intimacy and welcome."[12] And architects did that (and still do). But the danger here is evident: when liturgical art and architecture are unhinged from sacramental theology understood in light of received Tradition, the built form becomes the externalization of an individual's emotional response rather than the built form of universal liturgical and theological ideas.

In the early twentieth century, the Liturgical Movement faced a quite healthy artistic establishment. A bit derivative and prone to copyism, yes. But compared to today, standards of craft and design were quite high. Though there were many critics of the mass-produced plaster statues and the low level of architectural sophistication of many congregations, people had an intuitive sense that a church building was important, rooted in tradition, and needed to look like a church. A few strands of Romanticism had to be addressed to fine tune the architectural results in many churches. The Romantic sense of emotional response and adherence to precedent led to the moody quality of shadowy corners and deep chancels with altars set far behind screens and choir stalls. Architect Ralph Adams Cram argued that large stone piers were appropriate in a church nave even if a few people had to sit behind columns. The emotional satisfaction found in devotional statues and pious murals meant that they abounded, sometimes in disproportionate relationship to the altar and sanctuary. And of course, the great leitmotif of the Gothic Revival was the spikey, crocket-laden reredos over the altar, often sprinkled liberally with colorful saints, with the two doors of an embedded tabernacle beneath. These things were good, but the reformers of the Liturgical Movement thought they could be better.

Victorian exuberance in devotional imagery. Saint Mary's Church, New Haven, Connecticut, 1870s.

The early leaders of the Liturgical Movement had reasonable cause in calling for certain changes. The church renovations of the 1930s and 40s were not at all the wholesale emptying of churches as would come later. They desired instead fine tuning: making the altar and tabernacle more prominent, giving devotional images their own places, arranging sanctuary and seating so that all could see and hear the liturgical action, and allowing ample space in the sanctuary for liturgical processions. Baptistries, too, were given a renewed sense of importance. No longer portable fonts that could be stuck in a corner of the sanctuary, baptistry chapels were developed, and were often separated from the main building in imitation of the early Church, which saw the unbaptized as "outside" the Church. As Reinhold put it, "a Catholic church is a building for the liturgy first, and for private and extra-liturgical devotion in the second place."[13] Like others, he was not (yet) opposed to the use of historically derived styles, but he was disturbed that the Romantic mindset had made purity of architectural detail more important than the needs of the liturgy itself.

As early as 1929, architect Maurice Lavanoux showed his knowledge of the Liturgical Movement by asking that people become "imbued with the true spirit of the liturgy before inquiring into its historical or physical aspect."[14] Here

we see the reshaping of the historicist and Romantic spirit. Without denying the value of history, Lavanoux asks that the theology of the liturgy prove dominant over the emotional attachments to the past. He then went on to lament that so few architects or pastors read the Church's legislation on liturgical architecture, writing that he found an "amazing disregard for the decisions of the Sacred Congregation for Rites." He was particularly interested in renewing the sense of the altar, naturally a common theme for people desiring to restore the sense of the importance of the liturgical action. He quoted a book by an Irish priest, M. S. MacMahon, giving an insight into the period's view of what was often called the "liturgical" or "rubrical" altar:

> The tendency of the modern liturgical movement is to concentrate on the actual altar, to remove the superstructure back from the altar or to dispense with it altogether, so that the altar may stand out from it, with its dominating figure of the Cross, as the place of Sacrifice and the table of the Lord's supper, and that, with its tabernacle, it may stand out as the throne upon which Christ reigns as King and from which He dispenses the bounteous largesse of Divine grace.[15]

We find a wealth of implied theology here. "Putting first things first" meant that the primacy of the altar must be evident. Many nineteenth-century churches had fastened their altars to elaborate reredoses, so that one really only saw one-half to one-third of the altar itself. Critics of the time often complained that the altar had become a mere shelf attached to an elaborate screen of saints. They hoped to combine the understanding of the altar as place of sacrifice and the prophecy of the Last Supper with the notion of altar as throne, emphasizing Christ as priest, prophet, and king. And because the Eucharist is always associated with Christ's Passion, the altar and crucifix were never far from each other.

The form of a proper altar was promoted by several prominent architects, notably Geoffrey Webb, whose 1933 book *The Liturgical Altar* set the standard for the altars of the Liturgical Movement.[16] Webb's writings explain the importance of the altar quite clearly. He writes:

> The reason for [the Church's] meticulous directions is to be found in the supreme importance which the Church attaches to the altar in her liturgy. Not only does she consider it the central focus of the whole liturgy, the *raison d'être* of the building in which its stands; not only does she indicate that the church exists for the altar, rather than the altar for the church; not only does she look upon it as the sacrificial stone, upon which Christ, our Priest and Victim, offers Himself daily in His Eucharistic Sacrifice, which is the central act of her liturgy; but she has proclaimed again and again that in her mind the altar represents her Lord Himself. He is Altar, Victim and Priest; and the reverence for the altar, expressed in the restraint and dignity of its design, symbolizes the reverence due to Christ Himself.[17]

This is the context in which we should understand the terms *noble simplicity* and *noble beauty* as expressed in the time

Altar arrangements influenced by the Liturgical Movement, 1930s–1950s: prominent stone altar, veiled freestanding tabernacle, six candles, prominent crucifix, eschatological orientation, tester or baldachino.

Normative "liturgical" or "rubrical" altar from *Liturgical Arts*, 1931.

of the Council. Restraint and dignity did not indicate domesticity or mere plainness. It meant clarity of meaning. Though one might rightly claim that Webb's definition is a bit short on the "tableness" of the altar, that is, the concept of altar as table of the Heavenly Banquet (and therefore the earthly sacramental banquet), it clearly established the framework for many Liturgical Movement architects.

In the United States, the journal *Liturgical Arts* included instructions for a proper altar in its very first issue.[18] Referring often to the regulations of the Sacred Congregation for Rites, the altar emerges as a "first thing" once again according to Liturgical Movement principles: it is freestanding, made of fine materials, separated from its backdrop, given a tabernacle that can be veiled all around and not used as a stand for a statue or a monstrance, keeps the crucifix in proximity, has its six or seven well-designed candlesticks, and has a covering as either a **baldachino** or **tester**. How different this was from some of the churches of the day, where the tabernacle became

a little cupboard set in the elaborate backdrop or where multiple side tabernacles served as bases for statues.[19]

In response to this new understanding, a number of churches lost their Gothic reredoses in renovations long before the more general iconoclastic tendencies of the postconciliar years. But what replaced them was often more grand and more sophisticated. Saint Patrick's Cathedral in New York, for instance, had its white marble altar replaced with

baldachino: in popular use, the term *baldachino* is understood to mean an ornamented canopy supported by columns, though properly speaking, this is called a civory or ciborium.

tester: in popular use, the term *tester* usually refers to a canopy that is either hung over an altar or attached to the wall behind an altar. Although popular usage differs, this can also be called a baldachin or baldachino. For more on the tester and baldachino, see J. B. O'Connell, *Church Building and Furnishing: The Church's Way: A Study in Liturgical Law* (Notre Dame, IN: University of Notre Dame Press, 1955), 189–190.

Noble beauty and noble simplicity coexist under the influence of the Liturgical Movement. Church of Our Lord Christ the King, Cincinnati. Edward Schulte, architect, 1957.

Facing page: The *Christus totus*, or whole Christ, made knowable in liturgical art. Church of Saints Peter and Paul (now Church of the Holy Spirit), Norwood, Ohio. Edward Schulte, architect, 1934.

Maginnis and Walsh's Gothic bronze baldachino, which remains today. The cathedral in Wheeling, West Virginia, received its picture-perfect "rubrical altar," which it retains even after a recent renovation. Liturgical and architectural journals proudly displayed the "before and after" church renovation photos showing this new respect for altar, tabernacle, and devotional areas. All the way through the 1950s and early 1960s, this basic formulation remained dominant no matter how traditional or modern the architecture became. Before the radical re-definition of the church building as a domestic space, architectural styles with greater or lesser degrees of Modernism followed the basic premises of the Liturgical Movement: a church was sacred, the altar was primary, and devotions were secondary but important.

Liturgical Movement sanctuary arrangement in the early 1960s. Saint Patrick Church, Huntington, New York, 1962.

Tabernacle as statue base, a practice discouraged by the leaders of the Liturgical Movement.

Mediator Dei

In 1947, Pope Pius XII issued his encyclical *Mediator Dei*, which gave papal recognition to many of the ideas of the Liturgical Movement. In the manner common to encyclicals, Pius heartily endorsed many features of the movement and strongly criticized others, including ideas that related directly to liturgical art and architecture. In the minds of many today, 1947 sounds like long ago, while the time of the Second Vatican Council seems quite recent. But on many occasions, the Council picked up much of what Pius XII had done and written, taking lines from his writings almost word for word and incorporating them into Council documents. In many ways, reading *Mediator Dei* is to find the proper context for *Sacrosanctum Concilium*. Only 13 years before the opening of the Council, Pius XII had set the tone for liturgical renewal. Later he established a number of commissions for liturgical reform, which did significant preparatory work from which the Council benefitted, most notably the reform of the Easter Vigil.

Mediator Dei restated many of the Liturgical Movement's great points, emphasizing the primacy of the Mass as sacrifice and the liturgy as an exercise of the priestly office of Jesus Christ, writing that "there is no state of human life that has not its part in the thanksgiving, praise, supplication and reparation of this common prayer of the Mystical Body of Christ which is His Church!" (MD, 3). Here we see the language of the Mystical Body, which was so important to the liturgical renewal, and which became the premise for much of the proper theology of active participation. The Body worked in concert with its Head, each doing its part. Pius praised the leaders of the movement, especially the Benedictines, appreciating that through them "the majestic ceremonies of the sacrifice of the altar became better known, understood and appreciated." He went on to express his pleasure that "with more widespread and more frequent reception of the sacraments, with the beauty of the liturgical prayers more fully savored, the worship of the Eucharist came to be regarded for what it really is: the fountainhead of genuine Christian devotion. Bolder relief was given likewise to the fact that all the faithful make up a single and very compact body with Christ

Leaders of the Liturgical Movement desired to establish the preeminence of altar, tabernacle, candles, and crucifix, and critiqued many Victorian altars for being merely a "shelf for architectural virtuosity" or for reducing the tabernacle to a mere "cupboard." Left: Saint Mary's Church, New Haven, Connecticut, 1870s. Right: Saint Patrick's Cathedral, New York City, renovated sanctuary by Maginnis & Walsh, architects, 1942.

for its Head, and that the Christian community is in duty bound to participate in the liturgical rites according to their station" (MD, 5).

But Pius XII had serious warnings as well. And one of the great ironies of the mid twentieth century is that *many of those things which Pius XII warned against became almost universally normative in the time after the Council.* "Duty obliges Us," he wrote, "to give serious attention to this 'revival' as it is advocated in some quarters, and to take proper steps to preserve it at the outset from excess or outright perversion." Strong language, indeed. Ever cautious, Pius corrected both those who refused to acknowledge the value of the Liturgical Movement and also those who strayed too far:

> We are sorely grieved to note, on the one hand, that there are places where the spirit, understanding or practice of the sacred liturgy is defective, or all but inexistent, We observe with considerable anxiety and some misgiving, that elsewhere certain enthusiasts, over-eager in their search for novelty, are straying

beyond the path of sound doctrine and prudence. Not seldom, in fact, they interlard their plans and hopes for a revival of the sacred liturgy with principles which compromise this holiest of causes in theory or practice, and sometimes even taint it with errors touching Catholic faith and ascetical doctrine. . . . Let not the apathetic or half-hearted imagine, however, that We agree with them when We reprove the erring and restrain the overbold. No more must the imprudent think that We are commending them when We correct the faults of those who are negligent and sluggish. (MD, 8, 10)

So Pius finds the middle ground between excess and deficiency. We might call this the "spirit of *Mediator Dei.*"[20] Pius greatly praised the notion of exterior participation in the rites, but strongly stated that interior participation was more important, because "God cannot be honored worthily unless the mind and heart turn to Him" (MD, 26). He went on to praise devotional life and sacramentals as contributing to the building up of the piety of the faithful. He also defended the ministerial priesthood as well as the priesthood of the baptized,

Christ as King holding a model of the church building. Church of Our Lord Christ the King, Cincinnati, 1957. Pius XII's institution of the feast of Christ the King was meant to counter nationalistic ideologies that led to war in the twentieth century. Window by Esser Studios.

Facing page: Ideal "liturgical" altar at the Cathedral of St. Joseph, Wheeling, West Virginia. Edward Joseph Weber, architect, 1926.

and restated the need for a hierarchical understanding of the Church. Many of these ideas would become flash points after the Council, not because of the Council itself, but because they were already in dispute decades earlier. Pope Paul VI had to clarify similar exaggerations in his encyclical *Mysterium Fidei* in 1965 to combat "false and disturbing opinions" on the Eucharist. If there were any false and disturbing opinions that came to prominence after 1965, it is worth noting that they were probably there before 1947 as well.[21]

Pius XII emphasized the importance of liturgical art and architecture, reserving to the Church the right to determine their use, citing its responsibility to preserve matters of liturgy from error. This idea would be restated almost exactly in paragraph 122 of *Sacrosanctum Concilium*. Interestingly, he then spoke against an improper antiquarianism, which saw certain periods of the Church's history as somehow "golden," excluding the possibility that the Holy Spirit could inspire liturgical development in later ages. Pius's language was familiar to the Liturgical Movement, because a spirit of reform and continued inspiration was essential to the reform movement itself. While many liturgical scholars of the time criticized the Middle Ages as a deterioration of active participation for the faithful and favored some vision of the "pristine" quality of the early Church, Pius addressed them head on. The early Church had its virtues, of course, he said, but one could not deny the continued inspiration of the Holy Spirit in the development of the rites. Pius wrote: "The liturgy of the early ages is most certainly worthy of all veneration. But ancient usage must not be esteemed more suitable and proper, either in its own right or in its significance for later times and new situations, on the simple ground that it carries the savor and aroma of antiquity."[22] He called this tendency "excessive archaism" which had implications for the current practice. Returning to a vague notion of the house church was not considered a worthy goal, and therefore, he wrote, "one would be straying from the straight path were he to wish the altar restored to its primitive table form; were he to want black excluded as a color for the liturgical vestments; were he to forbid the use of sacred images and statues in churches; were he to order the crucifix so designed that the divine Redeemer's body shows no trace of His cruel sufferings. . ." (MD, 62). What Pius warned against only 15 years before the opening of the Council, strangely, became almost normative after the Council and remains operative in the Church today.

Pius XII truly acted as pontifex, building bridges between differing groups in the Liturgical Movement. Many theologians rightly wanted the faithful to understand the insights of the liturgy re-discovered by reading the Fathers of the early Church, wanted the altar to be understood as a heavenly banqueting table as well as place for offering sacrifice, and wanted to balance the Tridentine emphasis on the sacrifice of Christ (evident in the bloody, agonized Christ on the cross) with the glory of the Resurrection. These were laudable goals, but exaggerated positions were proposed that wanted to forbid certain things in a way that went beyond the "both/and" tension proper to Catholicism, just as some effectively "forbade" Catholic devotions instead of simply putting them in their proper place in relation to the liturgy. We are still trying to find this balance in the Church today; as such, we are still trying to understand the Second Vatican Council.

Pius XII's attitude toward "modern" art and architecture remained in continuity with the long Catholic tradition. In paragrah 195 of *Mediator Dei*, he argues that it was suitable for Catholic worship, not historic style, which would determine the right place of art in worship. "Recent works of art which lend themselves to the materials of modern composition should not be universally despised and rejected through prejudice," he wrote, leaving the door open for the work of the Holy Spirit in the modern age. In a phrase that would be adopted almost word-for-word in *Sacrosanctum Concilium*, he wrote: "Modern art should be given free scope in the due and reverent service of the church and the sacred rites. . . . Thus modern art will be able to join its voice to that wonderful choir of praise to which have contributed, in honor of the Catholic faith, the greatest artists throughout the centuries."[23]

Pius XII gave an important caveat, however, also echoed in *Sacrosanctum Concilium*. He could not help "deploring and condemning those works of art, recently introduced by some, which seem to be a distortion and perversion of true art and which at times openly shock Christian taste, modesty and devotion, and shamefully offend the true religious sense." These, he wrote, "must be entirely excluded and banished from our churches, like anything else that is not in keeping with the sanctity of the place" (MD, 195).[24] What exactly determines art as "perversion" is not explained explicitly because an encyclical is not the place to name names and give particular examples. But he does set the principles that make for proper liturgical art; namely, that they "preserve a correct balance between styles tending neither to extreme realism nor to excessive 'symbolism,' and that the needs of the Christian community are taken into consideration rather than the particular taste or talent of the individual artist" (MD, 195). Here we have a nice definition of any sacramental art. It must be naturalistic enough to be legible and abstracted ("symbolic") enough to be universal. Here again is the proper "both/and" found in Catholicism in general and the Liturgical Movement in particular. One can reasonably suspect that Pius was reacting to many of the abstract and expressionist painters who chose either to deny the value of the naturalistic form, or only see it as something to be distorted and broken.

In our day, the lessons to be learned from the Liturgical Movement are really the lessons to be learned from the Second Vatican Council. The best ideas of the movement, as properly filtered and promoted by Pius XII, give the proper context for the meaning of the Council texts themselves. Of course this does not mean that the authorities of the Church could not go farther than the limits set in 1947, because they can and they did. However, in an age that is still trying to figure out what the Council intended, one way of finding the proper middle ground is by understanding the spirit of the Liturgical Movement and the spirit of *Mediator Dei*, then examining carefully what we have experienced since the

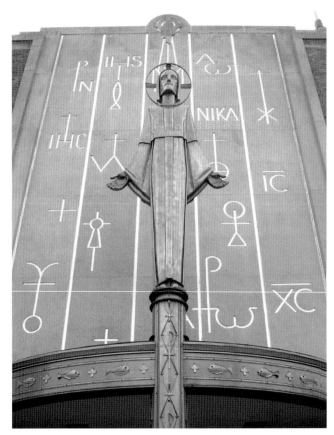

Pope Pius XII asked that sacred art avoid both "extreme realism" and "excessive symbolism." Saint Gertrude Church, Madeira, Ohio. Edward Schulte, architect, 1960.

Council. A spirit of continuity requires knowing what we are continuing, since the Church never does violence to herself, only grows in clarity and knowledge. The ideas of the Liturgical Movement are as valuable today as they were in 1960 because they call the Church back to fundamental principles. The exaggerations of the post-conciliar era have sent some of the faithful into the bunkers of antiquarianism circa 1962, or even possibly 1898 or 1570. And for others, exaggerations have become the norm, and they prefer to remain in their antiquarian bunkers circa 1978, seeing any attempt at pulling the liturgy back to the balance of the Council as some sort of "pre-conciliar" restorationism. The challenge for both extremes is to center themselves around the Council properly understood, in union with the Holy See, and look again for a liturgical understanding deeply rooted in the theology of the liturgy itself, understood not in opposition to the past or its fetishization, but as an organic, continuous growth revealed by the Spirit.

1. The Rev. William Busch, "Secularism in Church Architecture," *Church Property Administration* 19 (November–December 1955), 32–33. William Busch was a diocesan priest and faculty member at The Saint Paul Seminary in Minnesota. As something of the elder statesman of the American liturgical movement, Busch had been an advisor to Virgil Michel

as early as the 1920s, and together they planned the foundation of The Liturgical Press. Busch served as a translator for many of the European works the press published, particularly the German writings of Pius Parsch. Busch also helped form the League of the Divine Office, a group determined to help lay people pray the Liturgy of the Hours.

2. Robert Barron, *The Strangest Way: Walking the Christian Path* (Maryknoll, NY: Orbis, 2002), 29.

3. Alcuin Reid, *The Organic Development of the Liturgy: Principles of Liturgical Reform and Their Relation to the Twentieth Century Liturgical Movement Prior to the Second Vatican Council. Second Edition* (San Francisco: Ignatius Press, 2005).

4. For more on the Liturgical Movement, see the complete run of *Orate Fratres* Magazine, now called *Worship*. Secondary sources chronicling the movement include Keith Pecklers, SJ, *The Unread Vision* (Collegeville, MN: The Liturgical Press, 1998); Kathleen Hughes, *How Firm a Foundation: Voices of the Early Liturgical Movement* (Chicago: Liturgy Training Publications, 1990); Ernest Koenker, *Liturgical Renaissance in the Roman Catholic Church* (Chicago: University of Chicago Press, 1954); and Kevin Seasoltz, *New Liturgy: A Documentation, 1903–1965* (New York: Herder and Herder, 1966) among many others. For important primary source documents on the liturgical reform, see Virgil Michel, *The Liturgy of the Church* (New York: Macmillan, 1937), and also his translation of Lambert Beauduin's *Liturgy: The Life of the Church* (Collegeville, MN: Liturgical Press,1926).

5. "The Liturgical Movement," *The Liturgical Movement* (Collegeville, MN: Liturgical Press, 1930), 5.

6. "The Liturgical Movement," 5–7.

7. The Rev. H. A. Reinhold, "The Liturgical Church," *Church Property Administration* 5 (June–July 1941), 7.

8. See for instance, Romano Guardini's great work *The Spirit of the Liturgy*, originally published in 1930: "The claim that the liturgy should be taken as the exclusive pattern of devotional practice in common can never be upheld. To do so would be to confess complete ignorance of the spiritual requirements of the greater part of the faithful. The forms of popular piety should rather continue to exist side by side with the liturgy. . . . there could be no greater mistake than that of discarding the valuable elements in the spiritual life of the people for the sake of the liturgy . . . [but] it is still to liturgical worship that preeminence of right belongs." *The Spirit of the Liturgy* (New York: Herder and Herder, 1997), 20.

9. Authors spoke frequently of the reality that there were still "simple" people for whom even reading a vernacular missal would be impossible, so praying the Sorrowful Mysteries of the Rosary might in fact be for them proper participation in the Mass. This distinction between "devotional" and "liturgical" therefore needs to be discussed with great subtly of nuance.

10. Hans Urs von Balthasar, *The Glory of the Lord, vol. 1: Seeing the Form* (San Francisco: Ignatius Press/Crossroads, 1983), 98.

11. Hans Urs von Balthasar, *Explorations in Theology, vol. 1: The Word Made Flesh* (San Francisco: Ignatius Press, 1989), 125.

12. For more on the impact of the move to intimacy in Catholic liturgy, see M. Francis Mannion's masterful essay "Liturgy and the Present Crisis of Culture" in *Masterworks of God* (Chicago: Hillenbrand Books, 2004), 76–113.

13. Reinhold, 7.

14. Maurice Lavanoux, "An Architect's Dilemma," *Orate Fratres* 4 (14 July 1929), 277.

15. Lavanoux, 279–280, citing S. M. MacMahon, *Liturgical Catechism* (Dublin: M. H. Gill, 1926).

16. Geoffrey Webb, *The Liturgical Altar* (New York: Benziger, 1939), second edition of 1933 original.

17. Webb, *The Liturgical Altar*, 18–19.

18. Edwin Ryan, "The Liturgical Altar," *Liturgical Arts* 1 (Fall 1931), 29–33.

19. Maurice Lavanoux lamented that he once designed a "shallow tabernacle so that the back could be filled with brick as an adequate support for the statue." See "An Architect's Dilemma," 280.

20. For more on this topic, see Denis McNamara, "The Spirit of Mediator Dei," *Sacred Architecture* (Fall 2000), 13–18.

21. *Mediator Dei* refers to many abuses that became common after the Council, writing in paragraph 59: "The Church is without question a living organism, and as an organism, in respect of the sacred liturgy also, she grows, matures, develops, adapts and accommodates herself to temporal needs and circumstances, provided only that the integrity of her doctrine be safeguarded. This notwithstanding, the temerity and daring of those who introduce novel liturgical practices, or call for the revival of obsolete rites out of harmony with prevailing laws and rubrics, deserve severe reproof. It has pained Us grievously to note, Venerable Brethren, that such innovations are actually being introduced, not merely in minor details but in matters of major importance as well. We instance, in point of fact, those who make use of the vernacular in the celebration of the august eucharistic sacrifice; those who transfer certain feast-days—which have been appointed and established after mature deliberation—to other dates; those, finally, who delete from the prayer books approved for public use the sacred texts of the Old Testament, deeming them little suited and inopportune for modern times."

22. *Mediator Dei*, 61: "The same reasoning holds in the case of some persons who are bent on the restoration of all the ancient rites and ceremonies indiscriminately. The liturgy of the early ages is most certainly worthy of all veneration. But ancient usage must not be esteemed more suitable and proper, either in its own right or in its significance for later times and new situations, on the simple ground that it carries the savor and aroma of antiquity. The more recent liturgical rites likewise deserve reverence and respect. They, too, owe their inspiration to the Holy Spirit, who assists the Church in every age even to the consummation of the world. They are equally the resources used by the majestic Spouse of Jesus Christ to promote and procure the sanctity of man."

23. Compare to *Sacrosanctum Concilium*, 123: "The art of our own days, coming from every race and region, shall also be given free scope in the Church, provided that it adorns the sacred buildings and holy rites with due reverence and honor; thereby it is enabled to contribute its own voice to that wonderful chorus of praise in honor of the Catholic faith sung by great men in times gone by."

24. Compare with *Sacrosanctum Concilium*, 124: "Let bishops carefully remove from the house of God and from other sacred places those works of artists which are repugnant to faith, morals, and Christian piety, and which offend true religious sense either by depraved forms or by lack of artistic worth, mediocrity and pretense."

Chapter 12

The Texts of Vatican II: Looking Again at *Sacrosanctum Concilium*

Over forty-five years have passed since the fathers of the Second Vatican Council approved the text of *Sacrosanctum Concilium,* and the Church has been in a "post–Vatican II" mode of operation ever since.[1] The spirit of change has remained a driving force for those who remember the years before the Council, although the Council's primary contribution for the Church is a *text*, and, one might argue, a text that has at times either not been studied very carefully or studied as a recipe for change rather than a blueprint for continuity. In particular, much less interest has been expressed in the constitution's statements on liturgical art and architecture. The seemingly platitudinous nature of the document's short section on sacred art led many to believe that Vatican II had little to say on the matter other than a restatement of broad principles. For others, the document's statement encouraging the use of "the art of our own days" became a manifesto for the incorporation of *avante garde* forms from the secular art world.

With or without the guidance of *Sacrosanctum Concilium,* church buildings were often re-envisioned after the Council as "worship spaces" based on domestic rather than public buildings, with their actual designs of little or no import outside a perceived sense of hospitality, physical participation, and functional neutrality. In reaction, a movement toward a strong neo-realism in imagery and neo-traditionalism in architecture has grown up in recent years, aggressively battling the High Liturgical Modern of the 1960s and the folksy liturgical modern of the 1970s and 80s. Many architectural and theological theories not found in the texts of Vatican II itself have been dominating the world of Catholic liturgical art and architecture for some decades, and as the strength of the models of liturgical architecture popular in the 1970s and 80s has broken down, various other models have been emerging; everything from New Classicism to the nostalgic "Modernist Revival" of Rome's Church of 2000 or of Oakland, California's, Cathedral of Christ the Light (2008).

Unlike the supposed "spirit" of Vatican II, the texts of *Sacrosanctum Concilium* provide the normative teaching of the

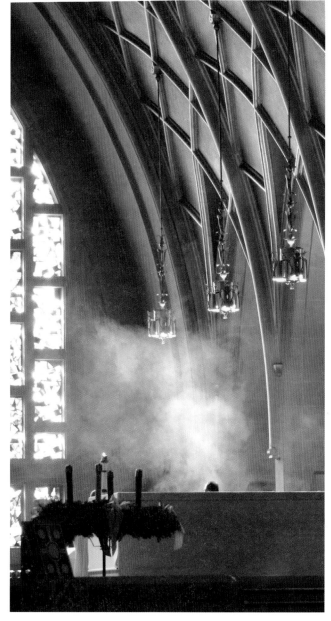

An architectural hermeneutic of reform. Cathedral of Saint Joseph the Workman, Lacrosse, Wisconsin, ca. 1962.

The heavenly liturgy persists in fittings noble, traditional, and modern. Tester, Cathedral of Saint Joseph the Workman, Lacrosse, Wisconsin.

magisterial authority of the Bishops in union with the Pope, which is guaranteed by the Holy Spirit. It is the sure guide for liturgical decisions as the Church goes forward into the second half-century after Vatican II. It deserves to be carefully read and understood. Another look at *Sacrosanctum Concilium's* teaching on sacred art and architecture might help elucidate the meaning of the words of the Council itself, and therefore aid in understanding the Council's great call for the Christian life to flourish again by drinking from the deepest wells of divine life found in the Church's Sacred Liturgy.

Sacrosanctum Concilium on Sacred Arts

Sacrosanctum Concilium's section on sacred art begins with the claim: "Very rightly the fine arts are considered to rank among the noblest expressions of human genius" (SC, 122). The document immediately speaks of the dignity of the vocation of the artist as one with whom to God shares his own creative powers. The artist, by virtue of his or her *imago Dei*, shares in the work of God, fashioning matter into things that are not only useful, but are given number, measure, and weight in order to make them reveal the spiritual realities they signify. The formlessness of inert matter is given shape and meaning in order to reverse the chaos that entered the world in the Fall. The artist sees beyond the fallen world and attempts to assist in God's salvific work by "undoing" the Fall, joining his or her efforts with the guidance of the Holy Spirit to assist in

God's plan of salvation by "creating" things that reorder the world back to what God intended. Although an infinite distance still exists between God and the artist because God can create something from nothing, and an artist fashions something out of preexisting matter, as a revealer of invisible spiritual realities, the work of the artist is primarily sacramental.

Sacrosanctum Concilium clearly emphasizes the sacramental nature of sacred art and presents it within the context of the long-standing tradition: "By their very nature, [religious and sacred art] are related to God's boundless beauty, for it is this reality which these human efforts are trying to express in some way" (SC, 122). God's Beauty pervades every aspect of the liturgy and precedes any particular liturgical experience. A God who desires to redeem his creation shares his Beauty with his creatures in order to divinize them by making them whole, turned toward him, and clearly conformed to the image of their maker. Art in the service of the liturgy would therefore imitate God's Beauty by being whole, ordered to its proper end, and transparent of the heavenly realities of eschatological perfection. In this way, sacred art does what its maker intended it to do: it gives a glimpse of a world transformed by grace, where the Fall is undone, and God is all in all. God's Beauty is full and complete, but in some limited way, artists participate in a partial revelation of his being.

For this reason, the next sentence in section 122 follows directly: "To the extent that these works aim exclusively at

Noble simplicity with dignified materials. Holy water font, 1962.

Noble and beautiful Christian simplicity across time: Saint Anne Church, Jerusalem (12th century) and Saint Gertrude Church, Cincinnati (ca. 1962).

turning men's thought to God persuasively and devoutly, they are dedicated to God and the cause of His greater honor and glory." Liturgical art properly leads human minds to contemplation of God. This happens, of course, when Beauty, theologically understood, is revealed. To review for just a moment, recall that Beauty is a quality of being in which the ontological reality of a thing under consideration is clearly manifested. This "flash" of the inner essential structure of a thing gives the perceiver a "window into heaven," a moment of understanding akin to the appearance of Christ at the Transfiguration on Mount Tabor. This Beauty is indeed the splendor of the Truth, which is also its attractive and persuasive power. It draws us out of ourselves and moves our wills toward contemplation of the Good. This movement of the will toward the Good is also a long-standing definition of love; so Beauty therefore leads us to love the thing revealed, and in liturgical art it is always the nature of the triumphant God that is revealed. Art that draws us to contemplate and love God is therefore intensely theocentric, and therefore dedicated to his honor and glory as well as a human being's sanctification. This view of the role of art explains why sacred art and architecture are essential and important, and why "Holy Mother Church has therefore always been the friend of the fine arts and has continuously sought their noble ministry" (SC, 122). According to the Council, art is more than pleasant enriching of a room or sign of earthly wealth and status; it is a ministry. *Minister* is a word that gets used frequently and lightly in parishes these days, usually understood as a "do-er" of something, but the word *minister* itself is etymologically related to the word *servant*. So art serves the liturgy, amplifies it, and supports it. It never draws attention to itself as a dead end of fashionable artists or trendy secular theories.

The general theological discussion of liturgical art is relatively easy to discuss. More difficult challenges arise when artists and clients must make actual artistic decisions. Here *Sacrosanctum Concilium* offers a set of principles for this decision making, which can be used to evaluate new artistic commissions. First, the document says that things used for worship should be "set apart," that is, distinct from everyday usage.[2] Vessels, vestments, books, and artwork for use in the Sacred Liturgy are indeed set apart by the level of will, intellect, elevated material, allusion, and craftsmanship applied to them. They therefore correspond most closely with the dignity of their use in the festive, sacrificial banquet of the Mass. On the earthly level, they speak of the best a community has to offer. From a sacramental perspective, they most clearly radiate the eschatological nature of the Heavenly Banquet of the Lamb, which the earthly Mass reveals and in which it participates.

These things set apart, then, have certain characteristics that make them different from the everyday, and *Sacrosanctum Concilium* uses the phrase "truly worthy, becoming, and beautiful, signs and symbols of heavenly realities," or in Latin, "*vere essent dignae, decorae ac pulchrae, rerum supernarum signa et symbola.*" Here the Council gives a wealth of ideas to consider. The words *worthy*, *becoming*, and *beautiful* mutually reinforce each other with subtle nuances of meaning. *Dignae*, or *worthy* gives us the words *dignity* and *dignified*, and it suggests suitability, propriety, and appropriateness. *Dignae* is about clarity of revelation, because any earthly thing that is *dignae* should be treated in a way that matches its inherent ontological dignity. Worthiness dilates and makes more penetrating the meaning of the object or act itself, so when a building, song, vestment, or vessel is worthy of the liturgy, it clarifies the importance of the liturgy by appearing different

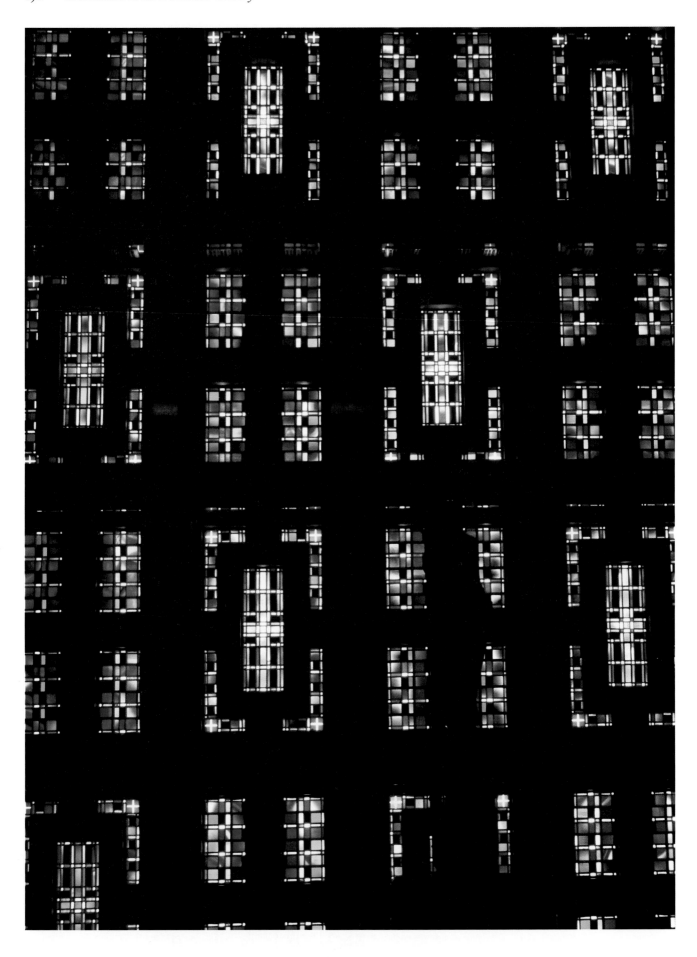

Noble simplicity combines with dignified beauty to evoke the table of the Wedding Feast of the Lamb. Cathedral of Christ the King, Lexington, Kentucky, 1967.

The use of modern trends in architecture need not rule out traditional imagery and theological understanding of the nature of the church building. Saint Patrick's Church, Huntington, New York, 1962.

Facing page: Gem-like walls of the heavenly Jerusalem. Cathedral of St. Peter in Chains, Cincinnati, 1957.

from and higher than secular things. Dignity adds to Beauty because Beauty always clarifies and makes attractive the Truth of the thing under consideration. Unworthy things appear to make the dignity of the liturgy less clear by presenting the transcendental and divine as humdrum and drab. Interestingly, the Germanic origin of *worthy* is *werden*, meaning "to become." A dignified thing poetically "becomes" the thing of which it is worthy by matching it closely in dignity.

The word *decorae* is translated as *becoming*, a slightly archaic word, which we still understand in the term *decorum*. A bride who wears jeans and sneakers at her wedding or says, "What's up?" upon meeting the Queen of England has broken decorum. Something *decorae*, that is, something decorous, like something *dignae*, is fitting, seemly, and proper but appears to take into account human convention about what the traditional usage of a thing should be. It is also related to the common word *decoration*, a word used earlier in architectural terminology to refer to revelation of structural clarity. Here, however, decoration suggests making *decorous* and is closer to the word *ornamentation* as an enrichment that clarifies the relative importance of a thing or act. A Christmas tree without this enrichment might be seen as deficiently ornamented because it fails to "speak" of the festivity and importance of the holiday. It suggests that the decorate-ors have not made the tree radiate with the *claritas* of the importance of the birth of Christ. Church buildings that are unornamented because of a fear of traditional things or a trendy industrial aesthetic might also be seen as unbecoming because they lack the sign and symbol value that speak of the festive, transcendental, and ultimately important nature of the liturgy.

The Council fathers also gave us the word *pulchrae*, or *beautiful*, as a quality of sacred art, and the rarely used word *pulchritude* remains in modern English. Beauty, as an attribute of being, arises when a thing participates most fully in and reveals the ontological or heavenly reality that lies behind it. In the earthly liturgy and the liturgical art and architecture that minister to it, Beauty is that which reveals the true nature of the liturgy most clearly. The liturgy is, as the great tradition of the Church teaches, an earthly presentation not only of the needs of the current day and personal experiences of the earthly congregation, but the anamnetic re-living of the one sacrifice of Christ as well as the anticipated foretaste of the Heavenly Banquet in which God is all in all and the new heaven and new earth are complete (*integritas*), fully ordered to God (*consonantia*) and radiant with the fullness of being (*claritas*). So *pulchrae* requests the fullness of the liturgy's artistic possibilities as known through John's visions in the book of Revelation: the one seated on the throne, the angels, the saints, the souls in purgatory, the Holy Spirit as the river of the water of life, the light-filled radiance of stained glass, golden vestments, and jeweled vessels. In architecture, it asks for signs of festivity and glory, a revelation of redeemed creation.

A rich iconographic program in a church presents the beauty of the liturgy because it presents the wholeness of the liturgy in as many of its earthly, heavenly, and cosmic dimensions as is decorous for the situation. Both the singularity of a cantor revealing the one voice of the Mystical Body or the complexity of a choir singing like the angels and saints at the throne of God increase the liturgy's *claritas* and *integritas*, conforming us to the "sound" of heaven. When the texts of liturgical songs are from, about, and to God rather than the earthly congregation alone, we know that they are whole and directed to their proper end. The "vesting" of the liturgy with music, art, and architecture follows a similar approach in relation to beauty: its purpose is to increase the claritas of the earthly, cosmic, and heavenly realities already existing in the

eternal liturgy.[3] Anything that distorts, distracts, or leads the mind elsewhere is foreign to the nature of the liturgy itself and is inherently not *pulchrae*. This would include cantors singing like Broadway divas or coffee house entertainers, priests changing the words of the liturgy on their own initiative, architects who choose a secular industrial aesthetic for a church building instead of the aesthetic of heaven, and so on. The problem in these instances is not style or modernity alone, but rather "un-liturgical-ness," things that either fail to reveal or reveal less clearly the nature of the liturgy. The primary job of liturgy that is worthy, becoming, and beautiful is not to be "post–Vatican II," "modern," or used to prove any inner-worldly theory of art or sociology. It might be or do those things, but primacy *always* remains with revelation of God's presence, for this presence is what divinizes the world.

Sacrosanctum Concilium on Beauty

Beauty and sacramentality are sisters because sacraments by definition make present and active the reality they represent, and Beauty is the attractive clarity of the Truth of that representation. A more full expression of a sacrament is one that more completely presents the reality of the sacramental thing itself. So *Sacrosanctum Concilium* tells us that the earthly liturgy is not only beautiful, but beautiful when it is composed of "signs and symbols of heavenly realities." Here again we are reminded that the liturgy is composed of signs and symbols that comprise God's "divine pedagogy of salvation" (CCC, 1145). So God chooses to communicate himself to us through signs (which convey information and refer us to some other reality) and symbols (sacramental signs which make present and active the very reality they signify). So if the signs and symbols that make up the liturgy are indeed God's method of conveying his divine life to us, it behooves us to make our liturgical decisions carefully so that this revelation is a complete, proportional, and clear revelation of "that heavenly liturgy which is celebrated in the holy city of Jerusalem toward which we journey as pilgrims. . ." (SC, 8). In other words, the job of every liturgical decision is to reveal both the earthly and glorified heavenly nature of the liturgy itself. The more clearly this is done, the more beautiful the liturgy and its allied arts will be.

The quest for the fullness and clarity of the liturgical experience make demands on every artistic choice made for the liturgy. The flooring of a church is meant to be transparent of the "streets" of the heavenly Jerusalem, described in the book of Revelation as pure gold and clear as crystal. Figural art in the liturgy is not only devotional, but makes present the heavenly beings invisibly participating in the one liturgy, earthly and heavenly. The altar is not only a memorial of the table of the upper room of the Last Supper, but prefigures the radiant table of the Banquet of the Lamb at the end of time when all has been glorified and is radiant with the light of Christ. The cup is indeed a precious chalice even though it keeps a deep connection to the simple cup of Christ's time on earth. Its sacramental role is to prefigure the glorious banquet of our heavenly future and be worthy, becoming, and beautiful by revealing a radiant flash of the transfigured heavenly perfection.

Sacrosanctum Concilium also gave the famous line: "the art of our own days . . . shall also be given free scope in the Church, provided that it adorns the rites with due honor and reverence," taken directly from Pius XII's encyclical *Mediator Dei*. This commentary on the art of our own days has frequently been misunderstood. Indeed, the Church believes that the Holy Spirit continues to inspire artists to reveal the Truth in our day as in the past. However, in the years after the Council, the beginning of this line from the Council was often quoted without reference to its qualifying proviso, and a supposed art of "our days" was often used in order to appear current and receive approval from the secular art and architectural critics. In many cases, hostile inner-worldly theories of liturgical art were promoted, much to the delight of many artists and architects and the confusion and dismay of the faithful. These aesthetic theologies, to use Hans Urs von Balthasar's terminology, have very often proven unbeautiful because they were not *dignae*, *decorae*, or *pulchrae*. They might have produced beautiful bus stations, efficient factories, or lovely meeting houses, but as churches they were deficient because they substituted secular art theories for proper liturgical theology.

A fuller sacramental understanding of liturgical art and architecture will often require things that are of great value: gold, silk, gems, marble, and the like. Does this not seem to fly in the face of the Council's supposed call for "noble simplicity"? A close reading of *Sacrosanctum Concilium* gives an answer. The document requests that the *rites* be characterized by a noble simplicity (SC, 34). Sacred art (as well as vestments and ornaments that are mentioned by name), were to have a noble beauty (SC, 124, *nobilem pulchritudinem*), with all of the implications already described above. This theological notion of beauty was clearly contrasted to "mere sumptuous display" (*meram sumptuositatem*). Often under the cultural bias for Modernist simplicity, many have understood this warning against *mere* sumptuous display as a call for the "earthy" and mundane in church architecture, effectively eliminating marble, gold, and ornament. Nothing could be further from the truth. *Sacrosanctum Concilium* simply asks that noble beauty not be overwhelmed by a merely earthly expenditure for the sake of empty lavishness. The word *sumptuous* finds its origin in the Latin *sumere*, "to spend," so an earthly display of mere spending without beauty—that is, without the radiant clarity of the ontological reality of the liturgy—becomes merely a senate aesthetic experience alone,

one that does not become a revelation of the heavenly Jerusalem. Mere sumptuousness becomes an earthly dead end of sensual pleasure and has no place in church buildings.

The word *noble* in "noble beauty" rescues us from this problem. *Noble* gives English its word *know* and finds its origin in the Latin *nobilis*, which itself comes from *noscere*, "to know." So a thing that is "noble" is in fact know-able. It reveals to the human intellect through the senses something of an object's inner spiritual logic, what theologian Jacques Maritain called its ontological "secret." This very revelation is what we call Beauty. So in a sense, "noble beauty" has a certain repetitive emphasis if not a redundancy. A beautiful thing is by definition knowable, and a knowable thing must possess Beauty. Unlike a mere earthly lavishness that only draws attention to itself, an extravagance that radiates the clarity of God and the glory of a divinized heaven and earth delights the senses in a way wholly conformed to God's divine pedagogy. All of creation finds its "liturgical end" in liturgical glory: gold, silver, limestone, marble, silk, gems, linen, wood, paper, leather, ink, and glass. The skill of the human voice, hand, intellect, and will are manifested, nourished, divinized, and transformed. All the while, God is glorified and creation is sanctified. Such is the sacramental understanding of the world and the divine pedagogy of salvation as evidenced in the Second Vatican Council's *Constitution on the Sacred Liturgy*.

---

1. Portions of this chapter appeared as an article in *Assembly: A Journal of Liturgical Theology* 33:6 (November 2007), 69–72.

2. The Latin text of the document uses the word *pertinentes*, which the Abbot-Gallagher translation of the Council documents translates as "set apart for." More literally, *pertinentes* means "pertaining to," though the idea expressed as "set apart" dilates the meaning in accord with traditional understanding of the word. *Per-* suggests *motion toward* and *tenere*, a holding fast to, through and through, in the sense of exclusive use. With gratitude to Father Samuel Weber, OSB, for assistance with translation.

3. For more on chant as "vesting" of the liturgical texts, see Marc-Daniel Kirby, "Sung Theology: The Liturgical Chant of the Church," Stratford Caldecott, ed., *Beyond the Prosaic: Renewing the Liturgical Movement* (Edinburgh: T&T Clark, 1998), 127–148.

Chapter 13

Meeting House or Church: The Hermeneutics of Discontinuity and Reform

It would be a mistake to arrange and decorate the interior of the church in such a way as to create the atmosphere of a comfortable and cozy bourgeois residence. . . . It should bespeak forcibly the grandeur of God which surpasses all earthly measure, so that it may exalt the worshipper above the sphere and atmosphere of his daily private life; and yet, it must still leave one with the friendly feeling of "the goodness and kindness of our Savior. . . ."

—The Rev. Theodore Klauser, "Directives for the Building of a Church," 1949[1]

We should no longer build places specifically devoted to the cultic event, or structures which have what is thought of as ecclesiastical character; . . . there can be no more church building in the sense that is meant when we talk about "houses of God," shrines, temples, naves, chancels or sacred edifices. We need to return to the non-church.

—Edward A. Sövik, *Architecture for Worship,* 1973[2]

In 1907 noted architect Ralph Adams Cram published a highly influential essay titled "Meeting Houses or Churches?" in which he tried to convince modern Protestant readers that church buildings were not meeting houses, but sacramental buildings.[3] His intended audience was the Reformation denominations that denied the deep sacramentality of liturgical art and architecture. Little did he know, that, had he lived another thirty years beyond his death in 1942, he would have had to try to convince many of the practitioners of the Roman Catholic Church of the very same points that he had aimed at Baptists and Unitarians at the time of World War I. The two excerpts cited above display the radical shift in the definitions of church architecture, which affected (and still affect) the Church after the Second Vatican Council. Solemn and public architecture gave way to intimate and domestic; and ecclesiastical architecture, as an inheritance of the entirety of salvation history, ceased to be part of an organically developing, continuous reform. It became something else. And this

Grandeur and approachability. Saints Faith, Hope & Charity Church, Winnetka, Illinois, 1962.

Pious skepticism, or architecture of continuity. Noble materials and recognizable conventions in a modernized form. Cathedral of St. Peter in Chains, Cincinnati, 1957.

Below: Though it made use of radically Modern architecture which gave up the articulate expression of traditional design, Otto Bartning's 1931 church in Essen, Germany (now destroyed), was understood as a church—solemn and public—rather than a domestic building.

"something else" has been the topic of discussion in church building committees ever since.

"Modern" Churches

People often call this something else "modern" for lack of better word. But quite often this is not a question of architectural style, or even of Modernism itself. Many churches built in the twentieth century were recognizably modern, yet still churchly. Many of architect Edward Schulte's churches, for instance, maintained their churchly character even as he drew more and more from contemporary trends. Ernest Pickering's book on architectural design from the 1940s shows a page with four church drawings, three of them quite daringly modern for the time, but all four fit quite convincingly under the heading "Ecclesiastical Character" (see page xiv). Even the most radical of the early Modernist church builders maintained this ecclesiastical character by designing buildings of a large scale, great height, and solid and prominent altar even as they made greater use of concrete and largely abandoned traditional styles. Into the 1950s and even into the early 1960s, many churches made use of differing degrees of "Modernism" as a stylistic choice, but always chose to maintain a churchly character.

We can find many reasons to discuss the appropriateness of Modernism as an architectural style for Catholic churches. Being rooted in socialist, rationalist, functionalist,

Above: Otto Bartning's Modernist church evoked the proportions of Gothic architecture and recalled the stained glass of the Sainte-Chapelle in Paris while absorbing the industrial aesthetic of the Bauhaus.

Right: Holy Cross Church, Frankfurt–Bornheim, Germany. Martin Weber, architect, 1929.

and revolutionary beginnings, it often does not provide an articulate architectural vocabulary for the church building. But for the most part, even the most modern churches of the first half of the twentieth century were intended to be *churches.* The best Modernist churches of the 1950s, for example, used a high level of craft, rich marbles, stained glass, liturgical imagery, and a hierarchical sense of progression from entry to nave to sanctuary and altar. They remained recognizably "modern," but they were decorated and ornamented and given the scale and material of public buildings. Just to be clear, it is perfectly reasonable to critique the philosophical underpinnings of many of the founding minds of Modernism, with their inherent anti-traditionalism and rejection of history. But most American architects building churches in the mid twentieth century were not doctrinaire about the philosophical roots of Modernism. They simply gave a parish a church in a "modern idiom," and the average passerby recognized it as a church. Even a church design published in 1957 based on the lines of the fallout patterns of an atomic bomb looked like a

Though Czech-American architect Antonin Raymond recommended the use of exposed concrete in this 1950 church proposal, it still retained a churchly presence, great height, public importance, and an eschatologically inspired mural reminiscent of the early Liturgical Movement. *Liturgical Arts,* August, 1950.

church![4] Moreover, where one might not recognize a building as a church, as with Marcel's Breuer's monastery chapel at St. John's Abbey in Minnesota, at least it looked *important*.

But a radical shift occurred after the Council, so much so that a Catholic liturgical journal could write the following about a Catholic church: "Saint Paul's is really a 'church house.' In spite of its particular function as a place of celebration, it remains on the same scale as the neighboring houses. Really a landmark of the church of tomorrow."[5] In 1968 Frederic Debuyst, editor of the influential journal *Art D'Eglise,* wrote, "The churches of tomorrow, if they are to be really good churches, will have to look more like houses than like

the churches of today or yesterday."[6] Nearly two decades later, another author praised a church building for being "virtually indistinguishable from common industrial structures."[7] Never did the Second Vatican Council or any of the Church's documents that led up to or followed it ever hint that a church should be radically redefined as either a private residence or a factory. But somehow the "spirit" of the Council became the catch-all for the adoption of ideas foreign to the Council itself. This "spirit" still lingers in our own time.

Today the field of Catholic liturgical architecture is dominated by competing approaches that tend to fall along lines that are often called "progressive" and "traditional," but the ideas they represent are much deeper than questions of architectural style or individual preference. Each represents a differing understanding of liturgical theology, though both claim to be adhering to the same Second Vatican Council. The first approach sees the church building as primarily domestic in inspiration, a neutral, comfortable, hospitable

When a church is thought of as a house rather than a sacramental building, utilitarian objects tend to fill the area that should be a sacramental icon of heaven.

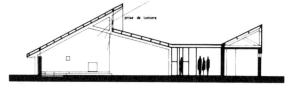

Above: Saint Paul Church, Belgium, Jean Cosse, architect, from *Liturgical Arts,* August, 1971. The building was described as a "church house" on the "same scale as the neighboring houses" which provided an atmosphere "very close to a domestic celebration."

Left, top and bottom: When church buildings are understood as houses, they lose their place in the architectural hierarchy as well as clear expression of their nature and purpose. *Liturgical Arts,* February 1972.

Legible and illegible use of simplicity. Above: Mission San Diego de Alcala, San Diego, California, founded 1769. Below: Cathedral of Our Lady of the Angels, Los Angeles. Raphael Moneo, architect, 2002.

"environment" where the primary symbol is the people celebrating, with a theological basis believed to be drawn from the supposed house churches of the first and second century. The other sees the church building as fundamentally public in nature, with a grandeur and dignity rooted in the traditional architecture of history, which must "look like" and "feel like" a church.

Pope Benedict XVI spoke of this sort of "either/or" dichotomy as one of the primary obstacles to the serene reception of the liturgical reforms of the Council. He pondered the question: Why has the implementation of the Council thus far been so difficult in large parts of the Church?[8] He cited a quote from Saint Basil, who, after the Council of Nicea in 325 spoke of "the confused din of uninterrupted clamoring," which had "filled almost the whole of the Church, falsifying through excess or failure the right doctrine of the faith." Does this not sound like the discussions of liturgy in recent years, which have earned the deeply oxymoronic name "liturgy wars"? How could that which is supposed to be the source and summit of the Christian life, the bringer of *cosmos* to chaos, become the source of "war"? Benedict's answer: In the implementation of the Council, two contrary hermeneutics—that is, two methods of interpreting the meaning of the Council's texts—came face to face, and differing theological understandings resulted from the one Council. And since church architecture is the built form of theology, it should come as no surprise that differing architectural theologies emerged as well.[9]

Benedict called one way of interpreting the Council the "hermeneutic of discontinuity and rupture." The other he called a "hermeneutic of reform." Importantly, in this document he does not use the phrase "hermeneutic of *continuity*." In each approach, liturgical reform is intended and taken for granted in light of the Liturgical Movement, of which the young scholar Ratzinger was a proponent. But the hermeneutic of discontinuity and rupture, he said, risks "ending in a split between the preconciliar church and the postconciliar church."

The hermeneutic of discontinuity argues that the texts of the Council cannot really be trusted to express the "spirit" of the Council because the texts were results of compromises between liberal and conservative bishops. The Council documents, then, are thought best understood as only imperfectly expressing the Council's goals. Therefore, the "true" spirit of the Council is not found in the texts, but in the impulses toward the new that are contained in them. Thinking of the Council's texts as somehow hobbled and limited means that one needs to "go courageously beyond the texts" to understand the Council. The problem here, he says, is not the attempt to discern the meaning of the Council's texts, but the nature of the method itself. Going "beyond" the Council means that "a vast margin was left open for the question of how this spirit should subsequently be defined, and room was consequently made for every whim."[10] It is hard to deny that

the "expression of every whim" has been all too true in liturgical matters in recent decades.

Benedict claims that the hermeneutic of discontinuity is not simply one interpretive method among many equals, but a fundamental misunderstanding of a Church council, as if it were some parliament that removed the old regime and replaced it with a new mandate. Seeing the Church this way is not right, he argues, because the basic nature of the Church comes from the Lord and does not change in its essentials. The Church indeed adapts from time to time for better sacramental and pastoral understanding, but it does not cease to be what it was and become something else. Therefore its fundamental Truths and liturgical expressions maintain considerable stability.

By contrast, Benedict claims, the hermeneutic of reform is the proper key to understanding the Council. This approach sees that renewal comes through clarification of inherited Tradition in continuity with the Church founded by the Lord. Benedict reminds us that the defining characteristics of this hermeneutic were expressed by Pope John XXIII at the opening of the Council when he stated that the goal of the Council was to "transmit the doctrine, pure and integral, without any attenuation or distortion." The doctrine of the Church, liturgical and otherwise, is not to be locked up in a cage as if the Holy Spirit was no longer at work in the Church. The "precious treasure" of the Faith, therefore, should indeed be reappraised in light of the current age with adherence to all the teaching of the Church "in its entirety and preciseness." So what we have here is indeed a **pious skepticism**, trustfully holding on to that which is old, but still seeking to see new facets of the same inherited gem. Importantly, the hermeneutic of reform is decidedly *not* an antiquarian restorationism, but a proper understanding of the Council and its intentions. By definition, a reform combines continuity and discontinuity, since any reform requires that something old is replaced or fulfilled by some new insight. But reform always presumes substantive continuity with that which came before, both in externals and spirit.

---

pious skepticism: Pious skepticism, a term used by architectural historian C. W. Westfall, indicates an approach to inherited tradition which assumes a pious or fundamentally reverent attitude toward things carried forward from the past as trustworthy. At the same time it carefully inspects and adapts them for current-day usage. A *pious piety* accepts the inheritance of the past without the possibility of change or organic growth. A *skeptical piety* assumes a fundamentally skeptical approach to the inherited tradition while assuming the possibility of some value being found there. *Skeptical skepticism* assumes no value for the current day can come from the inherited tradition. The apostolic nature of the Church and its theology of unfolding knowledge of God over time place it in greatest sympathy with the approach of pious skepticism.

A 1971 article in *Liturgical Arts* magazine proposed using the suburban house as the model for the "small church of the future" where the "stylistic triumphalism of the past" would "give way to a more sensible and human solution." Although the adaptation of houses for church use proved unrealistic and therefore uncommon, the intellectual notion of the church as house persisted through the 1980s and 1990s.

This line of inquiry leads to concrete responses in liturgy and its architecture. Even though the hermeneutic of discontinuity is so strongly entrenched that the average person sees an air of casualness, liturgy in the vernacular, the priest "facing the people" as the defining features of Vatican II, Benedict recalls that the Council itself says nothing of the direction of prayer or congregational creativity, and that *Sacrosanctum Concilium* states that Latin is to be conserved while vernacular may be given wider scope.[11] In fact, he writes, if Mass were said *ad orientem*, in Latin with some vernacular, using Gregorian chant, it would take a liturgical scholar of significant sophistication to even notice that the current Missal of Paul VI were being used at all.

The solution to the liturgy wars, he proposed, is to look again with gratitude at the Second Vatican Council and interpret and implement its texts with a proper hermeneutic. Since a lesser hermeneutic has operated in differing degrees in the last fifty years or so, a fresh look is needed to determine how we can enter a more mature stage in understanding Vatican II. Those attached to the hermeneutic of discontinuity will no doubt find this difficult. Those who genuinely oppose the reforms of the Council will find this difficult as well. In either case, those who build churches today need some way to assess the meaning of the Council's teaching on liturgy and to discover that it was the entire tradition of the Church, polished anew by the Liturgical Movement, which gave us *Sacrosanctum Concilium*. The hermeneutic of reform will always work in concert with this inheritance.

THE HERMENEUTIC OF DISCONTINUITY AND THE HOUSE CHURCH

For a time, a major publisher of Catholic liturgical materials published a series of booklets about Catholic churches called "The Meeting House Essays." One author entitled her book *Shaping a House for the Church*, another called his *From Temple to Meeting House*, and yet another, *God's House Is Our House.*[12] Cardinal Joseph Bernardin of Chicago wrote in 1984 that a church building was "a kind of living room of the family of God, . . . our room when we assemble as the Church. Here we are at home."[13] Others consciously refused to use the word *church* to refer to a church building because of its supposed origin in secular houses of early Christians. Edward Sövik's

·ECCLESIASTICAL· °°DOMESTIC···

·FIG·ⓒ·CONTRAST·OF·CHARACTER··°

"Contrast of Character" from Ernest Pickering's 1947 book *Architectural Design*.

hugely influential book, *Architecture for Worship*, called for a "return" to the "non-Church," which he chose to call a "centrum" so that he wouldn't have to use the word *church* at all. His writings advocated every possible device to prevent these "centrums" from acquiring a sacral character. Though an Evangelical Lutheran himself and convinced of Lutheran principles about sacramental theology, his writings and ideas were espoused by Catholic architects and theologians. The 1978 document of the United States Bishops' Committee on the Liturgy called *Environment and Art in Catholic Worship* embraced much of his philosophy and showed buildings designed either by Sövik's office or under his inspiration. A prominent priest and liturgical consultant dedicated his most recent book to him.[14] One author praises Sövik's St. Leo's Catholic Church in Pipestone, Minnesota (1969), as an example of a non-church built for a Roman Catholic congregation, which reflects the "concerns present in the wake of post–Vatican II developments" because it places the clergy in the midst of the laity and *avoids* an "altar-dominant space."[15] Yet another author praised this same church for avoiding "pompous, authoritarian otherworldliness" because of its squat form and its lack of ornamentation![16] Others found it a sacred duty to remove old high altars as signs of a "pre-conciliar" ritual sacrality and radically re-order the plan of the church so that the people are "gathered" around the "table" in imitation of a secular dinner party in a private home. Purifying the sacred vessels became known unofficially in sacristies and seminaries as "doing the dishes."

Within this theological and architectural milieu, the priest-celebrant was consciously referred to as a *presider*, because "presiding" was thought more accurate than "celebrant."[17] The role of the "presider" was not understood as a continuity with the very same priesthood of only fifteen years earlier, but involved a "whole new job description."[18] Images of butterflies, dandelions, ceramic chalices, and leavened bread appeared in liturgical books and hand missals. All traces of connection to the *Christus totus*, the whole Christ which includes the liturgy of heaven, was abandoned, or nearly so, in favor of the notion that "the human community assembled is the most important liturgical reality in the environment."[19] Liturgical architecture was no longer thought of as sacramental or having holiness proper to itself by virtue of its consecration, but instead it acquired "sacredness from the sacred action of the faith community" that used it.[20] The subject of the liturgical action was redefined to be the congregation alone, no longer understood as the exercise of the priestly office of Christ to whom the church was grafted as a Mystical Body. In certain writings, even the *object* of worship, God the Father, was neglected in favor of a truly striking anthropocentrism.

But these ideas were not simply coming from people on the margins of experimental theology. The aforementioned document on liturgical architecture, *Environment and Art in Catholic Worship*, called the gathered assembly *the* most important symbol in the liturgy.[21] Because the congregation alone was redefined as the most important symbol, the building in which it met could be redefined as a non-didactic "environment" or "worship space," just as a hothouse serves as an environment for a plant. It provides the air, humidity, and moisture but is otherwise neutral. Therefore, the primary concern for a church building was making people feel comfortable and welcome in a climate of hospitality that reminded them of their own homes. The building itself was radically desacramentalized, being called a "cover for enclosing the architectural space" in order to give it no theological import whatsoever. And in perhaps the single most damaging line written about liturgical architecture in the twentieth century, a church was called a " 'skin' for liturgical action which need not 'look like' anything else, past or present."[22] Because "the most powerful experience of the sacred" was claimed to be found in the persons celebrating, "that is, the action of the assembly," the authors of the bishops' document said, churches should be "designed as general gathering spaces."[23] This document, now replaced and completely rewritten, proposed a truly amazing revolution in the theology of church buildings.

There have been many arguments made for and against *Environment and Art in Catholic Worship*, and the goal here is not to treat it unfairly.[24] Understanding its emphases, however, provides one of the clearest guideposts for understanding much of the church architecture of the last thirty years. Its choices are highly biased and romantic, somehow envisioning the so-called "house church" as an ideal model, and therefore re-imagining the "environment for worship" on flawed premises. One need not vilify proponents of these differing positions even as we evaluate their ideas. The questions raised in the 1960s and 1970s are worth noting, evaluating, and purifying— exaggerated as they often were—because revolutions do not arise from a vacuum. People of genuine good will believed that reform was necessary. However, as time passes, a certain clarity arises as the liturgical reform passes through its adolescence. The old "either/or" categorization so crucial to a generation that came of age in a time of clericalism and ritualism simply does not apply today, and the last few generations have been living in the counter-balancing excesses of the period.

One might argue that the excesses after the Council were like what antibiotics are to an infection. Medicine is foreign, but it kills the bacteria, and for a short time it is necessary even as it can bring on unpleasant side effects. Whatever "disease" of liturgical misunderstanding was present before the Council often caused a corrective *in extremis* on the local and individual level. But in our day the disease is gone, and it is time to resume healthy liturgical living once again. This may not sound like good news to people who have grown used to either liturgical sickness or the feeling of the medicine's side effects. But it must be done. This is the hard work of agreeing on the hermeneutic through which to properly understand the Council.

The great challenge today is not to reject out of hand all recent discussions—including the "revolutionary" tone of

several decades ago and the so-called "restorationist" tone of more recent years—but to bring a proper sense of wholeness and balance to the issue of liturgy and liturgical architecture. Restoring the sacral character to the liturgy and the church building does not mean that "participation" will be taken from the people or that people will sit behind columns. In fact, we must be on guard against an uncritical return to pre-conciliar conditions. But, conversely, understanding that individual Christians offer the Mass with the priest as baptized members of the Mystical Body does not mean that the ministerial priesthood must be diminished. *Sacrosanctum Concilium* tells us that liturgical participation requires precisely the exercise of the baptismal priesthood, which is more than a mere external busyness. Taking a cue from *Mediator Dei*, it also states that the faithful should "not be there as strangers or silent spectators," but "should give thanks to God; by offering the Immaculate Victim, not only through the hands of the priest, but also *with* him, they should learn also to offer themselves; through Christ the Mediator, they should be drawn day by day into ever more perfect union with God and with each other, so that finally God may be all in all" (SC, 47).

Offering the self as a victim to Christ means participating actively as part of the Mystical Body, being joined to the Son who offers himself to the Father through the exercise of his priestly office in the liturgy so that God's presence might bring unity, peace, and the fulfillment of the history of salvation. *Here is active participation in the mystery of the liturgy!* And how much more it is than arguments based on political terminology of "pre" and "post" conciliar language about the "bad old days" or the "good old days." Our job is to glorify God and be transformed by divine life *today*, and our liturgical art and architecture ought to show this glorification now, because "in a church, everything is different from that which we constantly see around us and in our homes. . . . The walls are painted with sacred images; everything shines brightly; everything raises the spirit. . . ."[25] Quite often we are still circling around the fringes of the Council's treasures. It is time to drink deeply from its wells.

Our challenge now is to assess today's prevailing principles in light of a proper reading of the Second Vatican Council. Actually *reading* the great scholars of the Liturgical Movement and understanding its reforms in liturgical art and architecture makes clear that we have often betrayed the intentions of Vatican II through an antiquarianism that overly glamorized the house church. Re-balancing liturgical priorities is right and just, and grows from a hermeneutic of reform. Radically redefining the nature of church buildings is a thought process rooted in a hermeneutic of discontinuity. Nothing in the Council documents, *Mediator Dei*, or in the mainstream Liturgical Movement argued for the redefinition of liturgical architecture as something that was to avoid otherworldliness or emulate industrial buildings. In fact, the whole point of the Liturgical Movement was to *increase* the notion of otherworldliness so people would know they were part of a Mystical Body that participated in a sacrifice that was an exercise of the priestly office of Jesus Christ with the heavenly hosts of angels and saints.

One is reminded yet again of the Council's call for art and architecture to be "signs and symbols of heavenly realities" (SC, 123) and help the faithful understand that they shared "in that heavenly liturgy which is celebrated in the holy city of Jerusalem" with the "warriors of the heavenly army" (SC, 7, 8) for the glorification of God and the sanctification of the faithful. Here is the language of the Liturgical Movement. Here is the reality in which people were meant to participate actively, consciously, and fruitfully; both internally and externally (SC, 11, 19). For this reason the altar, tabernacle, and crucifix were made more prominent, sight lines were improved, and the vernacular were given wider scope. A "noble beauty" (SC, 124) was intended to make these realities more compelling by being complete, ordered to God, and radiantly clear. Devotional images were to be retained but in appropriate places. Art of the modern day could be used if it adorned "the sacred building and holy rites with due honor and reverence" (SC, 123). Sacred furnishings were not to be disposed of, for they were understood as "ornaments of the house of God" (SC, 126).

Read again the words of Vatican II: *God's beauty. Holy rites. Sacred building. House of God. Sacred images.* And yet we were (and are still) asked to build empty dining rooms with wooden tables for altars. Worse yet, we were asked to build the "non-church." All in the name of the Second Vatican Council, which proposed the very opposite!

Outside of the theology of the Reformation, the church building has never been understood as a home grown large. In the time of the Acts of the Apostles, the early Christians repeatedly returned to the temple for prayer, as scripture tells us. Their public singing of hymns and psalms in the Acts of the Apostles has clear ties to the worship of the temple and remains in the Mass to this day. The church more likely grew from the synagogue tradition as well, as Louis Bouyer has written: "The New Testament was born not only out of the Old but from it. . . . And the Church, the material temple in which this assembly of God is to meet . . . had its immediate preparation in the Jewish synagogue."[26] The synagogue was a ritually public building of significant architectural import, not a domestic building. But in a sense, this line or argument is a straw man, because the validity of ecclesial action does not depend solely on an antiquarian precedent. Certainly the Church looks to her tradition to find inspiration and understanding, but clearly eschews antiquarianism and trusts that the Holy Spirit gives new insight to the Church in different ages.[27] Our age is no different. The Church welcomes the offerings of the age, but always checks them for appropriate-

ness for sacred worship. Sometimes this takes thirty or forty years to sort itself out.

Indeed, the church building is a place where people meet, but churches are "not simply gathering places" (CCC, 1180), but are places that show us how God's dwelling with humanity looks now and will look at the end of time when the plan of salvation is fulfilled. The justification today for building glorious churches is not the shadowy typology of the Temple of Solomon or the ordinariness of a private home. Because we exist in the time of the Resurrection, where the veil is torn, we can know the realities of the heavenly Holy of Holies by way of sacramental image. The church is also a house, but it is more akin to a palace to which we are welcomed as a royal people with the King. Aquinas tells us that even though Christ and the apostles met in a secular house for the Last Supper, we still need a consecrated church building because the building signifies the Church, "and is termed a church; and so it is fittingly consecrated, both to represent the *holiness* which the *Church* acquired from the Passion, as well as to denote the *holiness* required of them who have to receive this sacrament."[28] The building is not a neutral meeting hall, but a signifier, and an incredibly important one.

The Old Testament speaks repeatedly of the temple as God's "house," where God dwelled. And though it started in the tent of Moses' tabernacle, it was no ordinary tent; its symbolic richness and complexity were clearly revelatory. God himself asked for a temple of serious public architecture where every detail had a meaning as a typological precursor to Christ. The subsequent move of God's presence from the limitations of the temple to the "living stones" of the *ekklesia* does not abolish the law of liturgical architecture, but fulfills it. The church building became a sign of the *ekklesia*, an icon of the people restored, filled with divine life, doing something different, important, and heavenly. As such, it garnered the architectural symbolism of decoration, ornament, and building types proper to its day. It also revealed an eschatological dimension that required the assistance of "high" art, with systems of structure (decoration) and meaning (ornament), showing restoration on the natural level and the presence of the heavenly beings on the supernatural level.

The church building is indeed the *domus ecclesiae*, the house of the People of God, the place where they know they belong because they have become God's adopted children. However, it is also the *domus Dei*, because it is still the place where God dwells, not only in the people who gather there as part of the Mystical Body, but in the Word enshrined there and the priest who acts *in persona Christi*. Moreover, the Blessed Sacrament reserved there in a tabernacle completes and fulfills the notion of God's abiding presence on the *kapporeth* of the Ark of the Covenant without taking anything away from the presence of Christ in his people who need to take the message to all nations. "The Eucharistic Presence in

Uneasy dialogue with Modernity. Church of the Holy Sepulcher, Jerusalem.

the tabernacle does not set another view of the Eucharist alongside or against the Eucharistic celebration, but simply signifies its complete fulfillment."[29] To deny this theological and artistic richness is to deny the very heart of active participation to the faithful and smacks of elitist neo-clericalism and snooty professionalism.

So our building is still temple and synagogue. We participate in the Liturgy of the Word as a fulfillment of the synagogue, then we move to the Liturgy of the Eucharist where the Victim is offered by the faithful with the priest as a Mystical Body in the unbloody offering of the Holy Sacrifice of the Mass. This liturgical reality makes demands on us as

people who offer it in spirit and in truth as one unified body welcomed into this mystery. But we also remember we are hospitably welcomed into the sacrificial offering of Christ, which returns to us transformed as a glorified, festive banquet of the Eucharist. This new reality, though offered once and for all, has yet to bear all of its fruits in time and space. The "already but not yet principle" remains at work. To say it one more time: In the time of image, the building remains an image of the fullness of the time when all is restored and divinized.

Precisely because the church building is so multivalent, it is easy to become "caught" on only one of its many strains and carry it to exaggeration. What an individual thinks of the

Innovation within tradition: the architectural hermeneutic of reform. Cathedral of Saint Joseph the Workman, Lacrosse, Wisconsin.

Theological confusion leads to architectural confusion: tabernacle, piano, and font compete visually with each other and with the main altar.

temple's influence on the origins of Christian worship will be a highly important factor in what kind of church building he or she finds suitable. After the Council, many thought that the notion of church building as synagogue and welcoming "house" was important, and indeed it was. But to limit the church building to just one of its facets is to do it a disservice, as it denies the faithful full participation in what is rightly theirs: all of the facets of the liturgy. Any early Christian

knowledgeable in the entire biblical tradition would never have seen the Eucharist as a mere fellowship meal in a secular dining room.

This notion of continuity provides the reason why Eusebius could rejoice in the early fourth century over a highly developed sense of ritual that flourished under Constantine. It did not, and certainly could not have, sprung up *ex nihilo* at Constantine's conversion, nor could its art and architecture. In describing church buildings, Eusebius can speak simultaneously of the Temple of Solomon, the temple of living stones and the heavenly city of Jerusalem. He sometimes called church buildings "houses of prayer," or "houses of the Lord," but almost as often called them "temples." Echoes of the temple are heard as he calls the altar the "Holy of Holies" and the bishop who built it the new Bezalel and Zerubbabel, the builders of the Temple of Jerusalem named in scripture. Moreover, he calls the Church the "living temple" composed of "living and moving stones," well-built on the foundation of the apostles and prophets and with Christ himself as cornerstone. Going even further, he compares the building of a church to the building of the temple, which was made "after the heavenly types [were] given in symbols," calling a church built in his own time the "magnificent temple of the highest God . . . corresponding to the pattern of the greater as a visible to an invisible. . . ."[30] The making of a church, then, was to make an image of the heavenly temple. Here we find shadow, image, and reality understood in terms that would later be called sacramental theology. Today we can call it architectural theology.

We can learn from Eusebius as we can from all intervening generations. Each epoch in history, either by its virtues or failures, has something to teach us about the inexhaustible nature of God and the demands of proper worship. The early Christians and the Byzantines gave us a vision of architectural glory that was deeply rooted in biblical ideals. John Damascene clarified the great theological gift of the icon. The medievals gave a distinct sense of the heavenly Jerusalem as transcendent and deeply incarnational, adding much to the understanding of the saints and the sacraments. Trent further opened up liturgical symbols to the people in rich iconography and dramatic architecture. The nineteenth-century revivals, while often overly focused on architecture rather than theology, nonetheless brought with them a highly developed sense of semiotics and churchliness. Various popes have further commented on the liturgy and church buildings as the need arose, picking up speed in the twentieth century with Pius X's claim that active participation in the liturgy would be manifested by singing the liturgy and receiving the Eucharist frequently. Pius XII further urged liturgical clarification and attempted to curb the excesses of the reform movement. Any art history book can chronicle the many styles and expressions that have graced the Church over the millennia, but every way of building is either useful to us now—or not—because of its theological continuities with apostolic tradition, not because of its architectural innovation.

The word *style* has been used infrequently in this book, for the very reason that "styles" are composed of a set of facts that are themselves contingent, changing, and time-bound. Style is the way *claritas* manifests itself in time and place. Some styles are better at *claritas* than others by virtue of how well they express theological realities, while other styles remain highly dependent on the conventional understanding current at a place in a specific time. Some are more self-conscious of being "about" time and place than others. But style should always remain secondary to proper liturgical theology, and proper liturgical theology always comes from the inspiration of the Holy Spirit with the approval of the Church. Understanding the church building properly means understanding the liturgical and theological tradition of the Church in light of its continuities, then focusing those Truths so that the eye may see them better. Here we find the hermeneutic of reform, not the hermeneutic of discontinuity. And here we find the path to the serene reception of the Second Vatican Council in art and architecture as well as the liturgy in general. An era of liturgical and artistic beauty is ready to flower, the energy of its petals bursting through the plump buds loaded with the *integritas* of right belief so as to reveal the *claritas* of right praxis.

1. "Directives for the Building of a Church," composed by The Rev. Theodore Klauser, Rector Magnificus of the University of Bonn, by order of and in cooperation with the Liturgical Commission established by the Catholic bishops of Germany. It appeared first in English in *Orate Fratres*, December 1949, and was also included in J. B. O'Connell, *Church Building and Furnishing: The Church's Way*, University of Notre Dame Liturgical Studies Series, v. 2 (Notre Dame, IN: University of Notre Dame Press, 1955).

2. Edward A. Sövik, *Architecture for Worship* (Minneapolis: Augsburg Publishing, 1973), 7, 39.

3. Ralph Adams Cram, "Meeting Houses or Churches," *The Gothic Quest* (New York: Baker and Taylor, 1907).

4. Architectural Record, *Religious Buildings for Today* (New York: F. W. Dodge Corp., 1957).

5. "St. Paul's Church, Waterloo, Belgium," *Liturgical Arts* 39 (August, 1971), 115.

6. Frederic Debuyst, *Modern Architecture and Christian Celebration* (London: Lutterworth Press, 1968), 30.

7. Michael De Sanctis, "Renewing the City of God: The Reform of Catholic Architecture in the United States," *Meeting House Essays* (Chicago: Liturgy Training Publications, 1994), 20, 23.

8. Address of Pope Benedict XVI to the Roman Curia, December 22, 2005, reproduced in *Origins: CNS Documentary Service* 35 (January 26, 2006), 536.

9. Cardinal Joseph Ratzinger has addressed the differing theologies of worship, noting in particular that the notion of the Christian liturgy as sacrifice has been under attack in recent years. He chronicles how the clarity of the Mass as sacrifice grew in the early Church under figures such as Saint Clement and was eventually canonized at the Council of Trent. "In consequence," he writes, "it is said there is an urgent need for firm action to counteract the dogmatization of this error in order that desacralization may finally be accomplished; that the sacramental ministry may be replaced by a functional one; that the still flourishing remnants of the former magic—sacrifice—may be banished; that a nonmagical, rationally structured "efficient" office [*Amt*] that will at last achieve what Jesus intended may be established in the spirit of Jesus." He continues: "It's real goal—often scarcely realized by—is to free itself from the burden of history. . . ." See Joseph Ratzinger, *Principles of Catholic Theology* (San Francisco: Ignatius, 1987), 250–251. With this premise in mind, we can see that many of the theological premises of "progressive" Catholicism (and therefore church architecture) have direct ties to this anti-historical, anti-sacral way of thinking. We might also recognize that the Modernist movement in architecture grew from similar principles; namely, an Enlightenment-inspired desire to be free of history and any trace of the "magic" of non-discursive thought.

10. Address of Pope Benedict XVI, 536.

11. Cardinal Joseph Ratzinger, Conference on the Tenth Anniversary of the *Motu proprio Ecclesia Dei*, October 24, 1998.

12. Marchita Mauck, *Shaping a House for the Church* (Chicago: LTP, 1990), Harold W. Turner, *From Temple to Meeting House* (The Hague: Mouton Publishers, 1979), and Richard Vosko, *God's House Is Our House: Re-imagining the Environment for Worship* (Collegeville, MN: Liturgical Press, 2006).

13. Cardinal Joseph Bernardin, *Our Communion, Our Peace, Our Promise* (Chicago: LTP, 1984), 7. No one is in a position to judge these individuals except God himself, despite some of the heated rhetoric that has emerged from all of the players in this debate. These authors, and many others, we must presume, are people who offer their best efforts at implementing the Second Vatican Council. Vilifying those with whom we disagree is not a Christian endeavor.

14. Vosko, *God's House Is Our House*, xvi. It should be noted that *Environment and Art in Catholic Worship* was a publication of a subcommittee of the Bishops' Committee on the Liturgy, and was never taken to a vote of the full body of bishops. It was replaced by *Built of Living Stones* in 2000.

15. Mark A. Torgerson, *An Architecture of Immanence: Architecture for Worship and Ministry Today* (Grand Rapids, MI: Eerdmans, 2007), 174.

16. De Sanctis, "Renewing the City of God," 20, 23.

17. Robert W. Hovda, *Strong, Loving and Wise: Presiding in Liturgy* (Washington, DC: Liturgical Conference, 1976), viii.

18. Hovda, *Strong, Loving and Wise*, 3.

19. Hovda, *Strong, Loving and Wise*, 49.

20. Bishops' Committee on the Liturgy, *Environment and Art in Catholic Worship* (Washington, DC: NCCB, 1978), par. 41, hereafter cited as EACW.

21. EACW, section heading II, par. 28–29.

22. EACW, 42.

23. EACW, 29.

24. For more on EACW, see Denis McNamara, "Can We Keep Our Churches Catholic?" *Adoremus Bulletin* (February–March 1998), and many others, especially Michael Rose, *Ugly as Sin* (Manchester, NH: Sophia Institute Press, 2001).

25. Alexis, Patriarch of Moscow, "Paschal Message to the Rectors of the Churches in Moscow (1947)," cited in Leonid Ouspensky, *Theology of the Icon* (Crestwood, NY: St. Vladimir's Seminary Press, 1978), 36.

26. Louis Boyer, *Liturgy and Architecture* (South Bend, IN: Notre Dame Press, 1967), 8–9.

27. Pius XII, *Mediator Dei*, paragraph 63: "Clearly no sincere Catholic can refuse to accept the formulation of Christian doctrine more recently elaborated and proclaimed as dogmas by the Church, under the inspiration and guidance of the Holy Spirit with abundant fruit for souls, because it pleases him to hark back to the old formulas. No more can any Catholic in his right senses repudiate existing legislation of the Church to revert to prescriptions based on the earliest sources of canon law. Just as obviously unwise and mistaken is the zeal of one who in matters liturgical would go back to the rites and usage of antiquity, discarding the new patterns introduced by disposition of divine Providence to meet the changes of circumstances and situation."

28. Thomas Aquinas, *Summa Theologiae*, tertia pars, q. 83, art. 3.

29. Cardinal Joseph Ratzinger, *The Spirit of the Liturgy* (San Francisco: Ignatius Press, 2000), 89–90.

30. Eusebius, *Church History*, X.4.25–26.

Conclusion: *Urbs Beata Jerusalem*

Jerusalem, heavenly city, blest vision of peace! Built from living stones, you are raised on high to the heavens and attended, like a bride, by countless thousands of Angels.

How happy the bride of such a favored destiny! Your rich endowment is the Father's glory and your comeliness is from the Bridegroom's grace—queen most beautiful, bride of Christ the King, radiant city of heaven.

In this city the gates of glittering pearls stand open for all to enter; for every man that follows the path of virtue must come to those gates—every man that endures sufferings here for love of Christ.

Its stones are fashioned by many a stroke and blow of the Savior-mason's hammer and chisel. Thus shaped they go to the making of this mighty structure, each being fitly joined to each and finding its appointed place in the whole building.

Let due glory be given to the Father most high, to His only Son and to the renowned Paraclete. To God be praise, power and glory through everlasting ages. Amen.

—*"Urbs Beata Jerusalem,"* from First Vespers of
the Common of the Dedication of a Church[1]

White-robed multitudes from the book of Revelation made knowable to the senses. Cathedral of Saint Joseph, Wheeling, West Virginia. Felix Lieftuchter, muralist.

Truth, Goodness, and Beauty appear everywhere in individual versions of things, and they are united by the overarching principle that gives them significance: the mind of God. Transcendentals deal with infinite ideas which have a limitless number of earthly manifestations. So the Truth of one thing is clarified by the Beauty of another and the Goodness of yet another. Right belief and right praxis find their expression in all things liturgical, whether it be ritual, vestments, art, architecture, music, proclamation, or any of the myriad things of this world elevated to its liturgical end in Christian worship. In each case, Beauty, theologically understood, becomes the lens through which we know what is right. In Beauty we find the mean between excess and deficiency. We find that nothing needs to be added or taken away or changed. In Beauty we see the wholeness of things. In Beauty we orient things toward their proper end. In Beauty, things "ring true" for us as they shed the light of clarity in which our minds can rest in a brief experience of relief from the effects of the Fall. In

Beauty, we see again some semblance of the order God desires us to have. In Beauty we are called to that which is Good, and therefore good for us.

In Beauty we find the Church, the revelation of God's continuing presence with us, based on Christ's own promise:

> "I will not leave you orphaned; I am coming to you. In a little while the world will no longer see me, but you will see me; because I live, you also will live. On that day you will know that I am in my Father, and you in me, and I in you. They who have my commandments and keep them are those who love me; and those who love me will be loved by my Father, and I will love them and reveal myself to them." (John 14:18–21)

So seeing and loving Christ requires obedience to his teaching, now given through the Church. We still see Christ in the Church, in Church councils, in the Petrine Office, in the sacraments, in those who act *in persona Christi*, and in one another. But seeing the Lord requires *claritas*, and *claritas* requires *integritas*, and *integritas* requires obedience to Truth. It is by doing what Christ asks that *claritas* takes shape. By obeying the Lord's revealed commandments we become *claritas* for others and others see Christ in us. Seeing Christ is to see Love, because Love means willing the good of the other, even unto death. So the rule of Love is the rule of revelation, and revelation is at the heart of *claritas*. The rule of Love is therefore also the rule of Beauty. Yet Beauty begets Love by causing a movement of the viewer's will toward the Good and to be transformed by the Truth it finds there. The one transformed then spreads the Truth beautifully, and before long the cycle starts again, and, at some point, the reign of God will be complete.

In the meantime, we lurch forward in fits and starts in this quest for Beauty, which is a quest for clarity, which is a quest for Truth, which is a quest for Goodness, which is a

Newly crafted baldachino at the Shrine of Our Lady of Guadalupe, Lacrosse, Wisconsin. Duncan Stroik, architect, 2008.

Mural of the heavenly Jerusalem, detail. Eugene Nitikin, EverGreene Studios, 2009.

quest for Love, which is a quest for God who is Love. Liturgical art and architecture, as constituent elements of the liturgical rites, can and should become a revelation of that Love which no longer calls us slaves but friends, no longer separated from God but united to him, no longer lawless but ordered, no longer abandoned but shepherded, no longer helplessly fallen but with the promise of glory. Liturgical art does what Christ does: fulfills the typologies of the past, abides with us in the present, and reveals the promise of divinization—all in loving obedience to the Father.

Of course, we still see through a glass darkly, and even the liturgical beauty of this life is infinitely less than the beatific vision. But at the same time, Christ's presence is not a vaporous, gauzy concept known only in the haze of emotion. We make Christ present by doing real, earthy, and specific things: consecrating bread and wine, cleaning the wounds of the injured, wiping the brow of the sick, preparing food for the hungry, writing icons, and building churches. Building a proper church means obeying the liturgical understanding revealed by Christ and governed by the Church. We take the material of the earth and offer it in sacrifice for transformation. We make hillsides into stone blocks, stone blocks into columns, and columns into the sacramental pillars of the Church. We make trees into boards and boards into carved angels. We make the soil's minerals into pigments and pigments into icons, which reveal heaven to us. *Creation is good*, and in the Spirit it becomes the vehicle for revelation. The

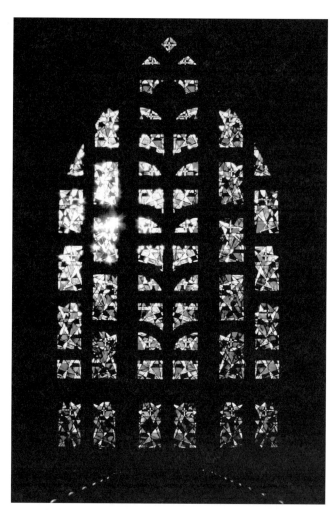

West window, Cathedral of Saint Joseph the Workman, Lacrosse, Wisconsin.

Second Vatican Council reminds us that "redeemed by Christ and made a new creature in the Holy Spirit, man is able to love the things themselves created by God and ought to do so" (*Gaudium et Spes* [GS], 37). Architect, artist, bishop, pastor, and parishioner work in concert to hurry us along on our earthly pilgrimage to the things of heaven by letting us see our heavenly goal in sacramental form. "By denying their love of self," and therefore any artistic and architectural theories not in conformity with the liturgy itself, church builders take up "all the earth's resources into the life of man," reaching out to the future "when humanity itself will become an offering acceptable to God" (SC, 38).

An artist or architect who submits his or her will to the Holy Spirit will not be left unaided. The Second Vatican Council reminds us that Christ "is now at work in the hearts of men through the energy of his Spirit" (GS, 38), and our minds and bodies make this work of God present in the world. Our desire for Beauty in liturgical architecture is more than an earthly aestheticism. Like our desire for justice, it arises from our hearts, souls, and minds because Christ awakens in us "a desire for the age to come," the time of the glorious

future when God is all in all, the time of reality, which we now understand in image in the Age of the Church (GS, 38). The creative gifts of artists, architects, theologians, steelworkers, stained glass makers, and stone carvers come from the Spirit. Their work gives "clear witness to the desire for a heavenly home," and moreover, keeps "that desire green among the human family." So we build as we believe, and our arts encourage others to renew their belief by what they see. God summons the artist and architect "to dedicate themselves to the service of men here on earth, preparing by this ministry the material of the kingdom of heaven" (GS, 38).

The famous hymn, "*Urbs Beata Jerusalem*," or "Jerusalem, Heavenly City," sung during First Vespers at the dedication of a church, opens up for us the theology of the church building. Though a sacramental bearer of our heavenly future, the church building maintains its roots in the biblical concept of God's presence, from Moses' desert tabernacle to the great temple building in Jerusalem. In the Old Testament, the earthly city of Jerusalem with its temple served as a typological precursor of the heavenly city, the new Jerusalem of peace, where God's presence restores all to right relationship with him. At first, the mystery of God was made known in veiled typological shadows, in the slavery of the Old Law. The letter to the Hebrews notes that even Moses was afraid to touch the holy mountain where God was made known through blazing fire and thunder. Here the fear brought by the Old Law was necessary to keep his people from straying further from him.

However, in the time of image, we have gone beyond the shadows and live in the time of Christ's Easter victory, where the New Law is written on our hearts. The veil of the Holy of Holies is torn. In the church building with its liturgy, we *see* an image of that heavenly reality available to us, and we enter into its glorious presence to be renewed by God. We build in glory because we participate in glory. In the time of image, the Sacred Liturgy and its sacred art bring us visually to the city of the living God, "the heavenly Jerusalem, to myriads of angels in festal gathering, to the assembly of the first-born in heaven, to God the judge of all, to the spirits of the just men made perfect, to Jesus, the mediator of a new covenant" (Hebrews 12:22b–24a). If we follow Christ in loving obedience to his precepts, Saint Athanasius says, "we shall be allowed, even on this earth, to stand as it were on the threshold of the heavenly Jerusalem and enjoy the contemplation of that everlasting feast, like the blessed apostles. . . ."[2] The presence of God is holy and confers holiness; the glory of God draws us to this life, and those who encounter God receive divine life.

Knowing that we have access to the heavenly city, we rejoice, and ornamenting our voices, we sing the praises of the heavenly city of peace: *"Jerusalem, heavenly city, blest vision of peace! Built from living stones, you are raised on high to the heavens and attended, like a bride, by countless thousands of Angels."* The church building gives an anticipated experience of that

St. Michael the Archangel Church, Leawood, Kansas. David Meleca, design architect, 2009.

heavenly city of Jerusalem, the fulfillment of God's promises to Israel, a blessed vision of peace where sin and death no longer cause anger, pain, strife, or discord. The heavenly citizens live *with* one another, not in fearful isolation, but as one body raising its voice to God. These living stones form the city, each a being created and divinized to give God glory and share his love. They are raised up by God to the heavens through his free gift of grace, a grace which works with our nature to transform our bodies, the world, and the cosmos. Even the angels minister to the Bride, the Church, who is divinized, beautified, transformed, ornamented, and ready for the Bridegroom.

"How happy the bride of such a favored destiny! Your rich endowment is the Father's glory and your comeliness is from the Bridegroom's grace—queen most beautiful, bride of Christ the King, radiant city of heaven." This divinization and beatification is the source of our joy. Once we were fallen and left to our own inadequate devices. But God, the loving Father, endowed us with a richness we did not merit: his own glory, restored for us by the Son. The Church is this beautiful, royal Bride, the queen most beautiful for which the Virgin Mary served as typological precursor. Christ raises up the Bride to be worthy of himself by sharing his divine life with her. The two that were separated—God and humanity—become one in a glorious unity. The bride is transformed to take on the very dignity of the King, and is welcomed in his palace, the radiant city of heaven.

"In this city the gates of glittering pearls stand open for all to enter; for every man that follows the path of virtue must come to those gates—every man that endures sufferings here for love of Christ." Before we reach for the kingdom of heaven, the pearl of great price, and before we "become" the city detailed so carefully in the book of Revelation, we must accept this grace. God compels no one to share his life. We journey as pilgrims through the fallen world with our eyes set on the goal, transformed by living a sacrificial life nourished by the sacraments. The gates

of this eternal city are the Sacred Liturgy and its rites, standing radiant and attractive; its beauty beckons us to come in. The radiant pearls call us: the Truth of the Gospel, the Goodness of Christ's love, and the Beauty of God's gracious plan. Christ is the entry to the Father, and every person must come to this gate. The journey to this gate includes both sorrow and joy, sharing in Christ's sufferings as well as his glory. It means offering oneself on the paten with the priest as Victim, sacrificing the self and trusting in transformation in glory.

"Its stones are fashioned by many a stroke and blow of the Savior-mason's hammer and chisel. Thus shaped they go to the making of this mighty structure, each being fitly joined to each and finding its appointed place in the whole building." If we are to be stones of the heavenly city, we therefore must become heavenly ourselves, molded away from our disordered selves and into the shape prepared for us before time began. We give ourselves over in trust to be fashioned by the blows of the Savior-mason's hammer, shaped in the easy embrace of palpable grace like water over rock, but shaped also in the difficult love of discipline, which sharpens us with quick blows. Here we find obedience, reminded that we are creatures who stand before God in love and awe. Here we root out our vices

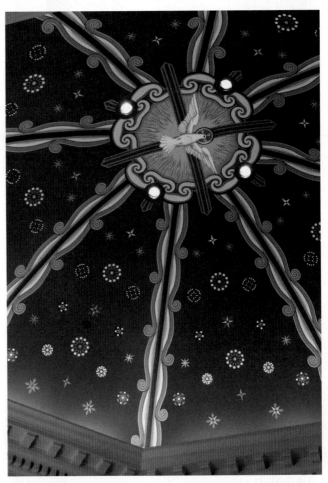

Baptistry mural, St. Michael the Archangel Church, Leawood, Kansas. EverGreene Studios.

Eucharistic Chapel, Cathedral of St. Peter in Chains, Cincinnati. Edward Schulte, architect, 1957.

and learn to love others as ourselves. Rightly shaped, we are then fitted into the golden, gem-covered walls of the heavenly city, made one with each other in a city in the "shape" of God. This stone-shaping occurs in the liturgy of the Church, where God, who made us from nothing, re-makes us into something glorified and like himself. We become Christ through Christ's donation of himself to us, and his glory radiates through us, and God is glorified because "the glory of God is man fully alive."

Here we find the role of liturgical art and architecture. When joined to the liturgy, it reveals to us our heavenly destination by showing us where we are, where we have been, and where we are going. It welcomes us to the Heavenly Banqueting Feast even as it reminds us that a banquet must come after the work of obedience to God's will. It shows to our eyes the glory of heaven and absorbs all good that has come before; from pagan, Jew, and Christian. In it we swim in the warm, effortless delight of the Sabbath, in the vision of freedom where all is from God, to God, and about God. We who had departed from God return to God glorified and transformed. Liturgical art and architecture, then, are part of the "practical application and fulfillment of the words that Jesus proclaimed on the first day of Holy Week, Palm Sunday, in the temple in Jerusalem: 'And I, when I am lifted up from the earth, will draw all people to myself'" (John 12:32).[3]

Let us, then, have truly liturgical art and architecture, an architecture of Beauty, an architecture of reality in the time of the image, an architecture of the Sabbath, a built theology of Love in the Age of the Church.

Apply this to Christ also when he comes along the roads as a pilgrim, looking for shelter. You do not take him in as your guest, but you decorate floors and walls and the capitals of the pillars. You provide silver chains for the lamps, but you cannot bear even to look at him as he lies chained in prison. Once again, I am not forbidding you to supply these adornments; I am urging you to provide these other things as well, and indeed to provide them first. No one has ever been accused for not providing ornaments. . . . Do not, therefore, adorn the church and ignore your afflicted brother, for he is the most precious temple of all.

—From a homily by Saint John Chrysostom[4]

1. Translation taken from *The Hours of the Divine Office in English and Latin*, v. 2 (Collegeville, MN: The Liturgical Press, 1964), 922.

2. Saint Athanasius, Easter letter, Ep. 14, 1–2: PG 26, 1419–1420. Translation taken from the Office of Readings, Fifth Sunday in Lent.

3. Cardinal Joseph Ratzinger, *The Spirit of the Liturgy* (San Francisco: Ignatius Press, 2000), 34.

4. John Chrysostom, Homily, Hom. 50, 3–4: PG 58, 508–509. Translation taken from the Office of Readings, Saturday of the Twenty-first week of the year.

Q & A

When I give presentations in parishes or teach in the classroom, I am often asked many intelligent questions by students, building committee members, architects, pastors, and parishioners. These questions have given me some insight into the needs and desires of the People of God, and in many ways they inspired me to write this book. The questions that follow are among those most frequently asked, and shorter summary answers are provided here for the reader's convenience.

1. Q: Didn't the Second Vatican Council do away with traditional, beautiful churches? What about "noble simplicity"?

A: The documents of the Second Vatican Council relating to art and architecture are in complete continuity with the Church's great tradition even as they set certain guidelines for the liturgical renewal. The document on the Sacred Liturgy, *Sacrosanctum Concilium,* asked that sacred art be composed of "signs and symbols of heavenly realities" that were meant to be expressive of "God's boundless beauty" (SC, 122). It also asked that all sacred arts be "in accordance with faith, piety, and cherished traditional laws" (SC, 122). It is interesting to note that despite the common understanding, the Council never used the phrase "noble simplicity" to refer to liturgical art and architecture. It actually asked that churches strive for "noble beauty" (SC, 124). The term "noble simplicity" was mentioned in the Council's documents in relation to the rites (SC, 34). So, Beauty is in fact the goal of new church architecture, according to the documents of the Second Vatican Council.

2. Q: Is it possible to build traditional churches today? Can we afford it? Does the architectural and artistic talent exist?

A: Since the advent of post-Modernism in the 1960s, the architecture world has been reexamining the place of traditional forms for new work. A large and flourishing movement generally known as New Classicism has been operating successfully for more than two decades. In recent years, designs for new traditional Catholic churches have been appearing

with greater frequency. The Shrine of Our Lady of Guadalupe in La Crosse, Wisconsin, the university chapel at Thomas Aquinas College in California, and the monastery of the Benedictines in Clear Creek, Oklahoma, have proven that traditional architecture is possible today. Scores of other projects are doing the same. The process of reaching backward to seek out high style, "star architect" Modernists has emerged as a strikingly outdated mode of building new churches.

Traditional architecture need not be more expensive than other quality ways of building. Cutting-edge Modernism is often extraordinarily expensive because of its demands for custom materials. Traditional architecture can be elevated with more elaborate designs and richer materials, or it can be reduced with simpler designs and materials that nonetheless partake of legitimate traditional design.

The most important consideration in building a traditional church is to hire an architect who specializes in traditional work. Many architects will promise something "traditional" to a church client by adding a few pointed windows or extra moldings to an otherwise Modernist design. This sort of design should be completely rejected or else the result will be the "strip mall classical" or "Disneyland gothic."

3. Q: Isn't using traditional styles for architecture just copying the past? Isn't there room for new development in church architecture?

A: There is always room for development in Catholic architecture just as there is always room for development of doctrine as we come to understand better the revelation of Christ. But simply absorbing current trends in theology is not an answer; they must always be tested against the inherited teaching of the Church. The same is true in architecture. The Church welcomes new technology and styles of the current day, provided that they bring due honor and reverence to the rites (SC, 123). Using "new" artistic and architectural conventions simply because they are new does not always engage a proper level of theological inquiry. Similarly, using old forms just to be antiquarian is not adequate either. New traditional architecture should never be an exact copy of an old building. The past serves as a treasury from which to draw, and we should not be afraid either to depart from it where necessary or use it quite faithfully when appropriate.

4. Q: Since the people are the "living stones" of the Church, why would we need anything other than a simple meeting hall for Mass?

A: The people are indeed the living stones of the earthly Church. However, the documents of the Second Vatican Council remind us that the Sacred Liturgy is an exercise of the priestly office of Jesus Christ, head, and members (SC, 7), where we "take part in a foretaste of that heavenly liturgy which is celebrated in the holy city of Jerusalem toward which we journey as pilgrims, where Christ is sitting at the right hand of God, a minister of the holies and of the true tabernacle; we sing a hymn to the Lord's glory with all the warriors of the heavenly army" (SC, 8). The job of liturgical art and architecture is to make a building that not only serves the needs of the earthly congregation, but also allows them, through the use of sacred images, to "see" the full community of the liturgy: angels, saints, the Trinity, and even the souls in purgatory. The building itself is a sacrament of the city of heaven, described in scripture as orderly, perfected, radiant, gem-covered, and golden. A church building, therefore, aids in our full, conscious, and active participation by showing us by way of foretaste the very realities in which we are participating. The church building not only shows us our earthly reality, but allows us to glimpse the realities of our destiny at the end of time when God has completely restored the world.

5. Q: The upper room of the Last Supper was a simple place for the Passover meal. Jesus never wore fancy vestments or drank from gold cups. Why should we do this in the liturgy? Shouldn't we give money to the poor instead?

A: Because the Sacred Liturgy is in one sense a memorial of the Last Supper, many people often think that the liturgy is supposed to imitate the earthly lifetime of Christ. However, it should be remembered that at the Incarnation, Christ veiled his divinity and power with only a few exceptions such as his miracles and the Transfiguration. The Catholic liturgy is not primarily a recall of the earthly Christ, but a foretaste of the heavenly Christ of the Second Coming. The fourth-century bishop Saint Cyril of Jerusalem wrote of Christ: "At the first coming he was wrapped in swaddling clothes in a manger. At the second coming he will be clothed in light as in a garment. In the first coming he endured the cross; . . . in the second coming he will be in glory, escorted by an army of angels. We look then beyond the first coming and await the second." The earthly liturgy recalls the shadows of the Last Supper and Passover, but more importantly, it serves as an image of the realities of the heavenly Wedding Feast of the Lamb. The earthly chalice is not only a recall of the cup of the Last Supper, but of the glorious, golden, radiant feast of heaven. Similarly, the church building should show us the order and perfection of heaven.

Building beautiful buildings should never be a substitute for feeding the poor and nursing the sick, but it is not an "either/or" question. The poor and the sick are also expected to participate in the liturgy and they deserve access to the foretaste of heavenly reality as much as anyone. Moreover, the poor are the least likely to have beautiful homes and personal artwork. A beautiful church gives them a refuge of beauty, which they need more urgently than do the wealthy. Serving the poor means serving their human need for liturgical beauty as well as food and shelter.

6. Q: Didn't the early Christians worship in simple private homes? Why, then, should we build elaborate public buildings?

A: Though scriptural evidence speaks of the earliest Christians "breaking bread" in their homes, it also speaks of them returning frequently to the temple for prayer. A number of the important discourses and cures in the Acts of the Apostles happen within the temple courts. Because Herod was a client-king of the Roman Empire, the temple was a grand, high-style architectural ensemble of the type common in imperial Rome. Christ and the apostles walked on the temple mount amid Corinthian columns, Classical moldings, and a large basilican hall called the Royal Stoa, which contained wood carvings and looked almost indistinguishable from early churches in fourth-century Rome. Christianity was not only born into Israel, but also the Roman Empire even before the emperor Constantine converted to Christianity and made it the religion of the empire.

But even if Christianity had been born in a cultural vacuum, it would still need to develop an art and architecture that could serve as sacramental bearers of the heavenly Jerusalem. So to revert to building churches as "houses" today is to embrace a false antiquarianism that says, "Older is always better." The church building is not primarily a house, but rather a ritually public and sacramental building where the many gather to anticipate the glory and perfection of heaven.

7. Q: What Church documents should I read to learn more about sacred art and architecture?

A: Paragraphs 122 through 130 from the Second Vatican Council's *Sacrosanctum Concilium* would be a great place to start (http://www.vatican.va/archive/hist_councils/ii_vatican_council/documents/vat-ii_const_19631204_sacrosanctum-concilium_en.html). A complete copy of this document is also included in an excellent study of *Sacrosanctum Concilium* entitled *An Abundance of Graces: Reflections on* Sacrosanctum Concilium by Pamela Jackson (Chicago: Hillenbrand Books, 2004). Pope Pius XII's encyclical on the liturgy, *Mediator Dei* (http://www.vatican.va/holy_father/pius_xii/encyclicals/documents/hf_p-xii_enc_20111947_mediator-dei_en.html), written only 13 years before the opening of the Second Vatican Council, gives specific guidelines for sacred art and architecture, which complement the Second Vatican Council beautifully. One might also read the *Rite for the Dedication of a Church and*

Altar to glean its theological underpinnings. An excerpt of this document is included in *The Liturgy Documents, Volume Two*, (Chicago: Liturgy Training Publications, 1999, pp. 323–342). Another important read is chapter 5 of the *General Instruction of the Roman Missal* called "The Arrangement and Furnishing of Churches for the Celebration of the Eucharist." This is available from the USCCB Web site (www.usccb.org). The introduction to the *Rite of Christian Initiation for Adults* (Chicago: Liturgy Training Publications, 2007) also includes a good amount of information useful for understanding and building baptistries. For American dioceses, the guidelines put out by the U.S. Bishops, *Built of Living Stones* (www. usccb.org), serves as a handy guide.

8. Q: What sort of theological questions should I ask a prospective architect in an interview?

A: Most architects are well-trained, insured, and have built buildings before. Follow up on their references and look at their previous work. Once you are satisfied with an architect's practical credentials, the first question to ask a prospective architect is: "How will you make our church a sacramental image of the heavenly Jerusalem?" Most architects will have no idea how to begin an answer to this question, yet it is the central question in church building. If this question stumps the architect, then ask: "What is your understanding of the nature of a church building?" If he or she says something similar to "meeting hall" or "gathering space" or "auditorium," move on to another architect.

Since most architects are not trained in theology, it is vital to find an architect that has an appreciation for its importance in church design. His or her lack of theological expertise, then, needs to be accounted for within your building team. It is important to have someone on the building team who understands the underlying sacramental theology of liturgical art and architecture, and not just the legislation on the topic. This might be an informed pastor or associate, or properly formed theologian. If you have a liturgical theologian on your team, ask the architect how he or she works with a consultant. Does he or she resent outside input or welcome it? (This is also a good question to put to the references.)

If you are seeking an authentically traditional church building, ask the architect if he or she has had training in traditional design. All architects want work and will promise the client almost anything to get a job. Don't be fooled by an architect who tells you that he can "learn on the job." One wouldn't tolerate that attitude from a brain surgeon and shouldn't tolerate it from an architect. Traditional architecture is a specialty, and as the owner of the project and as commissioner of the church building, clients should seek out a specialist.

9. Q: Who are some of the leading traditional church architects practicing today?

A: In the last ten years many traditional architects have developed their practices to include or specialize in ecclesiastical work using a genuine traditional architecture. A partial list of architects to consider is given below in alphabetical order. There may be others not listed here that have begun their practices more recently.

Ethan Anthony, Boston, MA
www.hdb.com

Franck & Lohsen, Washington, DC
www.francklohsen.com

William Heyer, Columbus, OH
www.heyerarchitect.com

Michael Imber, San Antonio, TX
www.michaelgimber.com

James McCrery, Washington, DC
www.mccreryarchitects.com

David Meleca, Columbus, OH
www.melecaarchitecture.com

Thomas Gordon Smith, South Bend, IN
www.thomasgordonsmitharchitects.com

Duncan Stroik South Bend, IN
www.stroik.com

10. Q: What are the ideas we should consider when thinking about the design of the altar?

A: In recent decades, the altar in a Catholic church has usually been described as a "table of the community." In one sense, this is true. A Catholic altar is indeed the table around which the earthly congregation gathers to worship God. But the altar is also a sacrament, a visible sign of otherwise invisible realities. And the prime reality is this: the altar is the glorified table of our future heavenly banquet as well as a symbol of Christ himself.

The book of Revelation tells us that the future holds for us an eternal celebration with God and the heavenly beings when the "rescue mission" of God is complete. God will be "all in all" and his divine presence will completely restore everything. The results of the Fall—death, sorrow, suffering, sin—will be overcome and God will be fully reunited to his creation once again; the two will become one. For this reason, the heavenly celebration is called the "Wedding Feast of the Lamb." Christ, the Bridegroom, has become one with the Church, his Bride. The heavenly celebration that ensues is not completely unlike the wedding receptions we have on earth, where festivity reigns and we share a banquet eaten on a beautifully decorated table, dressed with linens, candles, and flowers. But the altar signifies a feast of eternal, cosmic, and heavenly importance: Christ's mission to re-join God and creation is complete! So our worship is a celebration, a doing on earth what is done in heaven. The sacred meal of the liturgy, then, happens on a "table" in a church building that indicates eternal importance, permanence, radiance, and perfection. We become accustomed to heaven by doing the things of heaven, even while still on earth.

However, the celebration of Mass is also a sacrificial feast. It therefore requires not only a table, but also an altar as a place of offering. The feast is hosted by Christ whose body is simultaneously the "place" of offering (the altar), the offerer (the priest), and that which is offered (the victim). Christ then is the truest altar. Our earthly altar conversely signifies Christ and gives us the old expression "the altar is Christ," which is why the priest kisses it as he enters the church. To kiss the altar is to kiss Christ.

As a sacramental sign of Christ, the altar is treated in a way that makes its "Christ-ness" most evident. It is made of stone and is affixed to the floor, signifying the permanence and eternity of the Son of God. It is marked with five small engraved crosses indicating the five wounds of his body. When the altar is dedicated by the Bishop, it will again be treated as a body: sprinkled with holy water like a Baptism and rubbed with sacred oils in an anointing, which indicates Christ as "the Anointed One of God." It is then "dressed" in white linen altar cloths, signifying the white robes of heavenly beings, while at the same time showing that the "table" is prepared for the greatest feast ever celebrated. From this table is served God himself in the Eucharist.

11. Q: Where should the tabernacle be placed? Should it always be placed on the central axis of the sanctuary?

A: The ordinary place for the tabernacle is in the sanctuary, even on an old altar no longer used for celebration, as section 315 of the *General Instruction of the Roman Missal* states. However, more important than a dry rule is the principle that "the Most Blessed Sacrament should be reserved in a tabernacle in a part of the church that is truly noble, prominent, readily visible and suitable for private prayer" (GIRM, 314). So in cathedrals and places where many tourists might bring noisy disrespect for the reserved sacrament and those praying, a separate chapel is a permitted alternative. There was a time, however, when many theologians thought that the tabernacle was a distraction from the action of the Sacred Liturgy and needed to be removed to a separate room, even in a small parish church. This time has passed as we have understood better that Christ's abiding presence in the tabernacle does not compete with his presence in the liturgical rites.

The word *tabernacle* itself has its origins in the Latin word for "tent," so the tabernacle is indeed a small building

within the larger church structure itself. For many Catholics, the tabernacle seems to give a church its "glowing heart," the almost tangible knowledge of God's abiding presence in the reserved Eucharist, which is worthy of private prayer and devotion. But the tabernacle has a long history, starting with Moses, who was directed by God to build a tent-like building also called the tabernacle in which rested a gold-covered cedar box called the Ark of the Covenant. Atop this ark the presence of God came and rested as a burst of glory called the *shekinah*. The ark would later be brought to the great Temple of Solomon in Jerusalem, and God's presence moved to dwell there in the small room in the back of the temple called the "Holy of Holies." This room stood as an architectural image of heaven and is signified today by the sanctuary of a church. So our Father, "who art in heaven," nonetheless was also on earth, resting atop a golden box which indicated his presence. Like two circles that overlap in part, there was a common place where the God who dwells in heaven also rests in our midst on earth.

So today we see a tabernacle as more than a pretty container for storing the Blessed Sacrament until it is brought to the sick. It is the place where Emmanuel, "God-with-us," dwells on earth in our earthly image of heaven: the church sanctuary. Here the golden box of the Old Testament's Ark of the Covenant finds its fulfillment in sacramental life of the Church: God's presence abides with us even as it dwells within each and every Christian who takes that presence out to the world in evangelization, caring for the sick, the homeless, and even in the ordinary tasks of employment and raising a family. Pope Benedict XVI reminds us that in the humble tabernacle, God's presence really dwells with us, "in the humblest parish church no less than in the grandest cathedral."

12. Q: What issues should we consider when designing our ambo?

A: The origins of the ambo trace back to the early Church where it was set apart and reserved for the public proclamation of the scriptures and the subsequent preaching on those readings. An ambo, then, is more than a lectern or pulpit; it is something of a "sanctuary" for the word of God. As such, it is not only functional, but also a sign to those who see it that something important happens within it. Although it dropped out of use in the course of the Church's history to be replaced primarily by a preaching pulpit, in the years before the Second Vatican Council, the proper ambo was revived and the term came back into use. To say "ambo" is to use the very language of active participation in the public proclamation of scripture that the Second Vatican Council desired.

At the ambo we are spiritually nourished with the revealed word of God, just as at the altar we are nourished *par excellence* with the Body and Blood of Christ. For that reason, an ambo should exhibit a clear relationship in design and materials with the altar itself.

13. Q: What should we consider when planning our baptistry?

A: In the early centuries of the Church, baptistries were often buildings separate from the main body of a church. Those who were not yet baptized were not yet considered "citizens" of the Church, and as such received their Baptisms outside the Church, then processed into the church building in triumph. Many such baptistries exist to this day in the great churches of the world. As centuries passed, Baptism was often reduced to a pouring of water on the head of a child, and fonts began to shrink and lose their architectural significance. In the twentieth century, Baptism was understood anew as a sacrament of birth, death, and ritual washing. The fullness of the sign was seen as better expressed in immersing (immersion) the catechumen in water rather than a mere pouring (infusion), and the notion of larger fonts in which adults could walk became popular. In the years after the Second Vatican Council, a greater emphasis was placed on Baptism as an entry into the ecclesial community, and so baptistries became more prominent and were often located within the body of the church, sometimes at the rear of the church's central aisle. While this made baptistries more visible, it made it awkward for funeral and bridal processions. Because many pastors wanted their baptistries to be visible at the Easter Vigil, fonts were then often located in the front of the church.

There is no one "correct" place to put a baptistry in a church, but the placement should adhere to several principles. First, the location of the baptistry should suggest "entering" the church as one receives this sacrament of Initiation. The recent trend of putting baptistries in the sanctuary behind or next to the altar should by all means be avoided; Baptism signifies the entry into the church, not the final destination. Second, since Baptisms in large parishes usually involve many family members and multiple children, giving adequate seating and good sight lines to the baptistry is important, though not essential. Third, since Baptism is a preparation for fulfillment in the Eucharist, some connection with the altar is desirable, either in sight lines or materials.

The baptistry is a place of important sacramental activity, so its materials and design should announce that fact. The fiberglass tub baptistries seen in recent years should absolutely be rejected. The octagonal shape of the baptistry connects to a longstanding tradition of symbolizing the "eighth day," the day after God's seventh day of creation, signifying the eternal rest of the glorified paradise of heaven. Since Baptism provides the entry point to that paradise, the architecture itself should give a foretaste of that glory. But the glory of Baptism arises out of the symbolism of the baptistry as "womb and tomb." The centralized plan of the baptistry harkens back to the ancient form of tombs, which were often round buildings based on the shape of burial mounds. Baptism provides the entry to new life, but only as a "death" to the old self, where one descends down several steps, as if descending into burial. After the ritual cleansing with baptismal water, the newly baptized person then rises up the steps on the other side, indicating a rebirth as a new creation, out of the tomb, which is simultaneously like coming forth from a mother's womb, "born again," in the proper sense of the term.

14. Q: What is the place of devotional art in a Catholic church?

A: Devotional art is indeed welcome in Catholic churches, as strongly reinforced in the Second Vatican Council's document *Sacrosanctum Concilium*, which reads, "the practice of placing sacred images in churches so that they may be venerated by the faithful is to be firmly maintained" (SC, 124). Devotional art, as the name implies, is intended for use in devotional and para-liturgical activities. Devotional practices are generally private and allow for a wider range of expressive possibilities than liturgical practices, so permanent devotional art properly finds its home in a chapel or niche separate from the sanctuary. Devotional practices flow from and return to the Sacred Liturgy, but they should never be confused by or substituted for it.

15. Q: Do large murals still find a place in a Catholic church? Aren't they a distraction to liturgical participation?

A: Murals still belong in Catholic churches, but some careful theological consideration must go into their placement and content. If the subject of a mural is Christ in the carpenter shop or Saint Patrick driving the snakes from Ireland, then it is better understood as a piece for devotion or meditation on sacred history. As such, it should be treated as a devotional image. However, if the subject of the mural is the heavenly Jerusalem as derived from the book of Revelation, then the mural depicts the liturgy itself in its cosmic and heavenly dimensions, and rightly belongs in the sanctuary. To look at the cosmic and heavenly liturgy in addition to the earthly activity of the sacred rites is to participate even more fully and actively in the liturgy.

16. Q: Why did we build so many ugly churches after the Second Vatican Council? Why did we take out the marble high altars from older churches and paint over the murals?

A: In the early and mid twentieth century, the culture still had a great trust in Modernity and its notions of progress. The Church, too, desired to prove that the Faith could find expression in our own day as it had in other times, and was particularly eager to be a leaven for the world after two world wars, the Holocaust, the Great Depression, and the use of nuclear weapons. While the Church sought to be an antidote to the destruction of the early twentieth century, many strains of the art world moved toward a nihilistic or mechanistic understanding of technology as the answer to modern problems. In the elite circles of architectural philosophy and practice, the machine and the factory (and their materials of glass, steel and concrete) became the model for new buildings. Though this mechanistic understanding of buildings was often foreign to sacramental theology, building a church that embraced the modern world was often seen as a good by individual pastors and bishops. Only later did people start to see that some of the principles of Modernism needed to be rethought for ecclesiastical use. We are now living in that post-Modern time when many churches are reengaging with beauty and tradition once again.

Interestingly, after the Second Vatican Council, a strain of theology emerged in the Church that redefined churches as "meeting houses" and found its inspiration in the so-called house churches of the time of the apostles. Although this sort of uncritical antiquarianism had been widely condemned by Church authorities over the centuries, including Pope Pius XII in *Mediator Dei*, many Catholic theologians nonetheless argued that a church building had no import other than as a place of comfortable hospitality, a "skin for liturgical action," which "need not look like anything else past or present."

Though highly influential in the late 1970s through the 1990s (and even today in some circles), this is no longer the prevailing notion of church architecture. In fact, the *Catechism of the Catholic Church* specifically states that churches "are not simply gathering places, but signify and make visible the Church living in this place, the dwelling of God with men reconciled and united in Christ" (CCC, 1181). In other words, a church is an image that shows the realities of the heavenly future when God's reconciliation with humanity is complete.

In the late 1960s and forward, then, many people who accepted this redefinition of the church as a meeting house for the community's sacred meal then saw old altars, altarpieces, statues, and murals as relics of the "old" way of understanding the Church. In order to best express the new notion of a church as meeting house, they removed and destroyed many precious artifacts. Under Pope Benedict, the Church has come to understand better the Second Vatican Council as a call for reform within a hermeneutic of continuity rather than rupture, and people are learning to see the value of many traditional forms in the Church once again. However, it should be noted that an uncritical look at the past should be discouraged. There were in fact many reforms that were needed before the Council, and careful theological examination is required in "restoring" old forms in order to avoid simply repeating pre-conciliar excesses.

Index

Page 226: Virgin and Child, Cathedral of Saint Joseph the Workman, Lacrosse, Wisconsin. Leo Cartwright, painter

· FIG · (A) · EGG · AND · DART ·

· FIG · (B) · LEAF · AND · TONGUE ·

· FIG · (C) · TORUS · (GUILLOCHE) ·

· FIG · (D) · STELE ·

· FIG · (E) · HONEY·SUCKLE ·

· FIG · (F) · BAS·RELIEF ·

· FIG · (G) · EAGLE ·

· FIG · (H) · GRIFFIN ·

· CLASSICAL · ORNAMENT ·

· FIG · (I) · CAPITAL ·

· FIG · (J) · LION ·

· FIG · (K) · CAPITAL ·

· FIG · (L) · PANEL ·

· FIG · (M) · FRIEZE · DECORATION ·

· FIG · (N) · PANEL ·

· RENAISSANCE · ORNAMENT ·